ISAIAH–MALACHI

Morning Conversations

on the Prophetic Word

Days 680–929 of your
devotional journey through
the Old Testament with

JON R. ROEBUCK

© 2023

Published in the United States by Nurturing Faith, Macon, GA.
Nurturing Faith is a book imprint of Good Faith Media (goodfaithmedia.org).
Library of Congress Cataloging-in-Publication Data is available.

ISBN: 978-1-63528-224-5

All rights reserved. Printed in the United States of America.

Scripture quotations taken from the (NASB®) New American Standard Bible®, Copyright © 1960, 1971, 1977, 1995, 2020 by The Lockman Foundation. Used by permission. All rights reserved. www.lockman.org

Scripture quotations marked (NLT) are taken from the Holy Bible, New Living Translation, copyright ©1996, 2004, 2015 by Tyndale House Foundation. Used by permission of Tyndale House Publishers, Carol Stream, Illinois 60188. All rights reserved.

Scripture quotations marked (NIV) are taken from the Holy Bible, New International Version®, NIV®. Copyright © 1973, 1978, 1984, 2011 by Biblica, Inc.™ Used by permission of Zondervan. All rights reserved worldwide. www.zondervan.com The "NIV" and "New International Version" are trademarks registered in the United States Patent and Trademark Office by Biblica, Inc.™

Scripture marked NKJV taken from the New King James Version®. Copyright © 1982 by Thomas Nelson. Used by permission. All rights reserved.

Dedication

Prophets of God are called to perform two important roles. One is to "foretell" the future. Prophets speak of things yet to come, mysteries yet untold, and blessings not yet realized. Second, they also "forth tell" the message of God. Prophets are called to raise a powerful voice in response to God's leadership… a voice that is not always welcomed but important to hear. Every preacher I know stands in the pulpit each week to fulfil the prophetic roles to which God has called them. For over half my life I carried such a responsibility. I was carefully prepared for the prophetic task by "giants in the faith" who taught me well. By example and through instruction, I was taught to think critically, write with clarity, and proclaim boldly. Any success I have enjoyed in the discipline of preaching is due to their wisdom, insight, and prayerful support. This volume is dedicated to the women and men of our faith tradition who stand courageously, authentically, and compassionately in the pulpit each week to share the Word of God with those of us who constantly need the prophetic word.

Contents

Preface 1

Isaiah 3
    Days 680 through 745

Jeremiah 69
    Days 746 through 797

Lamentations 121
    Days 798 through 802

Ezekiel 126
    Days 803 through 850

Daniel 174
    Days 851 through 862

Hosea 186
    Days 863 through 876

Joel 200
    Days 877 through 879

Amos 203
    Days 880 through 888

Obadiah 212
    Day 889

Jonah 213
    Days 890 through 893

Micah 217
    Days 894 through 900

Nahum 224
    Days 901 through 903

Habakkuk 227
    Days 904 through 906

Zephaniah 230
    Days 907 through 909

Haggai 233
    Days 910 through 911

Zechariah 235
    Days 912 through 925

Malachi 249
    Days 926 through 929

Preface

Welcome to Volume 4 of a 5-volume collection of devotional thoughts drawn from the pages of the Bible. *Morning Conversations on the Prophetic Word* takes the reader through all the writings, proclamations, and predictions of the Major and Minor Prophets of the Old Testament. As in the previous volumes, I invite you to join with me in a fresh devotional read through the pages of the Old Testament text. My goal in writing is not to exhaustively interpret, translate, or provide full commentary on every chapter of the Old Testament, but to help you engage with the text and perhaps draw some meaningful application for each day. I have discovered many fascinating ways the truth of God's Word leaps off the page and into my own heart. It is my hope that some of my reflections will help you with your discovery of scripture and the role of faith in your life. I use the word "Conversations" with great intentionality. I think Bible study should happen that way. God is revealed to us through the stories in scripture, and then we reflect and offer back the thoughts of our hearts. It is a conversation… a back-and-forth dialogue. Conversations invite us to ponder, reflect, inquire, learn, and grow.

As you read these volumes, I hope you will take time, not only to read what I have written, but to reflect with me on what the ancients have written. Allow me challenge you each morning to take a few moments to read the suggested focus chapter from a trusted translation before you dive into the words I have written. Read and reflect. As you make your way through this book, and the other volumes in the set, you will discover a lot of my life story written into these pages. But more importantly, I hope you will discover a lot about God's story… the one carefully crafted and preserved for you. For in hearing God's story, you will hear the echoing refrain of God's desire to know you, to love you, and to redeem you. Welcome to the conversation.

Morning Conversations Volumes 1-5

Morning Conversations on the Creation of a People and Place is the first volume of a set that follows the natural order of the Old Testament canon, and spans the Biblical narrative from the opening chapter of Genesis to the end of the book of Ruth.

Morning Conversations on the Rise and Fall of Kings and Kingdoms continues the orderly progression, spanning the books of 1 Samuel through Esther.

Morning Conversations on the Wisdom of the Ages covers all five books of wisdom literature from Job to the Song of Solomon.

Morning Conversations on the Prophetic Word wraps up the Old Testament with a look at the books of prophecy, covering both the Major and Minor prophets, Isaiah through Malachi.

Additionally, *Morning Conversations on the New Testament* is the final volume of this collection.

Day 680 — Isaiah 1: A Promise of Renewal

> "Come now, let's settle this, says the Lord. Though your sins are like scarlet, I will make them as white as snow. Though they are red like crimson, I will make them as white as wool." Isaiah 1:18 (NLT)

Observation

The Book of Isaiah spans 66 chapters and three distinct periods of time. Chapters 1-39 tell of the Assyrian conquest of Israel (northern kingdom). Chapters 40-55 speak of the Babylonian destruction of Jerusalem. And chapters 56-66 describe a postexilic nation. The Jewish historian Josephus says that Isaiah "was a divine and wonderful man." There is some discussion that perhaps three different writers contributed to the book, but the Dead Sea Scroll discovery of an entire and complete version of Isaiah suggests it was written by a single author rather than cobbled together in a collection. The overall theme of the book is judgmental destruction and a confident and hopeful restoration of the nation after the period of the exile. It is the prophetic book most cited in the New Testament.

This opening chapter is part of the prologue to the overall book. The southern kingdom of Judah is chastised for her sinfulness. God calls the nation a "sinful nation, an evil people, and corrupt children" (v. 4). Isaiah offers the hope, however, that God will smelt away the dross of Judah's iniquity and restore her once again after a period of judgment.

Application

Our focus verse speaks of the hope of Judah. God longs for the moment when the nation will repent and seek righteousness once again. God promises to cleanse them of their sins, making scarlet sins white as snow. The crimson stains will become as wool. As I read these verses, I am reminded of God's ability to deal completely, powerfully, and historically with our sins. God will remove the darkest stain, redeem the broken life, and forget our insolence and mistakes. God hates the distance in relationship that sin creates. God longs to forgive, heal, and restore what has been marred. There is great joy in the knowledge that God is not a "one and done" type of Father. God grieves our sin yet loves us still. We are not cast aside nor viewed as "damaged goods." Instead, God claims each of us as a beloved child, cleans the stain of our iniquity, soothes the wounds of our scarred lives, and embraces us with joy. We do not have to live another moment under the shadow of guilt or the oppression of shame. God has offered grace that is sufficient to cover even our darkest transgressions. By God's love expressed through Christ, we are cleansed, forgiven, and healed.

Prayer

Father, remove our sins and make us new again...even this day. Amen.

Day 681 — Isaiah 2: A Loss of Pride

> "Human pride will be brought down, and human arrogance will be humbled. Only the Lord will be exalted on that day of judgment."
> Isaiah 2:11 (NLT)

Observation

This chapter begins the careful threading of a thought that will weave throughout much of the book. Isaiah prophesies consistently about the inevitability of God's coming Kingdom and the powerful day of judgment that will also occur. The pride of humanity will be destroyed, and the sovereignty and majesty of God will be exalted. Verses 1-5 speak of the elevation in Jerusalem's prominence. In the last days, the "mountain of God's house" will be the highest and most important place in the world. (In the culture of that time, the mountains were seen as the junction between heaven and earth. It makes sense, therefore, that on the day of God's judgment this spot becomes the most important place where heaven and earth meet.) On the day of judgment, nations will fully recognize God as the Lord who will judge the wicked and bring peace to the world. After a condemnation of human pride (vv. 6-11), the final verses tell of the prominent symbols of power and security that will be displaced when God's Kingdom comes in its fullness. The great cedars of Lebanon, the oaks of Bashan, the lofty mountains, the high hills, the fortified walls, the tall towers, and even the impressive ships will all be brought down. God's power will be displayed.

Application

Any fan of Southeastern Conference Football knows well the dangers of trash talk. It is a dangerous endeavor to talk "smack" before a big game. Bold predictions of a win can come back to haunt the fan whose team ends up stumbling. It's best to tread lightly and do your talking after the game. After all, who wants to be humbled by some erroneous boast that comes back to bite them?

Pride is a dangerous foe that all of us must battle. We take pride in things like our intellect, our wealth, our status, and our accomplishments. Sometimes we tend to forget that this is not our world to control; it is God's. Our pride can push us to depend more on ourselves and our savvy than on our God. Isaiah desperately tried to warn the people of the "overstep" pride was creating in their relationship with God. Their self-created idols had turned their hearts away from God, and judgment was coming. Whenever we substitute human pride for God dependency, surely a day of reckoning is about to unfold. We need the disciplines of confession and repentance. Each day, we need to acknowledge our sinful pride as we take definitive and careful steps to ensure that God is the only one who remains on the throne of our lives.

Prayer

Father, may you alone be exalted in our lives this day. Amen.

Day 682 — Isaiah 3: When All Is Lost...

> "The Lord, the Lord of Heaven's Armies, will take away from Jerusalem and Judah everything they depend on: every bit of bread and every drop of water." Isaiah 3:1 (NLT)

Observation
This chapter opens with a continuation of Isaiah's description of God's judgment on Judah and Jerusalem. Again, the key theme is human pride. God will strip away everything the city depends on—food, water, soldiers, heroes, prophets, and leaders. The nation will fall into disarray under the authority of poor leaders and rulers. The wicked will surely taste the fruit of their rebellion, while the righteous will know the fruit of their obedience. In verses 16-23, Isaiah includes a word of judgment on the women of Jerusalem and then on the city itself. The women of the city will discover a complete reversal of fortunes. All that has made them beautiful will be stripped away: earrings, bracelets, veils, perfume, etc. When all the men are killed in battle, the women will be left defenseless without husbands. Similarly, the beautiful city of Jerusalem will be stripped of her beauty and resources when God's judgment falls upon her.

Application
Sometimes all that we stand for, trust in, and anchor our hope on gets stripped away. Consider a dangerous wildfire that destroys homes, cars, and even human lives, leaving nothing in its wake. Or think of a tornado or hurricane that blasts across a region. Total destruction is the result, and all is swept away. People are suddenly left without shelter, without food, without work, and even without hope. Sometimes the devastation takes a different form, such as when divorce severs a family, when illness overtakes a life, or when job loss threatens stability. What happens when all seems lost?

In such moments, people are forced to do a little "asset mapping." Rather than dwell on what is gone, they must think in terms of what is left, the real things…the important things…the lasting things. Things like the love of family, the support of lifelong friendships, the presence, protection, and provision of God. If we have built our lives on the shifting sands of fortune, wealth, health, and self-sufficiency, then all can be lost in a moment. But if our lives are anchored to the solid rock of our faith in God's unrelenting love for us and constant vigil over us, then the storms become survivable. My pastor friend says, "Either we are heading into a storm, living in the midst of a storm, or walking out of a storm." He's probably right. Life presents a number of constant challenges. What holds us secure in such moments is the hope that is forever ours when Christ is Lord.

Prayer
Father, hold us close, secure, and safe…even this day. Amen.

Day 683 — Isaiah 4: Power Wash

> "The Lord will wash the filth from beautiful Zion and cleanse Jerusalem of its bloodstains with the hot breath of fiery judgment." Isaiah 4:4 (NLT)

Observation
The opening verse of Isaiah 4 finishes the thought at the end of chapter 3, where we learn that all the city's men will die in bloody battles and fierce fights. This paucity of men creates a problem for the women who remain. Isaiah writes that seven women will fight for every one man. These women will promise to bring food and clothing to the marriage; typically, the husband provided such things. The point is that these women longed to legitimize their position in society, and so they did whatever was needed to ensure a new marriage. The remainder of this short chapter reveals God's promise of restoration. God will not abandon the people. The remnant of Israel will be blessed. Punishment will turn to grace. God promises protection and presence.

Application
About once a year, I tackle the job of power-washing my front sidewalk. The "before and after" picture is always remarkable. Over the course of the year, the sidewalk dulls with dirt and grime, and when the water blasts it away, the result is a clean, pristine walkway that looks entirely different.

Isaiah writes that "The Lord will wash the filth from beautiful Zion...." He is referring to the Day of Judgment when the dirt and grime of sinful disobedience will be blasted away from God's chosen city and its residents. Notice that God is the one who will cleanse the city. Also notice that Jerusalem is still described as being "beautiful." The city is beautiful to God even beneath a veneer of filth. God will wash away the impurities and restore the city to pristine glory. Our lives are no different. Though we have marred the image of God with layer upon layer of sinful rebellion, God sees through the filth and declares that we are both beautiful and redeemable. God, through the provision of Christ's atoning death, will wash away our guilty stains and remove every dark spot. We will be restored, forgiven, and made new. We will once again become a glorious dwelling place for God's Spirit to reside.

On the days when I power-wash the walkway, it takes a lot of effort, toil, and sweat. There is nothing easy about it. And lest we slip into a false mentality that grace is easy for God to extend, let us remember that our cleansing is only made possible by the sacrifice of God's Son. There is nothing easy about it. God is compeled by unrelenting love for us to do whatever it takes to see the beautiful person emerge once again.

Prayer
Father, thank you for loving us enough to cleanse us and reclaim us. Amen.

Day 684   Isaiah 5: Baggage

> "What sorrow for those who drag their sins behind them with ropes made of lies, who drag wickedness behind them like a cart!" Isaiah 5:18 (NLT)

Observation
This chapter is sometimes referred to as "The Song of the Vineyard." It contains Isaiah's prophecy concerning the judgment and punishment of Israel and the strained relationship between God and the people. Verses 1-7 tell a parable of a vineyard in which God is the vinedresser and the people of Israel are the vineyard. The vinedresser cared for the vineyard, giving it everything it needed to grow and prosper, and yet it failed to produce good fruit. The "hoped-for" justice and righteousness never came about. Verses 8-23 describe six woes against the people of Judah, especially directed towards those who greedily consumed wealth and power. The word "woe" literally means "how sad for you." The six woes include pronouncements against the nation's greed, drunkenness, blasphemy, perversion of justice, arrogance, and corruption. The people became "heroes at drinking wine but failures at justice." They fully rejected God's wisdom and law. As a part of God's judgment, the surrounding nations would come quickly and powerfully to overrun the land.

Application
Isaiah describes the people of Israel "dragging their sins behind them with ropes made of lies." This is a keen insight into the way most of us deal with our sinfulness. Whenever we sin, our first impulse is rarely confession. In fact, until someone calls us on our sinfulness, we tend to move ahead as though nothing evil or wrong has taken place. But as our sins become exposed, we usually try to cover them up rather than confess them. We create a lie to present a false front of innocence. To perpetuate the lie, we tell a second lie and then a third. We sometimes think that we can outrun our sins if we tell enough lies to cover our tracks. We end up building a house of cards that God's scrutiny will quickly blow down. Doesn't it make better sense to practice honesty rather than deceit? What if, when we sin, we quickly begin the process of confession and of seeking forgiveness? What if we learned to say, "I was wrong and I am sorry," rather than pushing forward with layers of deception? The only people we really deceive with our lies is ourselves. God will not be mocked or fooled by our attempts at deceit. God stands ready to offer forgiveness and grace to our honest confessions and also allows us to bear the consequences of our actions if we choose the road of deception. Confession is the first step in restoration and healing. Practice it well.

Prayer
Father, forgive our arrogance that fails to make us confessional about our sins. Amen.

Day 685 — Isaiah 6: The Willingness to Serve

> "Then I heard the Lord asking, 'Whom should I send as a messenger to this people? Who will go for us?' I said, 'Here I am. Send me.'"
> Isaiah 6:8 (NLT)

Observation

As one of the more familiar chapters in Isaiah, chapter 6 describes the prophet's call to ministry. Because of Israel's sin, God sent this prophet to proclaim judgment and restoration. This passage includes a historical reference. Isaiah mentions that his "cleansing and calling" happened the year that King Uzziah died, approximately 740 BC. In his vision, Isaiah sees not only God but also seraphim or angels surrounding God's throne. They each have six wings, two of which cover their faces and two of which cover their feet. They cannot be fully exposed in God's holy presence. God is described with the words, "Holy, Holy, Holy." This triple phrasing underscores the depth of God's holiness. In every way, God is distinct and set apart from all that God rules. Isaiah recognizes his own sinfulness in the presence of God. To make him worthy for worship and service, one of the seraphim touches his mouth with a burning coal to cleanse his words and remove his sins. The passage closes with a declaration of the inevitability of God's judgment, as Isaiah laments the fallen state of Israel.

Application

With perhaps his most memorable words, Isaiah says in response to God's call for his life, "Here I am. Send me." It's no small thing to be called by God for a specific task. And it's no small commitment to say "yes" to such a task. In our willingness to surrender our lives completely to God's purpose and plan, we become the tools God uses. For most of us, the difficulty lies not in discerning God's call—God has many ways to get our attention and point us in a certain direction—but in our willingness to chase after this call with reckless abandonment. When we offer ourselves without reservation, without reluctance, and without personal regard, the wonder of a God-led life begins to unfold before us. The thrill and joy of being in the center of God's will awaits us all as we offer ourselves in service.

What holds you back this day? What keeps you from saying yes to God? Your reasons for not responding are likely bound up in fear, selfishness, distraction, or laziness. God is greater than any of those excuses, and if you are willing to jump into the flow of God's work, you will discover joy, peace, and assurance like you have never known. So say "yes." Go on the mission trip. Join the small group. Volunteer to serve at the nonprofit. Make that phone call or that visit. Say yes and see where the journey leads.

Prayer

On this very day, may we clearly see your plan and respond with a willing heart. Amen.

Day 686 — Isaiah 7: Sovereignty vs. Scarcity

> "But this is what the Sovereign Lord says: 'This invasion will never happen; it will never take place.'" Isaiah 7:7 (NLT)

Observation
Chapters 1-6 serve as an extended introduction to Isaiah, including Isaiah's call to prophetic ministry. Now, chapter 7 begins the main body of the book. As the narrative opens, chapters 7-12 tell of King Ahaz of Judah and his unwillingness to accept a sign from the Lord indicating God's protection. Oracles of judgment will follow his rejection of God's offer of a sign. Chapters 36-39 tell the story of King Hezekiah who chooses to trust in the Lord. Oracles of blessing will follow his story. More specific to chapter 7, the concept of a messianic sign is introduced. A child will be born to a virgin, and his name shall become Immanuel. Three interpretations have been offered in regard to Isaiah 7:1-16. One interpretation declares that these verses are a direct prediction of Mary's role and the coming of Christ. A second interpretation declares that the reference is purely historical, describing a child born to a "young maiden" and not a "virgin" in the eighth century BC. The third interpretation describes a dual fulfillment of prophecy that blends the first two. The narrative of Isaiah mentions the threat of an assault against Judah (the southern kingdom) made by an alliance of the king of Israel (the northern kingdom) and the king of Syria, who want to overthrow King Ahaz. Isaiah correctly and precisely predicts the downfall of the northern kingdom in 722 BC to the Assyrians.

Application
As context for our focus verse, Ahaz feared the invasion of an alliance between the northern kingdom of Israel and the nation of Syria. These two nations had conspired against King Ahaz and the people of Judah, including those living in Jerusalem. Speaking clearly through the mouth of the prophet, God told Ahaz that this invasion would never happen. As I read this passage, I am reminded of the constant battle within each of us between our fear of enemies and the promise of God's protection. We feel the struggle between God's sovereignty and the scarcity of our courage. If we would trust in the promises, nature, patterns, and presence of Almighty God, surely our fears and worries would flee from our hearts. How often have we worried about an invasion that never takes place? How often have we spent endless nights in worry, only to discover that God's presence continually defeats the toothless foe of fear and anxiety? Sometimes we need to be reminded that God is greater than the worst of our enemies, and God's peace is more powerful than the armies of worry that long to invade our souls.

Prayer
Father God, may we rest securely this day in the protection of your presence. Amen.

Day 687 — Isaiah 8: Guarding the Treasure

> "Preserve the teaching of God; entrust his instructions to those who follow me." Isaiah 8:16 (NLT)

Observation
As chapter 8 begins, Isaiah correctly predicts the Assyrian destruction of Damascus and Samaria. In just two years, the nations will be destroyed, and the riches of the nations will be carried away. He then focuses his prophecy on the destruction of Judah. Assyria will flood the land as a mighty river like the Euphrates. Because Judah has rejected the protection of God, soon everything will be laid waste. And Isaiah offers a hint that even in the midst of judgment, God will not completely forget or abandon the people. In verses 11-18, God encourages Isaiah to remain separated from the rest of Judah. He is not to get distracted by their conspiracy theories. In fact, according to our focus verse, God calls Isaiah to "bind up" or "preserve" God's instructions and teachings and entrust them to faithful believers who remain obedient to God.

Application
I recently saw a list of "Great Truths about Life that Little Children Have Learned." The list contained several great truths: "No matter how hard you try, you cannot baptize a cat." "When your mom is mad at your dad, don't let her brush your hair." "Never ask your three-year-old brother to hold an egg." "You can't trust a dog to watch your food for you." Most of us will appreciate these truths.

Notice what Isaiah teaches. God told him to preserve God's important teachings, and part of that instruction included sharing the teachings with people who remained faithful. We have the same commission from God. As believers, we are called to "handle accurately the word of God." We are to defend its veracity, never water down its authority, and carefully teach it to the next generation. We must ensure that the gospel message goes forth from age to age as we painstakingly, carefully, and consistently teach those who come after us about the things of God. It seems to me that earlier generations in our modern era took that responsibility more seriously than many do today. For example, I was taught the great Bible stories. I was challenged to memorize scripture. I was taken to church each week to hear the word of God proclaimed. Recent statistics show a sharp decline in church attendance, a staggering biblical illiteracy, and a terrible ambivalence for the authority of scripture among each emerging generation. We cannot and must not shirk our responsibility. We must lead by example, teach with patience, and love the Lord with all our hearts.

Prayer
Father, may we be committed to the task of entrusting your word to our children. Amen.

Day 688 — Isaiah 9: Freedom from Slavery

> "For you will break the yoke of their slavery and lift the heavy burden from their shoulders. You will break the oppressor's rod, just as you did when you destroyed the army of Midian." Isaiah 9:4 (NLT)

Observation

Isaiah 9 contains familiar verses that describe the promise of the coming Messiah. Phrases like "For unto us a child is born; those who walk in darkness will see a great light; he shall be called Wonderful Counselor, Mighty God, Everlasting Father, Prince of Peace" all appear in this chapter. These words indicate fulfillment of the promises of the Davidic covenant in 2 Samuel 7:12-16. The first five verses proclaim hope to those who have lived in accordance with the word of God, assuring them that they will find comfort. The "humbled" lands of Zebulun and Naphtali will be glorified. Using the imagery of light and darkness, Isaiah speaks of the salvation that will come to Israel. God will break the yoke of slavery caused by the invading armies. Verses 8-21 are an oracle of judgment. First, God will judge Israel for her lack of fidelity to God. And even though God will use Assyria as the instrument of judgment on Israel, Assyria will remain arrogant in her victories and fail to acknowledge the work of Almighty God. Thus, God will judge Assyria as well.

Application

While most of my readers will never experience the oppression of physical slavery, surely you will experience other various forms of slavery. Financial debt is one example. If we are not careful, it is easy to fall into the trap of living beyond our means. Suddenly we find ourselves spiraling into oppressive debt that consumes both our paycheck and our peace of mind. Another example is slavery to medicine. Sometimes our bodies don't function well and we become slaves to daily medications. Others are slaves to their schedules—meetings, events, and obligations. Calendars fill quickly as activities pile up. It seems that every moment is taken, and soon we have no time left for personal enjoyment or solitude.

Regrettably, we will fight some of these foes for years…maybe for a lifetime. But one enemy that seeks to enslave us can be completely defeated: the enemy of guilt and shame. Repeatedly, the scriptures remind us of God's grace and willingness to forgive our sins and wipe away even the memory of our transgressions. We have been set free forever!

Prayer

Father, thank you for the saving grace and freeing love of our Messiah. Amen.

Day 689 — Isaiah 10: Where Do You Place Your Trust?

> "In that day the remnant left in Israel, the survivors in the house of Jacob, will no longer depend on allies who seek to destroy them. But they will faithfully trust the Lord, the Holy One of Israel." Isaiah 10:20 (NLT)

Observation

Isaiah 10 speaks again of God's judgment on Israel and Assyria. Verses 1-4 reveal part of the reason for the judgment of Israel. The land is filled with unjust judges who have exploited and abused widows and orphans. These wicked judges will ultimately be among the captives from battle or will be slain in the destruction. Verses 5-34 concern the judgment of Assyria. Even while using this nation to judge Israel, God will also bring judgment upon the rulers and armies of Assyria. God will use them for a specific purpose, but they will overstep their role and suffer God's retribution. They will claim victory by their own power and wisdom. In failing to understand that their power comes not from themselves but from God, they will suffer. The chapter ends on a hopeful note, declaring that God will preserve a remnant of the people. God's purpose was never to annihilate them. God willed to discipline Israel, not destroy her completely.

Application

A remnant is a "small remaining quantity of something." I know people who go to the fabric store to buy "remnants." They put these small, leftover pieces together in a beautiful design. I know others who go to carpet outlets to buy carpet remnants for a kid's room or another small area in their home. While some may think remnants are just scraps to be discarded, others see great worth and gladly take them. In his prophecy, Isaiah speaks of the remnant of God's people. Once the destruction passes, God promises to preserve a small group of people who have trusted in God. Through this remnant, God will rebuild the nation and fulfill promises to Abraham and David. This faithful group will know that their survival depends not on their own strength or wisdom but upon God alone.

Trusting in God is not always easy. It can be difficult because it requires us to relinquish self-trust. It means yielding ourselves to God's way, will, and direction for our lives. We must trust when the destination seems uncertain. We must trust when the demands are arduous. We must trust when the resources seem too meager. We must trust when all the world tries to lead us in another direction. Notice in the biblical record that those who have final victory have placed their allegiance and trust in God alone. We can place our trust in many things or in many people, but only the Sovereign God can save us.

Prayer

Father, even this day, when choices come, may we place our trust in you alone. Amen.

Day 690 — Isaiah 11: Renewal

> "Out of the stump of David's family will grow a shoot—yes, a new Branch bearing fruit from the old root." Isaiah 11:1 (NLT)

Observation
In these early chapters of Isaiah, the prophet reveals a cycle of judgment followed by hope. Chapter 10 described God's judgment of both Israel and Assyria. Chapter 11, however, is alive with the hope brought about by the coming Messiah. Part of the imagery from chapter 10 spoke of a mighty forest, like the cedars of Lebanon, being cut off (vv. 33-34). Isaiah now continues that imagery by describing a "shoot" that will emerge from the stump of Jesse. A renewal is coming; the story of God's involvement with God's people is not ending. Isaiah speaks of Jesse here rather than his more famous son King David, probably to emphasize the humble ancestry of the Messiah. He does mention that the Spirit of the Lord will be upon this coming one. The Savior will have supernatural abilities, and his rule will be divinely ordained. The Messiah will have wisdom and understanding, counsel and strength, and knowledge and fear of the Lord. The word "fear" refers to a healthy and overwhelming reverence for God. This chapter closes with an idyllic picture of the reign of the Messiah where all those who were once at odds will be at peace once more. There will be harmony in the eternal reign of the Messiah.

Application
Years ago, I lived with my family on the outskirts of Birmingham, Alabama. A summer storm struck a large tree on the corner of our property, splitting it right down the middle. Because the dying limbs posed a threat to my back fence and roadway, I took a chainsaw and went to work. When I finished, all that remained was a short stump. By the next spring, several shoots of new life had begun to emerge from the stump. I recently visited our former home after a twenty-year absence. I noticed that a tall and towering tree, full of leaves and life, had grown from those early shoots that had emerged from the stump. I was reminded of Isaiah's message of renewal that can emerge even from the worst days.

Life has a way of sending a lot of storms into our lives. Even today, some of you may feel defeated, knocked down by life, maybe even destroyed. All that is left of your life is a ragged stump. But by the grace of God and through the love of Christ, renewal is possible. We rise. We live. We move ahead. God is never "finished" with any of His children. In our greatest defeats, lowest days, and fiercest storms, God is present. The Spirit remains alive within us and will call us to life over and over again.

Prayer
Father, may we know this day the renewing, life-giving power of our Savior. Amen.

Day 691 — Isaiah 12: Conversations and Connections

> "With joy you will drink deeply from the fountain of salvation!"
> Isaiah 12:3 (NLT)

Observation

The past few chapters have cycled between the pronouncement of God's judgment and the promise of restoration and salvation through the Messiah. Now Isaiah completes the section with a song of praise to God. This short chapter acknowledges that God will relinquish anger and offer the people the hope and comfort of salvific work. God is the only source of salvation. People should no longer look to other nations or political alliances to bring protection or security. God alone will restore and protect the people. In the final verses, they are admonished to tell the nations of God's mighty acts. God's praises are to be made known throughout the world.

Application

If you follow the same routine each day for years, you develop some relationships along the way. For nearly two decades now, my morning routine has included stopping at the local gas station to get a drink on the way to work. I'm not a coffee drinker; I get my caffeine from an ice-cold soda. Every morning I stop at the same store and speak to the same employees. Some have worked there for years and are now friends of mine. We exchange stories and concerns and show the latest pictures of our grandkids. We have even exchanged gifts through the years. At some point, I started getting my morning drink for free. When the line is long at the register, they just wave me out the door and yell, "See you tomorrow!"

There is a deep fountain at this store, and I enjoy drinking from it. I'm not describing the endless fountain of Mt. Dew that I enjoy each day (though the free drink is nice!) but the endless fountain of friendship that flows when we dare to intertwine our lives with others. That fountain springs forth in a lot of places. Some people at work refresh my soul and encourage my spirit each day. I have lifelong friends who text or call nearly every week. Familiar faces in all kinds of places offer me joy and happiness whenever I encounter them. I hope you have such a fountain of joy in your life. I hope you have established relationships that feed, nurture, and encourage you. If you don't have much of a fountain, you can take some steps to create one. Get the know the lady at the gas station. Speak to the produce man at the grocery store each week. Take a moment to step into your coworker's office and ask about their day. Talk to your mail delivery person. You don't always have to create deep, lifelong relationships; simple conversations and connections can help to get you through the day. Drink from that fountain, and share it with others.

Prayer

Father, with joy, may we drink from the fountain of our daily connections. Amen.

Day 692 — Isaiah 13: When Evil Is Defeated

> "Hear the noise on the mountains! Listen, as the vast armies march! It is the noise and shouting of many nations. The Lord of Heaven's Armies has called this army together." Isaiah 13:4 (NLT)

Observation

Chapters 13-35 of Isaiah pronounce oracles of judgment against the nations. Anyone who has either taunted or turned away from Almighty God will face consequences on the Day of Judgment. Part of this opening oracle may have served as a reminder to the people not to form alliances with evil and pagan nations. Chapter 13 speaks of the judgment to fall upon Babylon. Babylon came to prominence and power on the geo-political stage after the rise and fall of the Assyrian Empire. The judgment against her will be powerful and swift. According to verse 17, God will appoint the Medes as attackers. Unaffected by bribes, the Medes were ruthless in warfare. The closing verses of the chapter state that the fate of Babylon will be like that of Sodom and Gomorrah. The devastation will be so great that only the wild animals will inhabit the ruins of the city. (As a historical note, Cyrus of the Medes invaded and destroyed Babylon in 538 BC.)

Application

Years ago, I lived on the island of Oahu while serving as youth minister at a Baptist church in Mililani Town, Hawaii. The community of Mililani Town is located in the center of Oahu, just east of the mountain range that runs north to south. A number of people in our congregation were native Hawaiians who had lived in the area for many years. There is a pass in the mountain range named the KoleKole pass. Through that "cut" in the mountain range, the Japanese "Zeroes" slipped into the interior of the island and headed south to begin their destruction of Pearl Harbor. I was fascinated to listen to the stories of one old woman, a child at the time, who stated that she was awakened the morning of December 7, 1941, by the sounds of planes flying low overhead. She ran out to her front yard and watched as wave after wave of planes flew towards Pearl Harbor. With shock and horror, she watched the ships explode as the bombs struck their targets. She said it was a sound that she would never forget.

Isaiah challenges his people to listen to the sound of the vast Armies of God as they march across the mountains, signaling the end of evil and the triumph of righteousness. "Hear the noise on the mountains!" I hope none of us ever have to hear the sound of a great army invading our land, but I hope that all of us will listen for the sound of God on the march. The strongholds of evil will one day fall, and the people of God will rejoice with the sound.

Prayer

Father, may we hear, even this day, the faint whisper of your approaching victory. Amen.

Day 693 — Isaiah 14: The Testimony of the Trees

> "Even the trees of the forest— the cypress trees and the cedars of Lebanon— sing out this joyous song: 'Since you have been cut down, no one will come now to cut us down!'" Isaiah 14:8 (NLT)

Observation
As the oracle of judgment continues concerning Babylon, Isaiah interjects a brief word of encouragement reminding Israel of God's loyalty to them. The nation will one day taunt her oppressors. Verses 5-23 contain a particular word of judgment directed towards the king of Babylon. Rather than ascending to the heights of the gods, he will descend into Sheol, the place of the dead. All the rulers of Babylon will be humbled. Those who once mastered the earth will now be erased as they are buried in it. The final verses of Isaiah 14 offer a word of judgment against the Philistines. They are warned that the Assyrians will attack with speed and vengeance. True to this prophecy, King Sargon II of Assyria conquered the Philistines in 711 BC.

Application
The older I become, the more aware I am of trees. I can't explain it, but somewhere along the journey of growing older, a person learns the various types of trees. I can look at the bark or the shape or color of leaves and identify most any type of tree. I don't know where I obtained such knowledge; it just seemed to happen as I aged. And trees can tell a story. Those that stand tall and strong bear testimony of storms once weathered or fire that sought to destroy. When a tree is cut down, the stump tells its age and can even indicate the time frame of a great blight or storm that once attacked the tree. At my last pastorate, we had to get a tree removed from the church property. I counted the rings, and it was more than 250 years old! It could tell the story of the Civil War that was fought all around it, the farmers who once planted near it, and the children who once played beneath it.

In his prophecy, Isaiah insists that the trees of Israel, the cypress trees of the coastal plain, or the cedars of Lebanon will one day sing out the song of Israel's deliverance. At that time, when the warring nations are destroyed, there will be no one left to cut down the mighty trees. They will stand as a testimony to the greatness of God. Maybe we should listen to the trees, for they have a testimony to share. In their strength, we understand the power of God. In their shedding, colorization, and regrowth, we understand the creativity of God. In their roots that grip the soil, we remember God's stubborn love for us. In their towering branches that reach to the sky, we are reminded to extend our hands in endless praise of our Creator. All the earth should sing God's praises, even the trees.

Prayer
Father, thank you for the beauty of the trees that offer their silent testimony. Amen.

Day 694 — Isaiah 15: What We Choose to Carry

> "The people grab their possessions and carry them across the Ravine of Willows." Isaiah 15:7 (NLT)

Observation

Isaiah 15 contains the prophet's words of judgment concerning the nation of Moab. (This pronouncement of judgment extends into the next chapter.) The destruction will come quickly and with complete devastation. The land will be filled with mourners; every house will know grief and sorrow. Verses 5-9 offer an image of the people as they attempt to flee from the coming destruction. They quickly gather their possessions and scramble for a place of refuge, but it will elude them. The waters of the land, including various oases, will dry up. Both the northern and southern portions of the nation will endure the crisis. Even if people escape temporarily or remain in the land, God's wrath with hunt them down like a lion seeking prey. (The term "Ravine of Willows" in our focus verse is only referenced in this single place in scripture. It most likely refers to one of the borders of Moab.)

Application

Imagine fleeing from your homeland and attempting to find asylum in a different country, as many have been doing around the world. What if you could only take with you what you could literally carry on your back? Surely the scene at the United States' southern border must be heart-rending at times as families struggle to retain just a few meager possessions. What if you were forced to make such a decision? What would you carry if you "grabbed your possessions and carried them across the Ravine of Willows"? Some clothes, some cash, maybe a cell phone or a laptop, perhaps a few snacks, extra shoes or socks, sacred books and family photographs? It would be a difficult decision to make, and I hope none of us will ever face such a choice.

But let's turn our thoughts in a slightly different direction. What if the ravine we cross was not a physical location but a symbol of new beginnings? What if we think in terms of what we choose to carry forward into a new day, a new year, or a new relationship? Is there baggage we would leave behind? Are there suitcases of injury, regret, and pain that we could leave, or would we lug them into our future? The problem for many of us is that we haven't learned how to deal with guilt, shame, regrets, bitterness, or anger. We tend to carry such things inside of us into each new experience, relationship, or moment. If we carry these long enough, our hearts and minds will become jaded. When speaking about the oppressive weight of sin, Jesus said, "If the Son sets you free, you shall be free indeed!" (John 8:36). You don't have to carry unnecessary baggage any longer.

Prayer

Father, give us freedom from our past mistakes and crippling defeats. Amen.

Day 695 — Isaiah 16: It's Not Over...

> "A throne will even be established in lovingkindness, and a judge will sit on it in faithfulness in the tent of David; moreover, he will seek justice and be prompt in righteousness." Isaiah 16:5 (NLT)

Observation
Isaiah 16 continues the oracle of judgment against Moab. Because of the coming destruction, Moab seeks protection from Judah. Like fleeing birds that have no nests, the Moabites come to the borders of Judah begging for support. They hope to be covered by Judah's "shadow of protection" (v. 3). Verses 6-12 outline the extent of Moab's sinful pride. They will lose the security that has come from abundance and excess. They will offer ineffective prayers to their false gods. The glory of the nation will disappear, and the population will be decimated. The loss of prosperity and influence will be so great that even the prophet himself is brought to tears as he pronounces this oracle of judgment. The destruction was eventually fulfilled as predicted in the final verse. In 701 BC, Assyrian King Sennacherib completely destroyed Moab.

Application
Hope is a life-sustaining, life-giving force. It drives us ever onward in our noble quests. Sometimes, when I am switching through TV channels, I come across the film Apollo 13, starring Tom Hanks. I've watched it a dozen or more times, but each time it flashes by, I am drawn in and have to watch a little of it. Based on the true story, an onboard explosion threatens the life of the Apollo astronauts just hours into their mission. The entire mission to the moon has to be scrubbed and the new mission becomes bringing the three astronauts home safely. Against all odds, they survive and return to earth. Perhaps more than anything else, the hope of a possible safe return drives the NASA engineers and scientists to work.

In our focus verse, Isaiah speaks of the Savior's throne that will be established with justice and righteousness. He points, in hope, to a better day. The gospel is always forward looking. It gathers up the despair, pain, and fear of the present day and pronounces the hope that a better day is coming. The coming of the Savior reminds us that darkness will never triumph, evil will not win, and wickedness will never conquer. We need to be reminded of that good word of the gospel. No matter how desperate, how defeating, how lonely, or how dark your world may seem at this moment, have hope; this is not over. God has proclaimed through the prophets and enacted through the Son, Jesus Christ, a message of victory. We can survive the dark and scary moments knowing that God's Kingdom is indeed coming soon.

Prayer
Father, give us hope and encouragement as we live each day. Amen.

Day 696 — Isaiah 17: Handmade Gods

> "In that day man will have regard for his Maker and his eyes will look to the Holy One of Israel. He will not have regard for the altars, the work of his hands, Nor will he look to that which his fingers have made, Even the Asherim and incense stands." Isaiah 17:7-8 (NKJV)

Observation
Most of this chapter is devoted to words of prophecy against Damascus. These words of judgment are also directed towards the northern kingdom of Israel because of an alliance struck between her and Syria. The key issue raised by the prophetic words of judgment was the willingness of the nations to trust pagan deities and worship at their altars. Such practices were idolatrous before the Lord and ignored the Lord's sovereignty. True to Isaiah's prophecy, Damascus was swiftly destroyed by King Tiglath-Pileser III of Assyria. The final verses of Isaiah 17 speak about the threats made to Judah by the "roaring and raging" of the nations. These threats would prove no match for the Lord. Those who fought against Judah would eventually be subdued by God's sudden wrath.

Application
I wish I were better at making stuff. I envy people with well-equipped workshops where they can make tables and chairs and other kinds of furniture. I've made a few things—some Adirondack chairs and a few other pieces for the back deck—but that's about it. I don't have the tools or the experience to make much else with my hands. I once tried woodcarving, but too many finger cuts brought that career to an end… although a local, small-town paper once did a feature article on my wood carvings. (Don't even get my wife started on that story!) But what about making hand-created gods? I'm better at that, and you are too. All of us tend to create our own gods to worship. Maybe it's the god of our possessions. We desire the latest and greatest and spend too much on our worship of such things. But no matter how shiny or bright the latest gadget appears, our interest soon wanes as we look to the next big thing. Some of us worship our work. We sacrifice our health, our sanity, and even moments with our families for the sake of worshipping an unrelenting schedule or an impossible drive for success. We also worship the god of social media. We worship our looks. I know people who are absolutely chained to the local gym in an attempt to look fit and trim. Some worship alcohol. Others worship cars and houses. Some can't seem to stop paying for the next upgrade to their already lavish homes. How many gods can you create? And what lasting impact will they have on your life? None. It's better to worship the One, True, Eternal God.

Prayer
Father, forgive our foolish worship of things that don't matter. Amen.

Day 697 — Isaiah 18: Catching the Wind

> "Listen, Ethiopia—land of fluttering sails that lies at the headwaters of the Nile, that sends ambassadors in swift boats down the river."
> Isaiah 18:1-2a (NLT)

Observation

Isaiah 18 contains words directed towards Ethiopia. At that time, Ethiopia was a powerful nation with an impressive military record. In the Hebrew text, the words translated here as the "land of fluttering sails" literally mean "land of whirring wings." The interpretation is difficult. Most likely, Isaiah is referring to the speedy ships that sailed up and down the rivers of the nation. They skipped along the water's surface like "winged insects." Isaiah calls for messengers to go to Ethiopia to tell them that it will be foolish to prepare for battle or to make alliances with those who might oppose Israel. Anyone who joins forces to oppose God's people will discover greater destruction in the time of God's judgment. There is a hint in these words that Ethiopia may even choose to be an ally of Israel. There seems to be a "faithful remnant" of God-followers in that nation who will one day gather in Jerusalem to join with others in the worship of Almighty God.

Application

Have you ever done any sailing? I'm not experienced at all, but I have tried it. When I was a kid growing up in First Baptist Church, Rome, Georgia, summer youth retreats took place at an old YMCA camp near Panama City, Florida. There was a small lake on the property and the camp owned both canoes and sailboats. The sailboats were small, one-person crafts. Whenever I had free time, I sailed from one end of the lake to the other. I got pretty good at learning how to catch the wind with the sail in order to direct the boat the way I wanted it to go. It was exciting to harness the wind and feel its power.

It is equally exciting to feel the wind of the Spirit blowing in one's life. The wind, breath, or Spirit of God is always moving among us. It longs to direct our path and set the course for our days. When harnessed, the Spirit can lead us into an exhilarating life, full of God's power and presence. The problem is with our sails. I'm not sure that we always hoist them in the wind of God's movement. Instead, we try to force the direction for our lives. We long to chart our own paths and make our own choices. In fact, we often fight against the wind and flow of the Spirit's direction for our lives. But what if we held up the sails of our lives and prayed to God, "Take my life, fill my sails with your Spirit, and direct me to the places you would have me to go"? Could we even imagine the exciting rush that we would experience? We would be like "winged insects" skipping along the water's surface. This day, why not let the wind of the Spirit take you where it will?

Prayer

Father, may each of us be open to the leadership of your Spirit this day. Amen.

Day 698 — Isaiah 19: The Chaos of Disunity

> "I will make Egyptian fight against Egyptian—brother against brother, neighbor against neighbor, city against city, province against province. The Egyptians will lose heart, and I will confuse their plans."
> Isaiah 19:2-3a (NLT)

Observation
Now Isaiah turns his attention to the nation of Egypt. His words of prophecy about the nation fall into two sections. All of chapter 19 is devoted to what will happen at the end of the age when God's judgment is poured out on the nation. The other section extends into the first six verses of chapter 20. It speaks of a prophecy to be fulfilled in the short term. As Isaiah speaks of the Egyptian devastation to come, he mentions that the Nile will dry up along with all the other rivers. Worthless idols will be revealed. Turmoil will ensue as brothers fight against brothers. Many will consult mediums and those who call upon the dead, but to no avail. No answers will come. Foolish leaders will have the inability to govern well. Egypt will be like a "drunk who staggers in his own vomit" (v. 14). Isaiah also speaks, however, about the day when God will be worshipped in Egypt. The people will know and worship the Lord, even in the language of the Israelites.

Application
Have you ever watched a trail of ants? From time to time, especially in the summer months, our home is visited by a bunch of black ants until we spray them into oblivion. I always try to trace the source of their trail. I want to know where they are entering the house so that I can spray effectively. But every once in a while, I disrupt their carefully choreographed trail. As soon as the unity is broken, the ants scatter in a thousand different directions.

God intends for people to dwell together, work together, worship together, and "do church" together with a unified spirit. We are better at representing God's Kingdom when we avoid adversity, pettiness, back-biting, and gossip. When we march in cadence with one another, we are able to move the mission of the church forward. But unity is not always the watchword of the local church. Sometimes factions arise. Sometimes when people don't get their way, they begin sowing seeds of discord. Sometimes it's all about the money. Sometimes it's all about who holds power in the church. Sometimes it's about belittling the staff or starting rumors concerning a fellow church member. As soon as the unity is broken, the church loses its footing and God's Kingdom suffers. You have a role to play as a church member. Your task is to preserve unity with all your might. It means learning to devalue your own opinions, forgiving those who wrong you, stopping rumors in their tracks, and praying for everyone and complaining about no one.

Prayer
God, may we be good and faithful church members. Amen.

Day 699 — Isaiah 20: If God Commands...

> "The Lord told Isaiah son of Amoz, 'Take off the burlap you have been wearing, and remove your sandals.' Isaiah did as he was told and walked around naked and barefoot." Isaiah 20:2 (NLT)

Observation
In chapter 20, the narrative suddenly shifts away from prophetic words about things that will come "at the end of days," when all will acknowledge and worship the One True God of the Universe, and towards a more focused prophecy about a soon-to-come fulfillment of judgment against Egypt. Prophets often acted out or publicly demonstrated their words of prophecy. In one of the most dramatic displays of such actions, Isaiah strips off his clothing and walks around naked and barefoot for three years as a symbolic act of the devastation coming to the land of Egypt. Being naked and barefoot was a symbol of captivity and exile. Some scholars believe that Isaiah only stripped off his outer garment, but others argue for a more literal interpretation. Either way, the prophetic word held true as Egypt fell to the Assyrians in 711 BC. The overall theme is one of judgment because of a lack of trust in God.

Application
Sometimes God moves in a mysterious way. There are moments when God-followers are compelled to do something, say something, or believe something because of a careful and deliberate prompting of the Spirit. There are moments when God infuses a thought into the heart and mind of one of God's children, prompting that person to action. Sometimes, it is a "whisper of the Spirit," a gentle nudging, or a revelation from scripture that prompts an action. I have experienced times when I knew beyond the shadow of a doubt that God was urging me to do or say something at a key moment or opportunity. Maybe you have felt similar promptings of the Spirit.

Ponder this: What is God commanding you to do at this moment, in this particular "season" of your life? Are you willing to practice full obedience, offer full surrender, and live with an attitude of servanthood? More than likely, God is not going to ask you to strip off your clothes and walk around naked for the next three years to pronounce judgment on a nation. But God may call you to a new job, a new city, a new friendship, or a new perspective. God carefully arranges people, place, and circumstance to God's glory. There are things that God longs to accomplish through each of us. Only when we are willing to offer our full obedience to God's call—and sometimes it is a daily call—do we place ourselves in a position to speak to the world around us. There are lives and situations and ideologies that need to be changed. Are you bold enough to offer your life to get that done?

Prayer
God, let us hear your direction, and grant us the courage to respond. Amen.

Day 700 — Isaiah 21: Mindful Generosity

> "O people of Tema, bring water to these thirsty people, food to these weary refugees. They have fled from the sword, from the drawn sword, from the bent bow and the terrors of battle." Isaiah 21:14-15 (NLT)

Observation
This chapter includes oracles of judgment against Babylon, Edom, and Arabia. Verse 1 refers to Babylon as "the desert by the sea." This vague reference is likely a phrase meaning "armies that come from the desert like water from the sea," referring to the vastness of the Babylonian army. Isaiah predicts that judgment against Babylon will be harsh; the betrayer will be betrayed, and the destroyer will be destroyed. The prophet seems somewhat pained or even grieved by the vision of Babylon's destruction. Perhaps he fears the upheaval and change that will come when Israel's oppressors are themselves oppressed. It is apparent that Israel can no longer rely on Babylon's strength but must rely fully on the Lord for protection. Verses 4-12 mention both disaster and deliverance that are coming to Edom. The remaining verses speak about the judgment against Arabia. The people are directed to bring water and food to the refugees who are fleeing to their land.

Application
Isaiah offers a word to the people living in Tema. Tema was an oasis in northwest Arabia. The people were told to offer food and water to weary refugees who were fleeing from the terrors of battle. These words offer us some insight into the way God longs for people to treat refugees who come into their land. I think we often view the plight of modern-day refugees through a distorted lens. Rather than see them as oppressed people with great humanitarian needs to be met, we often see them as evildoers, exploiters, and terrorists who long to bring down the values and security of our nation. Refugees are just what the name itself implies: people seeking "refuge," a "safe place," a shelter from the storms of oppressive violence that many face. Uprooting their lives and their families, abandoning all that is familiar, is the last thing most want to do. But when the violence, terror, and oppression of their homeland becomes too great, there is no other option than to seek peace in another place. Haven't we all felt the same desires and emotions, at least on some scale? If pressures are too great at work, we seek new employment. If our children's schools seem unsafe, we explore other options. If relationships become caustic, we end them and seek healthier connections. So why do we view refugees to our land with such disdain? Those who are able to help must help. Those who are blessed must bless. Those who have been showered with endless grace must extend grace to others. Let's model both understanding and grace.

Prayer
God, burden us with the compassion to help those in need. Amen.

Day 701 — Isaiah 22: Wasted Effort

> "You survey the houses and tear some down for stone to strengthen the walls." Isaiah 22:10 (NLT)

Observation
Isaiah 22 is devoted to an oracle of judgment against Jerusalem. Verse 11 holds the key to the reason for her destruction: "But you never ask for help from the One who did all this. You never considered the One who planned this long ago." All of the city's defenses were flawed and tragically weak. The people depended on their own strength and resources rather than trusting in Almighty God. Their inappropriate reaction of non-repentance reflected disrespect for God that ultimately brought judgment. In verse 1, Jerusalem is referred to as "the valley of vision." The meaning is somewhat unclear. This is the only such reference in all of scripture. Normally, Jerusalem was referred to as a mountain, or mount, or even the hill of Zion. This reference could be to the Hinnom Valley, which is found to the south and west of the old city. It could be a reference to the Kidron Valley, which separated the city from the Mount of Olives. In addition to speaking of the destruction of both people and property, the chapter makes mention of the building of a reservoir. This refers to the well-known tunnel constructed through solid rock by King Hezekiah that linked the Gihon Spring to the Pool of Siloam.

Application
In his description of the destruction of Jerusalem, Isaiah mentions that the people even dismantled some of their homes to provide more stones in an attempt to fortify the city walls. It was a futile effort as the city soon fell to the invading forces. I wonder what we are willing to dismantle in our efforts to shore up our defenses. Many within our culture live with fear. In an attempt to offer some level of protection and peace of mind, people purchase handguns, live in gated communities, and arm their homes with alarm systems. They go to great lengths to "keep the evil out." And yet the fear remains. Like the ancient Israelites, many place their security in their own initiatives. Then the fear crops up in other areas: people try to protect their online identity, their passwords, even the ways they safeguard their wealth. But even the best-laid plans can't guard the things that matter most, like the human heart, the human will, the health of our bodies, or the salvation of our souls. At the end of the day, we remain solely dependent on the One who called us into being and who guards our coming and going each day. You have a choice to make: live in fear or live in faith. With faith placed not in our things but in our Creator, we begin to acknowledge that the intangibles that matter cannot be taken from us. Cling to faith and you will secure your life.

Prayer
Father, may we place our ultimate trust in your hands this very day. Amen.

Day 702 — Isaiah 23: The Use of Broken Tools

> "Yes, after seventy years the Lord will revive Tyre. But she will be no different than she was before. She will again be a prostitute to all kingdoms around the world. But in the end her profits will be given to the Lord. Her wealth will not be hoarded but will provide good food and fine clothing for the Lord's priests." Isaiah 23:16-17 (NLT)

Observation

In the final oracle of judgment and destruction, Isaiah turns his attention on the people of Tyre. Tyre was located on the Mediterranean shore, just north of Israel. It epitomized the arrogance and pride of the prosperous. In fact, according to verse 3, Tyre was the "marketplace of the world." Her trading commerce affected the entire Mediterranean world, especially places like Tarshish, Cyprus, and Egypt. So when Tyre fell, so did the economies of many nations. Tyre would be conquered and defeated by Assyria in 700 BC. Seventy years later, as predicted by Isaiah, she would rise from ruin and become prosperous again. God would use her economic power and strength to assist Israel in rebuilding the Temple.

Application

In my collection of tools in my garage, I have a big screwdriver—I mean really big… like more than two feet long. I happened upon it by accident. Years ago, I found it wedged between the engine and wheel well of a car I once owned. Apparently, when working on the car, some previous owner dropped the tool and never retrieved it. When I found it, most of the black plastic handle was broken off. Even though it is a "broken tool," I use it often for a distinct purpose. Whenever I am changing out the brake pads on my car, it is the perfect tool to help me push the hydraulic cylinder on the brake caliper back into place. (If I lost you in that description, just Google brake repairs and you will figure it out.) Here's the point: sometimes what is flawed or broken can be repurposed to do great and mighty things.

According to Isaiah, God was going to use the prosperity of Tyre for God's purposes. Tyre was going to aid in the rebuilding and ministry of the Temple. Something that had been corrupted by exploitation, greed, and deceit would find a place of use in God's work. God has a way of repurposing what is broken for God's glory, including people. Though we might discount our abilities to be used by God, He does not. He never looks to our past and declares us to be failures. He looks to our future and speaks of our potential. None of us get through life unscathed. We all carry around a little brokenness, a few flaws, and a backpack full of regret. And yet God continues the Kingdom-building work through people just like us. So if you are feeling a little worthless, broken, or torn, not to worry; God has big plans for your life.

Prayer

Father, mend our brokenness and use us to your glory. Amen.

Day 703 — Isaiah 24: The Abuse of Earth

> "The earth suffers for the sins of its people, for they have twisted God's instructions, violated his laws, and broken his everlasting covenant."
> Isaiah 24:5 (NLT)

Observation

Chapters 24-27 comprise a section of Isaiah sometimes referred to as "The Little Apocalypse." Judgment is pronounced on the whole earth. The perspective of the prophet changes from an immediate sense of judgment to more of a long-term prophetic word. Many of the key elements of Apocalyptic literature are contained in these chapters: things like the defeat of Leviathan, the reaction of moon and sun, and the theme of eschatological salvation. The key message to be conveyed is this: God will triumph, destruction will come to everyone who practices unrighteousness, and Israel will be restored. The people are reminded through these words, not to trust in the alliances they form with other nations, but to put their trust solely in the Lord. More specifically, this chapter speaks of the judgment of the entire earth. The use of the word "city" does not refer to a specific city or town, but rather, to the earth as a whole. Isaiah states that the earth will be emptied and looted... none will be spared. Yet the remnant of God's faithful people will worship as they witness the hand of God moving with power over the face of the earth.

Application

A word of insight from the first half of our focus verse is the phrase, "The earth suffers for the sins of its people...." We have been warned by environmentalists and scientists for years about the destructive nature of our actions in regard to the mistreatment of the planet and its natural resources. We have polluted our waterways and oceans. We have dirtied the air. We have abused and depleted many of our natural resources. We have warmed the atmosphere. In other words, we have not taken seriously the mandate to protect the planet. God created an amazing planet to sustain life and placed it in the hands of human beings to manage it carefully, till it properly, and care for it with sustainability in mind. And so the earth now suffers because of our sins of abuse, greed, selfishness, and wastefulness. Even in our politics, we sometimes choose self-interest over what's best for the earth. So what to do? I think we must learn to think globally and act locally. Recycle as often as you can. It makes a difference. Think about owning a car with better fuel efficiency, maybe even electric. Turn down the thermostat. Use food and drink containers that can be washed and reused rather than thrown into the trash. Support lawmakers who are championing renewable energy initiatives. We can make a difference. Let's live responsibly.

Prayer

Father, may we be faithful and good stewards of our planet. Amen.

Day 704 — Isaiah 25: The Victory of Hope

> "In that day the people will proclaim, 'This is our God! We trusted in him, and he saved us! This is the Lord, in whom we trusted. Let us rejoice in the salvation he brings!'" Isaiah 25:9 (NLT)

Observation

In chapter 24, the prophet Isaiah announced God's judgment of the earth. Now in chapter 25, Isaiah reports the response of God's people to the news of the impending judgment. The first response is that of grateful praise. Protection and care will characterize God's coming reign. The second response is that of triumph. God will bring comfort, will wipe away the tears of the people, will restore Israel, and will remove the reproach of the people from opposing nations. The third response is that of joy. The people will recognize the fulfillment of God's long-awaited promise of deliverance. The opposing nations will be brought low as Israel is restored.

Application

Hope brings joy to our longing and conviction about all that is to come. Hope allows us to live victoriously even in the midst of difficult times. Hope convinces us that God's promises will ring true, that God's plans will come to fruition, and that we live under God's constant watch care. We live in joy, in peace, and with a sense of victory because of our well-placed hope.

There is a vast difference between foolish hope and faithful hope. A child might foolishly wish for a present that neither Santa nor parents can possibly deliver. A struggling musician might hope for recognition that his talent and circumstance can never deliver. A businesswoman may sink a ton of money into an investment, hoping for a good but never-guaranteed result. Sometimes we hope for a situation to work out, knowing that the right factors are not in place to bring resolution. At times, we all foolishly hope for things that may or may not come to pass. Faithful hope, on the other hand, is based in the reality and promises of God. Faithful hope is not a fleeting "wish and prayer" but an assurance that is secure in the power of God's ability to bring the Kingdom to pass. We hope for a better day. We hope for salvation. We hope for deliverance. We hope for everlasting life. We hope for the forgiveness of sins. Such hope is based in a coming reality. It is not that God "might" bring about such answers to our prayers, but that God "will" bring such things to pass. Hope and waiting go hand in hand. We wait, but we know our waiting is not in vain. God is at work. God's Kingdom is coming. God's promises are being fulfilled. Isaiah's words hold true for us: "This is our God! We trusted in him, and he saved us! This is the Lord, in whom we trusted."

Prayer

Father, give us an unshakable, sustaining, joyful hope. Amen.

Day 705 — Isaiah 26: The Promise of Life

> "But those who die in the Lord will live; their bodies will rise again! Those who sleep in the earth will rise up and sing for joy! For your life-giving light will fall like dew on your people in the place of the dead!"
> Isaiah 26:19 (NLT)

Observation
Isaiah 26 points to the blessings of God's Kingdom that will follow the period of judgment described in the previous two chapters. The opening six verses are a "Song of Joy" as the people of Judah praise God for powerful acts. The city of God will be strong and secure because God will make it that way. The lowly and poor will trample the proud and mighty. This sense of lasting security is based on the people's continued trust in God. The next section of the chapter (vv. 7-11) discusses the importance of dependency on God while the people wait for the Kingdom to be established. The final verses describe the confidence that the people have in God's ability to renew them. They are confident that God will bring peace.

Application
Each fall, I take on the battle of the leaves. I have two large trees in my yard. One is a sycamore tree with huge leaves that the wind often blows across the yards of several neighbors. (Sorry, guys.) The other is a sugar maple that offers a beautiful blanket of yellow leaves across the front yard until they turn to a dull brown. And then it starts: the raking, mulching, and blowing of the leaves. It's at least a two-month process to collect them all—not because I am lazy about yard work but because they hang on for dear life, taunting me each time I gaze out at the yard. It's always interesting to me how different the trees look as they transition from the warm days of early summer to the cold days of December. In late spring, the trees look alive, vibrant, and healthy. But in late fall, they look bleak, dead, and sorrowful. And yet in the cold of the winter I do not grieve nor mourn their passing for I know that, in spring, the resurrection of life will occur and the trees will be full once more.

Isaiah speaks to his generation of the great promise of God's resurrection of the people. As a result of faithful living and continued trust in God as the giver of life, those who have died will live again. They will be raised to life and will sing with joy. That's an important word for us to hear. The promise of resurrection is powerful, hope-giving, and life-sustaining. Though we may grieve and even mourn the vitality and energy that age and circumstance drain from our bodies, we should rejoice knowing that what is lifeless about us will rise again and claim a place of beauty and grace in God's forever Kingdom. Our songs will not be filled with words of sorrow, regret, or even shame. We will sing with joy.

Prayer
Father, we praise you for the promise of the resurrection. Amen.

Day 706 — Isaiah 27: Feeding the Planet

> "The time is coming when Jacob's descendants will take root. Israel will bud and blossom and fill the whole earth with fruit!" Isaiah 27:6 (NLT)

Observation
Isaiah 27 continues the thought from the previous chapter in which Isaiah describes the destruction that will occur on earth on the day of God's judgment. The opening verse makes a reference to "Leviathan." Though a clear interpretation is not offered, typically when Leviathan is mentioned in scripture, it is associated with chaos and the sea. In slaying Leviathan, God will conquer the symbol of chaos and rebellion. The powers of the world will not stand. God will be victorious in the end, triumphing over all things. Those who have practiced rebellion will feel God's harsh rebuke. Verses 2-6 describe Israel as God's vineyard. God has carefully planted and protected the vines. "Thorns and briars," which represent any threat against Israel, will be struck down. The final verses, 7-13, begin with a rhetorical question: "Has the Lord struck Israel as he struck her enemies?" The answer, of course, is "no." Though Israel has received a harsh rebuke in the form of the exilic period, she will not endure the destruction that other nations will experience. The final verse mentions the "trumpet sound" of God, which will announce the return of the Israelites to Jerusalem.

Application
A neighbor has introduced me to the concept of "hay bale gardening." Rather than tilling his backyard, he lines up a number of hay bales in one corner. In early spring, he begins to fertilize and water the hay bales. After about a month, he inserts young plants or even seeds into the hay bales. There is no digging, no hoeing, and no effort. The seeds and seedlings quickly take root in the hay and begin growing. Within weeks the plants sprout straight and tall and soon yield their fruit. By the end of the season, the hay bales begin to deteriorate, and he simply spreads them out across his yard, where they are quickly absorbed. But here's what I like most about his garden: he shares the produce with his neighbors in the cul-de-sac. We all enjoy fresh tomatoes, squash, and even corn all season long.

Isaiah prophesied that the whole earth would be filled with the fruit of God's work in Israel. The descendants of Jacob would "bud and blossom and fill the earth." God is still in the business of impacting the entire world through the lives of faithful followers. With every faithful heart, every compassionate spirit, every generous hand, and every loving person, God brings goodness upon the earth. Even this day, as a representative of God, you bless the earth as you share your life with the people around you. Lives are changed, hurts are healed, broken lives are mended, and grace is extended as you and I choose to live as God's children.

Prayer
Father, use us this day to change the world by sharing your Spirit with others. Amen.

Day 707 — Isaiah 28: The Solid Rock

> "Therefore, this is what the Sovereign Lord says: 'Look! I am placing a foundation stone in Jerusalem, a firm and tested stone. It is a precious cornerstone that is safe to build on. Whoever believes need never be shaken.'" Isaiah 28:16 (NLT)

Observation

Isaiah 28 begins a section known as the Book of Woes (chs. 28-33). In this section, six woes are declared upon the leaders of Israel for their various sins. A "woe" is an interjection or exclamation of lament. Chapter 28 speaks directly to the sin of drunken mocking. In verse 1, Isaiah mentions the "glorious" or "proud" crown worn by the political leaders. The crown is a symbol of power and sovereignty. The drunken behavior of the leaders blinds them to the coming destruction. The city of Samaria is specifically named in this declaration of woe. The capital of the northern kingdom of Israel during the eighth and ninth centuries BC, Samaria will be powerfully destroyed by the Assyrians just as Isaiah has predicted. God will replace the corrupt priests and prophets with justice and power. A remnant of people will one day remain and will overcome their enemies. Verse 16 speaks of a strong cornerstone on which the nation and the salvation of her people will be built.

Application

On my travel "bucket list" is the abbey built on the island of Mont St. Michel. Situated on the island about a half-mile off the coast of Normandy, France, the abbey is one of the country's most recognizable structures. Mont St. Michel is a granite outcropping that rises about 300 feet above sea level. The abbey is built at the top of the outcropping and dates back many centuries. According to legend, the Archangel Michael appeared in that place and ordered the construction of the church. Pictures of the island are spectacular. Interestingly, the island can only be accessed during low tide. When the tide is high, water completely surrounds the island, cutting it off from the mainland and, in earlier times, from opposing armies. The people who first built structures on the island recognized the importance of building on the solid rock rather than the swampy marsh land that surrounded it.

Isaiah speaks of a strong cornerstone on which God will build the Kingdom. This is a messianic reference pointing to God's coming Messiah. As I read this passage, I am forced to consider my own life and the soil on which I place my foundation. Am I careful to seek solid rock, or do I willingly stand on the swampy marshland of culture and popularity? We'd better watch our footing as we traverse this life. Our values, our priorities, and our very lives must be founded on Jesus Christ. All other ground is sinking sand.

Prayer

Father, help us to distinguish the solid rock from the swampy soil. Amen.

Day 708   Isaiah 29: The Motions of Worship?

> "And so the Lord says, 'These people say they are mine. They honor me with their lips, but their hearts are far from me. And their worship of me is nothing but man-made rules learned by rote.'" Isaiah 29:13 (NLT)

Observation
Isaiah 29 opens with a second pronouncement of woe, this time directed towards the city of Jerusalem, particularly the leaders who have practiced religious hypocrisy. Jerusalem is called "Ariel" in the opening verse. Ariel refers to an altar for making sacrifices. Jerusalem will no longer be a city where feasts are celebrated; instead, it will become a place of lamenting and mourning. God will humble the city and the people will cry out from the dust. And yet, in spite of this severe punishment, the eventual punishment of her enemies will be greater. God will bring to the city both destruction and deliverance. According to Isaiah, the enemies of Israel can only "dream" of ultimately defeating Jerusalem. They will awaken one day to discover that their victories were short lived. This passage also notes the spiritual impairments of the religious leaders. Rather than seeing and hearing the movement of God, they have become deaf and blind. In verses 15-16, a third woe is pronounced upon the leadership for the ways they foolishly attempt to fool God. The chapter ends with a note of hope as Isaiah declares the eventual restoration of the land.

Application
To learn something "by rote" is to learn something by habitual or mechanical repetition. For example, most of us learned our ABCs by rote as we repeated them over and over again. Many of us learned our multiplication tables by a continual repetition of each equation. In college, one of the ways I prepared for tests was by going to an empty classroom, writing key points on a blackboard, erasing them, and then writing them again over and over until I knew the material. The repetition caused me to learn. In terms of our experiences of worship, repetition can be both good and bad. The repetition of some elements of worship teaches us to remember and value their content. For example, reciting the Lord's prayer teaches us to know the prayer and draw strength from it as we ponder it in our minds. On the other hand, repeating it too often could cause us to lose the depth of its meaning. The same could be said of Communion. Can we share Communion so often that we become guilty of going through the motions? Or is the repetition vital to serve as a constant reminder of Christ's sacrifice? Isaiah makes this point in his prophetic word: Worship must be more than a mechanical recitation of key prayers or well-known verses. It must be a fresh expression from our hearts, filled with thought, emotion, and praise.

Prayer
Father, may our worship be fresh, thoughtful, and deliberate. Amen.

Day 709 — Isaiah 30: Who's Calling the Shots?

> "'What sorrow awaits my rebellious children,' says the Lord. 'You make plans that are contrary to mine. You make alliances not directed by my Spirit, thus piling up your sins.'" Isaiah 30:1 (NLT)

Observation

Chapter 30 pronounces the fourth woe of Isaiah, this time directed towards Judah for stubborn rebellion displayed by a worthless treaty/alliance with Egypt. The chapter contains three sections. The first deals with a description of Judah's rebellion. The second deals with God's impending judgment because of the rebellion. The third deals with Isaiah's prophecy concerning the restoration of Israel after the time of judgment is complete. The key issue is that the leaders of Israel have been making plans and treaties without consulting God. Their rebellion reveals a lack of trust in God's ability to lead and protect the nation. They feel that their treaty with Egypt will help them survive, but instead the alliance will bring shame and not security. Even though Israel has invested a great deal of time and resources in the treaty, there will be no lasting results. According to verse 7, God gives Egypt the nickname "Rahab," which was a mythical creature of chaos, a "harmless dragon" according to the text. Israel has focused on self-security and self-reliance rather than dependency on God. This alliance will be like a "cracked wall" that will fall on the people rather than offering protection. Even with this warning, however, the chapter ends on a positive note as Isaiah insists that God will one day provide a Messiah along with an abundance of other provisions.

Application

Years ago, friends threw my future bride and me a party, celebrating our impending nuptials. As part of the festivities, guests were asked to write a piece of advice on an index card. I still remember one piece of advice some 35 years later. The card simply read, "Don't join a record club!" Record clubs were popular in the 1970s and 1980s. For a subscription fee, a person would receive a new record in the mail each month. The problem was not "joining" such a program but trying to "leave" such a program. It was hard to cancel a subscription, and many people battled such companies for years. (Obviously, whoever wrote the card that night had not enjoyed a good experience.)

Alliances can be tricky. Whenever we align ourselves with other people, organizations, or clubs, our success is determined by how well those entities fare. We are only as good as our alliances. The words of Isaiah remind us that the single most important alliance we can establish is with God alone. God's power is great. God's wisdom is supreme. God's love is enduring. Why cast our lot with anyone or anything else?

Prayer

Father, may we depend solely on you. Amen.

Day 710 — Isaiah 31: The God of the Second Chance

> "Though you are such wicked rebels, my people, come and return to the Lord. I know the glorious day will come when each of you will throw away the gold idols and silver images your sinful hands have made."
> Isaiah 31:6-7 (NLT)

Observation
Isaiah 31 proclaims the fifth woe of judgement upon Israel. The key theme is not trusting fully in God to protect and defend the nation. The prophecy includes two main components. The first is a word of condemnation for reliance on Egypt and not God. The second is a word of hope proclaiming that God will still fulfill all the promises to Israel, including sending a Messianic king. Isaiah reminds the people that the fast horses and strong armies of Egypt are no match for the power of the Mighty God. God will be a fearless and furious defender of Jerusalem. God will "pass over" the city. The phrase used in verse 5 is the same one used in Exodus 12 when God's angel passed over Egypt. It is a deliberate allusion to the redemption of God's people over and against the people of Egypt and other enemies who attempt to overthrow the city.

Application
I have a friend with a troubled son. He has been in trouble with the law, the authorities at his school, and certainly with his parents. Like many misguided teens, he has made a number of poor choices that have put him, time and again, on a dangerous path. And although he has rebelled against and betrayed his parents on many occasions, the father continues to tell me how much he loves and believes in his son. "We pray every day that he will know our love and will soon make better choices." This father has a stubborn and faithful heart. He believes in his son against all odds. He loves his son in spite of all the rebellion. He promises that his son will always have a home to which he can return when he finally makes the decision to leave his wayward choices behind.

Isaiah triumphantly proclaims the news that a glorious day is coming when the rebelling Israelites will throw away their false gods and prideful self-reliance and turn once again to the Almighty God. Though they are "wicked," the glorious day will come. Not a single person reading this devotion has lived a perfect life. All of us have sinned. All of us have rebelled against God's intention for our lives. Though we have sinned, God has not abandoned us, neglected us, or tossed us aside. In fact, we have been loved. And like a shepherd who tirelessly looks for the lost lamb, God searches for us, calling us home and welcoming us like beloved children. We've been given a second chance…and a third…and a fourth…

Prayer
Father, thank you for loving us in spite of our rebellious ways. Amen.

Day 711 — Isaiah 32: The Blessings of Generosity

> "But generous people plan to do what is generous, and they stand firm in their generosity." Isaiah 32:8 (NLT)

Observation

Isaiah 32 begins by speaking of Israel's ultimate deliverance as God establishes a Messianic king to rule the nation. Rather than an unsuccessful alliance with a foreign nation like Egypt, God's people will find a bright new future by trusting in God alone. In addition to this great king, righteous princes will rule under him. The new leadership of the nation will keep the people from harm and will be a healthy influence. These leaders will transform the culture, value system, and mindset of the nation. The second portion of this chapter reveals the harsh punishment and rebuke of God that will come to those who live in complacency and foolish security. They will discover the inadequacies of their defenses. They will learn that the land's prosperity and blessing are conditional upon the people's continued loyalty to God alone. God will be the source of abundance and well-being. The final section of the chapter ends on a positive tone of restoration, with God's blessing on both the people and the land.

Application

Certain people seem more generous than others. Some argue that generosity is a spiritual gift and that those who are generous possess more of that gift than other people do. Others suggest that generous people just have more to give away. "Make anyone wealthy and generosity will follow." Such a statement does not always hold true. Although it may be true that some people possess a special sense of giving, I think the heart of the matter is trust, and not in the abundancy of one's blessings. Whenever we place our trust in our own possessions, wealth, and connections, we tend to become selfishly stingy, clinging tightly to "our" things. But if we learn to trust in the One who owns all things, and if we recognize that we are to be conduits of God's abundance to those around us, how can we not practice generosity? The more we trust God, the more we are able to share what we have with others, knowing that God will continue to supply our needs.

Recently, I taught a class of undergrads at Belmont University in Nashville, Tennessee. A student responding to a question concerning ministry to the homeless offered this word: "What good is owning something like a house if I am not willing to share it with others?" Such a response comes from a heart of generosity. I hope you realize that everything you have is a blessing from your Father. God's desire is never for selfishness but for providing you with an opportunity to help others.

Prayer

Father, make us generous with the gifts you have given to each of us. Amen.

Day 712 — Isaiah 33: The God Who Visits

> "Though the Lord is very great and lives in heaven, he will make Jerusalem his home of justice and righteousness." Isaiah 33:5 (NLT)

Observation
Isaiah 33 describes the sixth woe delivered against the enemies of Israel. This particular pronouncement of woe is directed towards Assyria, although the words could be applied more generally to all who have assaulted Israel. According to Isaiah, the destroyer will be destroyed and the betrayer will be betrayed. As they wait for God's deliverance, the nation calls upon God to provide salvation and strength. They wait with eager anticipation, knowing that God will restore both Jerusalem and the land. Unlike the unpredictable alliances with other nations, God is both powerful and consistent. Verse 8 refers to a broken peace treaty. Most likely this refers to a peace treaty made with the Assyrian king Sennacherib. The agreement was to leave Jerusalem alone in exchange for a tribute to be paid. But even though the money was paid, the Assyrians attacked Jerusalem anyway. Amid hopelessness, the Lord promises that the enemies will fail, Israel will be purified, and the daily needs of the people will be met.

Application
In our "connected age," we have lost sight of what it means to "visit" with each other. We send emails, text our thoughts, and we display pictures on Instagram, but do we really connect? Remember the days when someone would drop by to visit? A visit meant sitting down to talk about everything or anything. It's how we truly stayed in touch. But people rarely do such things now, and we are lessened because of it. Many of us don't dwell in each other's presence. We don't relax and talk across the table or over a cup of coffee the way we once did. Sometimes here at work, a coworker will step into my doorway just to say "hello." It's hard to get them to sit and talk for a moment. And I'm just as guilty of doing the same. I'm always on the way to take care of the next thing and feel that I have little time to listen to others.

But notice what Isaiah states in our focus verse: "Though the Lord is very great and lives in heaven, he will make Jerusalem his home of justice and righteousness." Here's my translation: "Though the Lord is great and mighty and certainly separated from us by wisdom, strength, power, and love, He chooses to visit with us. He welcomes Himself to our table and sits on our sofa." What a joyful thought to know that God Almighty longs to visit with each of us. I invite you today to take a moment and welcome God into your world. Talk to God about your pressures, problems, and fears. Tell about your joys and sorrows. God welcomes the visit.

Prayer
Father, we thank you for your abiding presence in our lives each day. Amen.

Day 713   Isaiah 34: The Desolate Places

> "It will be called the Land of Nothing, and all its nobles will soon be gone. Thorns will overrun its palaces; nettles and thistles will grow in its forts. The ruins will become a haunt for jackals and a home for owls."
> Isaiah 34:12-13 (NLT)

Observation
Isaiah 34 and 35 provide a summation of the judgments and blessings described in the first half of the book. Chapter 34 pertains to God's judgment of the nations, while chapter 35 specifically highlights God's future blessings for Israel. In the narrative, the nation of Edom is singled out for destruction. It is likely that the story of Edom represents what will occur in every nation that denies Israel's God. It is a warning to all who oppose the Lord Almighty. With graphic language, Isaiah describes the destruction, noting that the mountains will melt away or erode because of the quantity of blood that will be spilled upon them as the enemies of Israel are slain. Our focus passage speaks of the devastation of Edom, where the once grand palaces and fine homes will be reduced to barren, desolate, and uninhabitable places.

Application
On a trip to Haiti, as the plane turned and made its final approach into Port-au-Prince, I was dumbfounded by what I noticed outside the airplane windows. I saw the mountains of Haiti. Since Haiti is an island resting in the warm, tropical waters of the Caribbean, I expected its mountains to be lush and green, much like I had seen on the Dominican Republic side of Hispaniola. Instead, the mountains were rust colored, completely stripped of forest and vegetation. I discovered that the bare mountains resulted from exploitive deforestation that stripped them of all trees and essential plants. This led to erosion that many believe is beyond recovery. It seems such a shame; here was a region that was once so full of life, vitality, and produce, and now it is all but uninhabitable. It's a desolate place, not unlike the way Isaiah describes Edom.

Yet for me, the saddest, most desolate place I know is the human heart. I think of God's purposeful creation of people. We were born for joy, for love, for peace, and for hope. And yet so many lives are devoid of such things. Hearts are made desolate when they shun the presence of Almighty God. Whenever we choose to live apart from God's purpose, plan, and provision, shunning the work of the Holy Spirit in our lives, we are left with desolate hearts. The good news, however, is that our hearts are not beyond recovery. God can make all things new, vibrant, hopeful, and life-giving. Let God transform your heart.

Prayer
Father, into the desolate, empty spaces of our hearts, plant a seed of hope and joy. Amen.

Day 714   Isaiah 35: Highway of Holiness

> "And a great road will go through that once deserted land. It will be named the Highway of Holiness. Evil-minded people will never travel on it. It will be only for those who walk in God's ways; fools will never walk there."
> Isaiah 35:8 (NLT)

Observation
Isaiah 35 highlights the blessings of God that will be poured out upon Israel. These blessings will benefit both the people and the land. The desert landscape will undergo spectacular and unexpected changes. What was once barren and arid will become lush, fertile, and productive. As people see the reversal of the desert, they should rejoice and find great comfort. In the coming Messianic age, God will do great and mighty things. The eyes of the blind will be opened. The deaf will hear. The lame will walk. The mute will speak. The entire created order will be transformed. Isaiah speaks of a "great road" that will appear in the desert. Called a "Highway of Holiness," it will lead the righteous people safely to worship at Zion. The reclaimed nation will be swept up in joyful singing and praise of God.

Application
When I was young, my grandfather often took me on long afternoon drives. When pulling onto a wide, smooth highway, he occasionally remarked, "This is a fine road." Now I find myself saying that from time to time. Recently, the city of Franklin, Tennessee, resurfaced the main road in our neighborhood. It's a fine road. When I was in college, I-65 was not complete through Birmingham, Alabama. Driving from Montgomery, where I worked in youth ministry, meant exiting onto old US 31 just south of Hoover. Now, when I blast through that part of the world, barely slowing to pass through town, I think, "This is a fine road." For me, a "fine road" is smooth and wide with little traffic.

Isaiah spoke of the smooth road that the people of God would one day walk as they made their way to Jerusalem. The "desert days" of hardship, exile, and discipline would be soon forgotten as they stepped into the presence of God. When most of us consider stepping into the presence of God, we imagine doing so with great trepidation. When we think of our mistakes, our rebellion, and our foolish ways, we sheepishly step towards God's throne, awaiting both rebuke and punishment. But it's not that way with God. We will walk on a fine road, made smooth by God's grace, compassion, forgiveness, and wide-armed welcome. We will step out of the desert of regret and shame and walk boldly onto the road of our acceptance. Having been reclaimed from our past, we will be swept up with joyful singing and join an everlasting chorus of praise. Until that day comes, our steps might fall on a lot of broken asphalt, puddles, and potholes. But just wait…soon we will walk that fine road.

Prayer
Father, we thank you that you long to welcome us into your presence. Amen.

Day 715 — Isaiah 36: God Told Me...

> "What's more, do you think we have invaded your land without the Lord's direction? The Lord himself told us, 'Attack this land and destroy it!'"
> Isaiah 36:10 (NLT)

Observation
Chapters 36-39 speak of the Lord's rescue of Judah from the hands of the Assyrians. As the narrative begins, the good and godly King Hezekiah reigns in Jerusalem. Unlike the former King Ahaz, whose story was told earlier (chs. 7-12), Hezekiah welcomes "signs and instructions" from God. The events described in this chapter occurred around 703 BC. Assyrian King Sennacherib, who is invading the land of Israel, sends a delegation to Jerusalem to demand the surrender of the city. He has already captured several of Judah's well-fortified cities. Hezekiah sends a high-level delegation to meet Sennacherib's chief of staff, who tries to deceive the delegates by telling them they should not trust in God to deliver them. The gods of the other conquered nations have failed to save them, says the chief of staff, so why should Israel trust in her God? The delegates return to Hezekiah in fear of all that they have heard.

Application
Some of the most deceptive words, often used by preachers, politicians, and people who long to manipulate and control others, are "God told me...." Have you ever been victimized by those deceptive words? Playing the "God Card" is always good theatre. If someone can convincingly argue that God has given key words of instruction, then who are mere mortals to dispute that? The problem is that often those who claim to have a word from the Lord have never actually received this revelation. They merely use manipulative tactics to impose their own will. Even while serving as a pastor, I was hesitant ever to present a "God told me" narrative to my church members. Yes, there were certainly times when I felt the leadership of God to preach a certain passage or to take on a certain ministry role. But I used such words sparingly, with authenticity, integrity, and also with a sense of fear and trembling. If I ever said, "God told me...," I wanted to be absolutely sure that God had indeed authored the thought or the instruction.

One of my life lessons is that God consistently communicates a message to both proclaimer and recipient. If God has truly compelled someone to proclaim a message, God has also opened the mind of the recipient to hear that message. Be careful when someone tells you that they have a word from the Lord. Test it. If it is an authentic word offered by a faithful spokesperson, listen to it carefully and obey it. If it is offered by a charlatan, ignore it.

Prayer
Father, grant us the wisdom to know truth from falsehood. Amen.

Day 716　　　　　　　　　　　　　　　Isaiah 37: God Dependency

> "After Hezekiah received the letter from the messengers and read it, he went up to the Lord's Temple and spread it out before the Lord."
> Isaiah 37:14 (NLT)

Observation
In the face of a looming Assyrian attack on Jerusalem, King Hezekiah tore his robes and put on sackcloth as a sign of mourning. He sent two of his trusted leaders, Eliakim and Shebna, to seek the counsel of God's prophet, Isaiah. Hezekiah hoped that God had heard the evil taunts of the Assyrians and would punish their king. Isaiah responded that the king of Assyria would be called back home and would fall by the sword. The city of Jerusalem would be spared. Later in the narrative, Hezekiah receives a letter from the king of Assyria (Sennacherib), offering continuing threats against Jerusalem. Hezekiah takes the letter to the Temple and spreads it out before the Lord. He prays that God will act in a way that shows God's universal sovereignty. God responds with a promise to be faithful to the people and to the covenant made with David. The next morning, as a result of the action of the angel of God, 185,000 Assyrian troops are found dead. King Sennacherib retreats to Assyria, where two of his own sons kill him.

Application
I like the image of King Hezekiah spreading out the Assyrian king's letter before the Lord. He literally unrolls the scroll in the Temple and prays to God for a solution. I see this as an act of total God dependency. Hezekiah is saying in essence, "I have no answer for this problem, Lord. I need you to see it, hear it, and respond to it." In Hezekiah's moment of humility and trust, God hears his plea and responds in a mighty way.

For most of us, it will take a lifetime of struggle to learn the lesson of God dependency. Rather than trust in God's wisdom, strength, and timing, we tend to try it alone. As we encounter problems, we lean into our own intellect and experience and move forward accordingly. And rarely do our problems find a lasting solution. I love the old, well-worn story of the little boy who was sent off to bed. His father said to him, "Be sure to say your prayers before you go to sleep." A few minutes later, the father walked past his son's bedroom and heard him reciting the alphabet. "What are you doing, son?" the father asked. The young boy replied, "Sometimes I don't know the words to say, and so I just say the ABCs knowing that God will put the right words together for me." Or, as Paul once wrote, "In the same way the Spirit also helps our weakness; for we do not know how to pray as we should, but the Spirit Himself intercedes for us with groanings too deep for words" (Romans 8:26, NASB). Stop depending on yourself. Lean on God, who wants to help.

Prayer
Father, may we substitute self-sufficiency with God dependency. Amen.

Day 717　　　　　　　　　　Isaiah 38: The Gift of Perspective

> "Yes, this anguish was good for me, for you have rescued me from death and forgiven all my sins." Isaiah 38:17 (NLT)

Observation

The stories contained in Isaiah 38-39 actually precede the events described in chapter 37. The lack of chronological order is intentional. It emphasizes the second half of the book, which describes the Babylonian assault. Isaiah 38 describes a terminal illness faced by King Hezekiah. Isaiah visits him and tells him to prepare for death. Hezekiah cries out to God about his condition, reminding God of his past faithfulness. God is moved by this prayer and promises him an additional 15 years of life. God also promises to defend the city against the Assyrians. A supernatural event affirms God's promise: the sun will move backward 10 steps on the sundial of Ahaz. The later part of the chapter describes Hezekiah's joy following his recovery. The illness had prevented him from worshipping in the Temple. Now that he is well, he can freely go and offer his praises. The final verses describe the treatment for a boil caused by his illness. He is to make an ointment of figs and apply them to the boil.

Application

In December 2015, I had double knee replacement surgery. It was quite the ordeal. I was in the hospital for four days, in rehab for four months, and on pain relief for ninety days. I learned a lot during that time. I learned a few things about myself, about the rigors of rehab, and about dependency on others. More than anything else, I gained a little perspective. I understand more of the emotional and physical stress of a major surgery. I understand more about offering empathy to those who undergo a similar experience. I understand more about pain, medication, and nutrition. As Isaiah wrote in our focus verse, "this anguish was good for me."

None of us welcome times of difficulty and hardship. We don't warmly embrace moments of suffering, grief, or anxiety. And yet these kinds of experiences can offer important lessons. We can gain insight in the "reflective space" we create in our minds. Reflective space helps us to ask, "What did I learn from this experience? What did God reveal to me? What did I learn that I can use as I move forward?" The problem is that most of us don't slow down long enough to be introspective and ask such questions. Don't waste such a teachable moment. Don't fritter away the opportunity to learn. As you walk away from the latest storm in your life, whether emotional, physical, or relational, take the time to learn from your anguish. Step into the "reflective space" and find the lessons that await you there.

Prayer

Father, help us to learn even from the difficult moments of our lives. Amen.

Day 718 — Isaiah 39: Caught Up in the Moment

> "Hezekiah was delighted with the Babylonian envoys and showed them everything in his treasure-houses—the silver, the gold, the spices, and the aromatic oils. He also took them to see his armory and showed them everything in his royal treasuries! There was nothing in his palace or kingdom that Hezekiah did not show them." Isaiah 39:2 (NLT)

Observation
In this short, eight-verse chapter, King Hezekiah exhibits a lack of judgment when envoys from the king of Babylon visit Jerusalem following the king's illness and recovery. Their visit drips with suspicion. The king of Babylon may have good intentions and wish Hezekiah well in the hopes of establishing an alliance. Or perhaps the Babylonian king simply wants to assess the wealth and strength of the nation. At first, it appears that Hezekiah is motivated by pride. He gladly shows his visitors all the nation's treasures. It could be a sense of pride in the blessings God has showered upon them. Maybe Hezekiah just gets caught up in the joy of his recent deliverance. With a giddy attitude, he shows little restraint in revealing all of the treasures. He is definitely short-sighted. He tends to celebrate the here and now without giving much thought for what needs to happen in the future. If the reason for the Babylonian king's visit is indeed for the purpose of an alliance, Hezekiah should know that an attempt to place trust in any nation or leader besides God will surely cripple Israel.

Application
Recently, a friend of mine was chosen from the audience to be a participant on the TV game show The Price Is Right. He outbid his fellow participants and made it onstage. Later, as the show continued, he had a chance to spin the "Big Wheel." As luck would have it, the wheel stopped on the $1 mark, winning him both a thousand dollars and a chance to play in the Showcase Showdown, which he did not win. But in the euphoric moment of spinning the Big Wheel and watching it land on the dollar mark, my friend temporarily lost his mind! He screamed, shouted, and dove onto the floor! He got caught up in the moment…and who could blame him? Have you ever gotten caught up in a moment that was too big for you to handle? I'm not talking about a joyful reaction after winning a big game or watching your team score a touchdown. I'm talking about being so overwhelmed by temptation that your actions are controlled by a lack of judgment. Sometimes the lure of temptation causes us to lose our better judgment, forcing us to act poorly. Lack of self-control reveals misguided trust. In such moments, we tend to rely on our own strength and judgement and not God's. We lose our minds and our better selves. Game over.

Prayer
Father God, deliver us from evil and even from ourselves. Amen.

Day 719   Isaiah 40: The Greatness of God

> "Who else has held the oceans in his hand? Who has measured off the heavens with his fingers? Who else knows the weight of the earth or has weighed the mountains and hills on a scale?" Isaiah 40:12 (NLT)

Observation
Isaiah 40 begins the second of three major sections contained in the book of Isaiah. This section spans chapters 40-54. In contrast to the first third of the book, which emphasizes God's judgment on the unfaithful, attention now shifts to oracles of blessing, particularly focused on the nation's deliverance from Babylon. There are two divisions within the second section of Isaiah. Chapters 40-48 give specific attention to God's exiled people who lived in Babylon. Chapters 49-54 gives emphasis to Jerusalem. Isaiah 40 begins with a word of comfort. God has instructed Isaiah to speak this word. He is to remind the people that God will bring peace, forgiveness, and restoration. God will remain faithful to the covenant made with Israel. Though the exilic period has been harsh, God promises that it will not last forever. The nation is to prepare for the coming glory of God. God's word is eternal in nature, unlike the false claims of pagan gods, and what God has promised will come to pass. God will shepherd the people.

Application
My wife and I are longtime fans of the old Andy Griffith Show. We have seen every episode and can recite almost every line of dialogue. Even in our day-to-day conversations, some expression occasionally emerges from the words of Barney or Andy. With the recent news cycles filled with anger, hostility, and false claims, sometimes we have to take our attention off the news reports and seek some light-hearted, sane, rational diversion. Sometimes we just need a little Andy Griffith to calm our nerves and restore a sense of gladness to our hearts, and so we tune in to an episode.

Sometimes, as believers living in a hostile, violent, and oppressive world, we need a little encouragement…a little peace…a little grace. Isaiah 40 can offer the solace we need. These words continue to speak comfort to the people of God in any age. Take the time today to read the chapter slowly and carefully. The words may be familiar to you. They are echoed in song, poem, and memory. They speak of hope, of God's power, of God's continual concern and redemption of God's people. In them we find new strength and hope. Let's be honest: this world can be harsh. We often live as though exiled from all that is good, peaceful, and loving. Yet God promises to restore God's rule and reign and will carefully watch over all of us. So, clear a way for the coming of the Lord. Shout to the world that our God is coming in victory and triumph. Speak comfort to those who are struggling and hope to those who are bewildered. May the promises of Isaiah 40 bring gladness to our hearts.

Prayer
Father God, we welcome you into our world. Come in power and might. Amen.

Day 720   Isaiah 41: The God Who Is with Us

> "Don't be afraid, for I am with you. Don't be discouraged, for I am your God. I will strengthen you and help you. I will hold you up with my victorious right hand." Isaiah 41:10 (NLT)

Observation
Isaiah 41 speaks of God's powerful deliverance. It is both a call to the nations to recognize God's power and a call to Israel in particular to remind her of God's special relationship to her. In these words, God is identified as the author of all things, the one who controls all the events on the world's stage. It is clear that God, in the orchestration of world events, has not forgotten the covenant with Israel. The first seven verses speak about the role of King Cyrus of Persia. God will use him as a political servant. He is indeed a rising star on the world's political stage. God will use Persia to bring the restoration of God's people. This chapter also gives attention to calling out "false idols" for what they are. They are meaningless and without power. And, for the first time in the book of Isaiah, the prophet uses the word "redeemer" to refer to God's action towards Israel. God will reconstitute the scattered nation. Israel is commanded not to fear.

Application
Years ago I became a blood donor. To be honest, I began the process with a lot of fear and trembling. I was squeamish about donating blood. How would I feel afterwards? Would I pass out? Would I feel weak? But one determined member of my church convinced me to give. She was a crusader for blood drives and encouraged me to host one in our fellowship hall. And then, to get me to donate, she said, "I will walk with you through the whole process. I will sit with you while you register, stay with you while you are having your blood drawn, and even hold your hand if needed." She also promised to sit with me for the few minutes of recovery after donating just to make sure I was okay. Her presence made all the difference in the world. I felt confident and encouraged.

    I love these words of Isaiah. He instructs us not to be afraid or discouraged because God will be with us. God will strengthen us, sustain us, and be ever present with us. God sits with us in our fear. God counsels us as we make choices. God walks with us through every experience. God holds our hand through the darkest nights and longest days. God is with us. God named the Son Immanuel, which means "God with us," to remind us of that truth. Life can be daunting. It can stretch us to our limits and fill us with fear, anxiety, and life-draining hopelessness. But amid all the "scary stuff," let's remind ourselves that God is indeed with us always and will strengthen us.

Prayer
Father God, thank you for being present with us each day. Amen.

Day 721 — Isaiah 42: Responsibility

> "God, the Lord, created the heavens and stretched them out. He created the earth and everything in it. He gives breath to everyone, life to everyone who walks the earth. And it is he who says, 'I, the Lord, have called you to demonstrate my righteousness.'" Isaiah 42:5-6a (NLT)

Observation

Isaiah 42 describes the work of God's chosen servant (whom we know as the Messiah). The chapter begins with the words, "Behold my servant" or, in some translations, "Look at my servant." These words focus the reader's attention on the future work of the Messiah, who will bring universal justice and an everlasting covenant between God and God's people. Isaiah states "I will take you by the hand and guard you" (v. 6). There is power in such language. What is guarded by God will never be brought down by evil forces. Verse 3 speaks about God's involvement with a "weakest reed or…flickering candle" This is a reference to those who have all but lost their faith and hope in God. The Messiah will redeem them and encourage them. In contrast to King Cyrus, who is mentioned in chapter 41 as bringing political deliverance to Israel, the Messiah will deliver Israel from sin. When the work of the Messiah is completed, all the nations will sing a song. God's glory will be revealed, and all the world will know it. In the latter part of this chapter, a word is offered concerning the reasons for the period of exile. The people of God had been deaf to God's warnings and blind to God's plan. The exile brought correction and renewal to the people.

Application

Our focus verse says that God has given "life to everyone who walks on the earth." This reminder should cause us to reflect on the value and worth of every single life. There are no "second-class citizens." There are no "inferior races." We have all been deliberately created by a God who celebrates the diversity of creation. Made in God's image, every person on the planet should be afforded a sense of respect, civility, and dignity. The focus verse also says that God has "called [us] to demonstrate my righteousness." The people of God are charged with the responsibility of liberating, affirming, and including all of God's children. It is a grandiose and lofty idea to say that all should be afforded a sense of respect, civility, and dignity. It is an equally grandiose and lofty idea to state that the people of God must lead the way in efforts of offering inclusion, fighting for dignity, and forging respect among all people. We are not only made in God's image; we are also made as God's image. We are to bear God's witness before the nations. We cannot be identified with racism, prejudice, hatred, abuse, or slander towards people of different races, faiths, ideologies, or political persuasion. That kind of behavior does not reflect the image of God.

Prayer

Father, forgive us when we neglect our crucial role as your image bearers. Amen.

Day 722   Isaiah 43: God's Grace

> "I—yes, I alone—will blot out your sins for my own sake and will never think of them again." Isaiah 43:25 (NLT)

Observation

Isaiah 43-44 contain God's comforting assurance to Israel, reminding her that God will protect God's people. The passage begins with the phrase, "Thus says the Lord...." This speaks to both the authorship and reliability of the prophetic word. The promises will certainly be fulfilled. God speaks of those whom God has "created" and "formed." Like a potter molding clay, God has purposefully and decisively brought the nation into being. They are not to be fearful of the future, for God has ransomed them. God speaks of protection in verse 2: "When you go through deep waters, I will be with you. When you go through rivers of difficulty, you will not drown. When you walk through the fire of oppression, you will not be burned up." These words are references to the Red Sea deliverance from Egypt and the fiery furnace in Daniel's day. These reminders seem to contrast with what God says in verse 18. In verse 18, God tells the people to forget God's mighty acts in the past. The point is that these things done by God's power in the past will be insignificant when compared to the future Kingdom of Glory that God will establish. God will choose to save and forgive the people.

Application

In our focus verse, God promises to blot out our sins and never think of them again. God does this "for my own sake." Let's unpack that. When children are disobedient or unruly, their behavior often reflects on their parents. Have their parents raised them well? Have they disciplined them carefully and helped them to make better choices? If my children behave poorly, it can mar my reputation as a parent. In other words, my kids can make me look bad. Is God willing to blot out our sins to look better? Does God think, "My kids are embarrassing Me"? Is that what God means by blotting out our sins for God's own sake? I don't think so. It's not about God's reputation; it's about the distance that sin creates. God knows that sins disrupt relationships and that our sinfulness separates us from God's presence. God doesn't like the distance. To hold us close as beloved children, God removes our sins so that nothing separates us from God's presence. It is for God's "own sake" that the sin is removed. It's a selfish desire on God's part to love us intensely and without distance, even though we live with an imperfect past. And of course, it's for our sake as well. Without God's love, grace, and mercy, we would be forever distanced from God's presence. Once again, the Lord asks us to forget all that has come before in order that we might embrace the joy-filled, freed-from-shame life that God longs for us to know.

Prayer

Holy Father, we praise you this day for the complete removal of our sins. Amen.

Day 723 — Isaiah 44: Refreshment

> "For I will pour out water to quench your thirst and to irrigate your parched fields. And I will pour out my Spirit on your descendants, and my blessing on your children. They will thrive like watered grass, like willows on a riverbank." Isaiah 44:3-4 (NLT)

Observation

The prophetic word of Isaiah offers further comfort and assurance to Judah. God offers hope to God's "beloved"—"Jeshurun" in the Hebrew language. This word for beloved is only found in Isaiah's writings. Again, God counsels the people not to be afraid. God promises to pour water on the thirsty land—meaning God's Spirit will be poured on God's children. They will be refreshed like "luxurious grass." God is also described as a rock, which offers the image of stability and protection. A large portion of this chapter is devoted to condemning idols. God warns about the absurdity of worshipping metal and wooden objects. How, God asks, can the same piece of wood be burned in a fire for warmth while the other end is fashioned into an idol to worship? The people worshipped objects made from God's creation rather than worshipping the Creator. The chapter ends by naming King Cyrus as the person whom God will use to bring about the people's liberation.

Application

Several years ago, while leading a mission team in the Dominican Republic, I caught a stomach virus. I was violently ill for most of a day, with no cool or comfortable place to rest and recover. I became dehydrated, and for the first time in my life I fainted. Feeling the "lights go out," I called out to a friend. He caught me as I slumped forward in my chair and carefully laid me on the ground. A moment later, I came back to consciousness, and my friends decided to take me to a clinic for IV fluids. But even before that, a friend rushed up and handed me an ice-cold Coca-Cola. To this day, I have no idea where he got it. It was the most refreshing drink I had ever tasted. The cool, sugary liquid soon helped bring my body back to a relative sense of normalcy.

From time to time, we all need a little refreshment. Life can drain every bit of energy from our bodies. We stagger through a long day as though we're attempting to traverse a dry and arid desert. We long for a quiet moment, a respite, a little renewal. This is when we need to be reminded that God pours out the Spirit on us, like water on a parched land. God's Spirit encourages, revives, renews, strengthens, and pushes us forward. There is strength for the journey. God's Spirit resides in us.

Prayer

Holy Father, send your Spirit our way this day so that we might find refreshment. Amen.

Day 724   Isaiah 45: Called to Service

> "And why have I called you for this work? Why did I call you by name when you did not know me? It is for the sake of Jacob my servant, Israel my chosen one." Isaiah 45:4 (NLT)

Observation
This chapter highlights the work that God will call King Cyrus of Persia to do. Verse 1 calls Cyrus the "anointed one" or "Messiah" of God—an unusual term for a pagan emperor. Under the sovereignty of God, even foreign rulers can be conscripted into service. This passage presents a hopeful future that will come to Israel through the establishment of the Persian Empire. God will use Persia as a tool to restore Jerusalem. Even if Cyrus does not acknowledge God's leadership, Persia will prosper through God's power alone. After warning those who trust in idols, the chapter will again focus on the work of Cyrus. It offers more words of great hope for the Israelites. The prophetic word indicates that one day Egypt, Ethiopia, and Yemen will bring tribute to Israel. Further, the prophet claims that all nations will one day acknowledge and revere the God of Israel. Every knee will bow before the Lord (v. 14), and every tongue will swear allegiance (v. 23).

Application
Years ago, as a student at Samford University, I was called to a moment of service that I did not expect. It happened during StepSing week. StepSing was a singing and dance competition that involved every major organization on campus. It was a big deal, with lots of work and lots of reward if your organization won. I was standing with my Sigma Nu fraternity brothers just outside the Wright Performing Arts Center on campus. We were third in line to perform. Suddenly a frantic-looking woman ran up to me and said, "Here, hold my baby! I've got to get to a restroom really fast!" I don't recall having held a baby before that point in my life. I looked at her and said, "Who, me? You want me, a perfect stranger, to hold your baby?" It scared me to death! She returned a few minutes later and I was extremely relieved.

    Sometimes we feel unqualified for the tasks to which we are called. We worry about our abilities and strengths. We fear the unknown. We sometimes want to say to God, "Are you sure you want me for that task? Am I your best choice?" But I have discovered along the way that God knows exactly what's best. God equips us, trains us, and positions us in ways we might not perceive. Though we might question our suitability for a task, God doesn't. When God calls, it is never a question of ability or qualification. It is always about obedience. Listen well today. God may have a special task in mind for you.

Prayer
Father, thank you for preparing us for the work you have in mind. Amen.

Day 725 — Isaiah 46: Take Your Gods and Go

> "Bel and Nebo, the gods of Babylon, bow as they are lowered to the ground. They are being hauled away on ox carts. The poor beasts stagger under the weight. Both the idols and their owners are bowed down. The gods cannot protect the people, and the people cannot protect the gods. They go off into captivity together." Isaiah 46:1-2 (NLT)

Observation

Isaiah 46-47 describe God's immediate judgment on Babylon and the Babylonian empire. Babylon is not the invincible power that she appeared to be. Because of her idolatry and unjust practices, God will judge her. Hearing this would have encouraged the people of Israel and given them hope. Two Babylonian gods are mentioned in this passage: Bel and Nebo. Bel is probably a reference to the Babylonian god named Marduk. Nebo is the son of Marduk. Animals will carry off the statues of these two gods, for they are totally worthless and powerless as objects of worship. In fact, they will be a burden to those who carry them. In contrast, Isaiah's prophetic words celebrate the power of God. God alone is able to uphold, defend, and restore the people. God's sovereignty is described in the second half of chapter 46, which says that God will summon a "bird of prey" or "man of My purpose" (v. 11) to bring about the destruction of Babylon. This is another reference to Cyrus, king of Persia.

Application

Long ago, when I served as a youth minister, I often used a simple illustration in my teaching. In the center of a clean sheet of paper, I drew a small black dot. I held up the paper in front of the group and asked them to tell me what they saw. Invariably, they described the black dot. They readily saw the dark stain but never mentioned the 99 percent of the paper that was clean and white. People tend to see the negative much more quickly than the pure, good, and noble characteristics of a person's life. I used this illustration to remind my students of the importance of being consistent and Christlike in all they did.

The Babylonians were guilty of horrible idolatry. They fashioned gods with their own hands and bowed down to worship them. In judging their actions, God reminded the people that the things that are false, evil, and soiled cannot stand in the place of what should be spotless, clean, and pure. Whenever we attempt to position our self-created gods alongside Almighty God, we present them as equals. Such positioning is an abomination before God. God alone is worthy of our praise, attention, pursuits, admiration, and longing. Let us cart off our false gods so that it is apparent to all whom we truly serve.

Prayer

Father, forgive our foolish creation of false gods. Convict us and correct us. Amen.

Day 726 — Isaiah 47: The Mighty Have Fallen

> "Come down, virgin daughter of Babylon, and sit in the dust. For your days of sitting on a throne have ended. O daughter of Babylonia, never again will you be the lovely princess, tender and delicate." Isaiah 47:1 (NLT)

Observation
Isaiah 47 speaks about the imminent fall of Babylon. Though God once used the nation to punish Israel and bring her to repentance, Babylon overstepped her authority and acted cruelly towards the Israelites. God will punish her for this. Babylon is depicted here as an arrogant woman of great beauty who will quickly lose her status among the elite and grovel as a slave. No longer will she be "loving, tender, and delicate." She will leave her throne and sit in the dust as a sign of mourning and humility. The once-proud centerpiece of the Babylonian empire will be shamed. God will show no mercy or pity—only wrath. The judgment will include a loss of security, and the land will gain widows and lose children in a single day. The magical incantations of Babylon's pagan priests and the worship of idols will prove useless. Babylon has failed to realize that God gave her strength and power. Now God will quickly come and take both away.

Application
For a successful game of football, players must work together as a team. In order for the quarterback to have sufficient time to complete a pass, he needs a pocket of protection around him to keep the defensive linemen at bay. The offensive line drops back and forms this "pocket." The quarterback steps up into the pocket and finds time to throw. But if a player misses a blocking assignment, the wall of protection is destroyed and the quarterback is vulnerable.

In the words of Isaiah's prophecy, Babylon learns that her once-strong defenses will be overrun. The nation will fall into ruin. Disobedience and idolatry before God will bring this downfall. Similarly, we will fall whenever we fail to acknowledge the sovereignty of God in our lives. Whenever we usurp God's authority, ignore God's word, and disregard God's counsel, we lower the wall of protection that once kept us safe. We expose ourselves to every temptation, every intent of evil, and every foolish distraction. The key is to rest secure in God's pocket of protection. We discover that place of security through attention to our faith disciplines: spending the necessary moments in prayer, immersing ourselves in God's word, looking and listening for the prompting of God's Spirit. God's will carefully shepherd us if we will simply listen. Don't become vulnerable. Become faithful.

Prayer
Father, protect us, even from our foolish ways. Amen.

Day 727 — Isaiah 48: No Room at the Top

> "I will rescue you for my sake—yes, for my own sake! I will not let my reputation be tarnished, and I will not share my glory with idols!"
> Isaiah 48:11 (NLT)

Observation

After predicting the destruction that would befall Babylon, the prophet Isaiah turns attention back to the Israelites living in exile. The people of God also need correction. Israel must move beyond obstinance towards God and instead display obedience. Isaiah calls the people "to hear." The phrase is used ten times in this passage. The people should pay close attention to what God has done and what God now promises to do on their behalf. It is important that God reveals plans for the future so that when those predicted things happen, the people cannot give credit to their false idols and pagan worship practices. Only God can control events in the future and correctly predict when they will happen. Clearly there is no other God like the Lord. With clear language, God indicates the plan to use Cyrus of Persia as an instrument of judgment against the Babylonians. The chapter ends on a positive note as God promises to restore the people to their place in Israel and to provide for their needs.

Application

Part of parenting is teaching children to share with others. We instruct our children to share their toys, their blankets, and maybe even their snacks with the boys and girls around them. We view generosity and sharing as noble qualities. Even as adults, we are reminded of the importance of sharing our possessions with those in need. We know that it is right to give to the needy and to bless those who have less than ourselves. And certainly, God has shared resources, attributes, and mercy with all of us. We learn generosity from God's example of grace.

Our focus verse indicates one thing that God is unwilling to share. God will not share glory with idols. God refuses to yield any honor to false gods and manmade idols. If we co-opt the praise and glory that our hearts should offer to God and give it to other things, then we make those things the objects of our worship rather than the Lord God. "I don't serve false gods," you may say. "I don't offer glory to an inanimate object." Are you sure? Consider your spending. Where does the bulk of your income go—to the things you think are necessary to make your life better or to the things that build the Kingdom of God and make the lives of others better? Maybe your generosity should increase and your selfishness should decrease. Consider reprioritizing your allegiances. We need to glorify God and not ourselves.

Prayer

Father, forgive us when we offer praise to "things" and give them priority over you in our lives. Amen.

Day 728 — Isaiah 49: The Liberation of the Lord

> "I will say to the prisoners, 'Come out in freedom,' and to those in darkness, 'Come into the light.' They will be my sheep, grazing in green pastures and on hills that were previously bare." Isaiah 49:9 (NLT)

Observation
Isaiah 49-57 comprises an important section in the book of Isaiah. This major section emphasizes Israel's deliverance from Babylon and from sin. It also contains three of the four "Servant Songs" in the book of Isaiah. Chapters 49-52 speak to the impending gloom of the nation's anticipated captivity by offering the promise of deliverance and restoration. Chapter 49 speaks of the role of "God's special servant" who will speak to Israel and to the nations. Scholars debate the identity of this servant. Some suggest it is Isaiah himself, King Darius, the nation of Israel, or even the Lord God. Regardless of the servant's identity, it is clear that the message of redemption and salvation is directed to the heart of the nation. As Israel continues to reject the full implications of the message, God will extend it to Gentile nations as well. The final section of this chapter offers great encouragement. Even though the exile is coming, God will not forget or forsake the people.

Application
With a clear sense of God's calling to prepare for pastoral ministry, I worked hard to complete my education. I went from college straight into graduate school to earn my master's degree. As soon as I completed that degree, I forged ahead until I had earned my doctorate by the age of 28. It was a grind. That season of my life represented hard work. When I finally completed all the papers, all the writing, all the books, and more, a huge weight lifted off my shoulders. I felt free. Of course, there is no adequate comparison between my experience and what the ancient Israelites endured while living under the oppression of the Babylonians. But God faithfully promised that one day they would experience freedom once again and would return to their homeland. In our focus verse, Isaiah speaks of walking out of the darkness and into the light. Sometimes we need to view our life experiences as seasons. Some seasons may be difficult and painful, while other seasons bring greater enjoyment and less stress. But the promise made to the ancient Israelites is also made to us. In the midst of every season, God is present. And seasons don't last forever. If you are living in a difficult time, the day will come when this season draws to a close. That's a promise.

Prayer
Father, we praise you for your continued presence and grace through every season.

Day 729 — Isaiah 50: Determined

> "Because the Sovereign Lord helps me, I will not be disgraced. Therefore, I have set my face like a stone, determined to do his will. And I know that I will not be put to shame." Isaiah 50:7 (NLT)

Observation

Isaiah 50 continues to encourage the people of Israel. In preparation for the dark days of exile that lie ahead, the prophetic word challenges the nation to look to the example of the Suffering Servant who will emerge victorious. God has not "divorced" the people or "put them away" forever. Instead, God promises to be faithful to the remnant that will return after the exile. God will redeem, or "buy back," those who have sold themselves into the slavery of exile because of their sins. Verses 4-11 contain the third Servant Song in Isaiah. God awakens the servant to hear what God has to proclaim. In describing the servant as "putting his back to those who strike him" and "not hiding his face from shame and spitting," Isaiah speaks directly to the fulfillment in Jesus' actions leading up to the crucifixion. The passage ends on a triumphant note as it promises that the enemies of God will be judged.

Application

What are you determined to do? What goal have you set that will occupy your thoughts and energy until you reach it? In his words of prophecy, Isaiah spoke about the Suffering Servant (later identified as Jesus Christ) who would work toward our redemption through his complete obedience to the will and purpose of God. Jesus "set his face like a stone, determined to do God's will." Consider the short-term goals we often set for ourselves. Sometimes the goal is to "get back in shape." Maybe the goal is to shed a few pounds, read a certain number of books, write encouraging notes, or memorize a few verses of scripture. These goals are certainly worthy of time and attention. To accomplish any of them takes dedication, a little planning, and maybe a workable strategy. They may also require consistency: do the right thing over and over again until the goal is accomplished. There are also loftier, greater, and more important goals. We are placed on the planet to bring honor and glory to God. Therefore, we must dedicate ourselves to that task with obedient behavior, dedicated resolve, and purposeful action. If we take seriously the Great Commission (to make disciples) and the Great Commandment (to love people), we will be forced to live with greater determination. We must become intentional about our faith development, Kingdom-building relationship development, and sacrificial lifestyle development. We must learn how to give ourselves completely to our God-given tasks.

Prayer

Father, may we have a determined resolve to live fully for your purposes. Amen.

Day 730 — Isaiah 51: Finding Comfort

> "I, yes I, am the one who comforts you. So why are you afraid of mere humans, who wither like the grass and disappear?" Isaiah 51:12 (NLT)

Observation

Isaiah 51 records words that remind Israel of God's promise of deliverance and restoration. It begins with a call to remember. The people are reminded to remember Abraham and Sarah and how God once worked in their lives. Abraham was only one man, but from his descendants came a great nation. The promise is that God will do it again. Israel will rise from the ruins. "Songs of thanksgiving will fill the air" (v. 3). God's righteous rule will never end. In verse 9, the dialogue shifts. Now God is called to awaken and be clothed with strength. God is called to act on behalf of the people. Verse 14 promises God's deliverance: "Soon all you captives will be released! Imprisonment, starvation, and death will not be your fate." The people will "drink no more of his fury" (v. 22).

Application

There are a lot of spiders on the planet. If one of them invades our house, we launch a full-scale assault. It begins with a strong summons from my wife. "Jon!" Through all the years of marriage, I have come to recognize the subtle differences when she calls my name. "Must be a spider," I say to myself. Quickly I am off the couch and on my way to kill the beast. Then, it's off to grab a can of Raid so that I can thoroughly soak the house with insecticide. I always find it interesting that something so small can wreak such havoc.

God wonders the same thing, according to our focus verse. Why do we fear frail, weak, and misguided humans when the Almighty God protects our lives? How can something so small frighten us when something so big surrounds us? God promises to comfort us, to be with us, to deliver and protect us. What can "mere humans" do to us?

We fear a lot of things that people bring into our lives. We fear hatred. We fear embarrassment. We fear abuse. We fear belittlement. The problem is that the pressures of everyday life sometimes obscure the length of eternity. Nothing about this life is permanent; fear, anxiety, anger, abuse, scorn, oppression, and condescension are temporary. The day will surely come when our powerful and saving God will call us near. We will rest secure forever in God's arms of protection. We will wonder why the pressures and anxieties of life ever seemed so big. I hope that you will spend this day not in endless fear and worry but in the hope of that coming day.

Prayer

Father, deliver us from evil and fill our hearts with hope. Amen.

Day 731 — Isaiah 52: Time to Wash Up

> "Get out! Get out and leave your captivity, where everything you touch is unclean. Get out of there and purify yourselves, you who carry home the sacred objects of the Lord." Isaiah 52:11 (NLT)

Observation
Isaiah 52 calls the Israelites to awaken and "put on strength." In other words, "be encouraged." They are to clothe themselves with beautiful garments and celebrate because the days of oppression and exile are drawing to a close. The unclean and godless pagan people will no longer enter the city of Jerusalem to bring it harm. God will redeem Israel and punish her oppressors. The people are called to remember their time of oppression under the Assyrians and Babylonians. In poetic language, the watchman over the city is told to look out and see the restoration of Jerusalem. God will bring about the return of the exiles by God's "Holy Arm." The people are called to leave Babylon along with the Babylonians' pagan practices. The last portion of the chapter records part of the fourth Servant Song, which describes in vivid language the suffering and redemptive work of the Messiah, later fulfilled in the work of Jesus.

Application
As a child who often played for endless hours in the dirt and dust of the backyard, I can remember hearing my mother call me inside to get cleaned up for supper. "It's time to wash up," she would say. When the activities of the day render us a little too stained and soiled, we still need to wash up in order to make ourselves presentable. I have a friend who is a judge here in the city of Nashville. He deals with some of the more heinous crimes of our city. He gets rape cases, abuse cases, assault cases, and even human-trafficking cases. I asked him once how he handled the day-to-day stress of the job and still functioned as a loving family man at home. He told me that as soon as he got home each evening, the first thing he did was take a shower. He said, "I know the water can't wash away all the dark deeds described in my courtroom, but symbolically, I need to wash away those things from my mind so that I can be fully present for my family." The prophet Isaiah instructed the people of God who returned from the Babylonian exile to purify themselves. Everything they had touched was unclean. They were to remove the impurities from their lives so that they could return to God's presence. All of us have sinned and fallen short of the glory of God. Our walk-through life has left us soiled and dirty. If we are not careful, we will allow some of the world's stain to remain with us as we move forward into the next chapter of our lives. It's time to wash up. It's time to walk away and start again. We must leave the impure behind and find the joy of forgiveness.

Prayer
Father, teach us how to remove the impurities from our lives that sin has caused. Amen.

Day 732　　　　　　　　　Isaiah 53: The Great Atonement

> "But he was pierced for our rebellion, crushed for our sins. He was beaten so we could be whole. He was whipped so we could be healed."
> Isaiah 53:5 (NLT)

Observation
Isaiah 53 continues the best-known and most-cited Servant Song in the book of Isaiah. The fulfillment of this prophetic word is stunningly portrayed in the life and death of Jesus. The passage begins with a rhetorical question, asking who will believe the message God has revealed to the believing remnant in Israel. The prophet speaks of the Messiah who will rise like a tender plant in the dry ground of rejection displayed by Israel. Verse 3 mentions that the suffering servant will not be beautiful or majestic. Christ will not possess a majestic manner. He will not look like royalty. "He will be a man of sorrows." This does not mean that Christ will have no joy or zest for living but rather that he will know better than anyone else the havoc that sin brings into human life. He will bear the grief (pain) and the sorrow (sickness) of shame and remorse that are the result of sin's consequences. He will suffer in our place, bearing the weight and punishment of our sins. Verse 10 points out that Christ's atoning death is part of God's eternal plan for the redemption of humanity.

Application
Years ago, a friend of mine was on the interstate behind a flatbed truck loaded with Port-A-Potties. The driver had obviously picked them up from a concert site or something similar and was taking them back to the company. My friend noticed that the one nearest to the back edge of the flatbed was starting to wobble, dancing its way off the back of the truck. He swerved to avoid a potential problem, and sure enough, the Port-a-Potty fell from the truck, smashing into a thousand pieces, spilling who-knows-what all over the road. When my friend passed the truck, he looked at the driver. The driver just shrugged his shoulders and kept driving as though nothing had happened.

Sometimes we leave a mess for others to clean up. Look at the use of the pronouns in our focus verse: "He was pierced, he was beaten, he was whipped." This happened because of "our rebellion, our sins, our need for healing." Christ stood in our place. He took on our punishment. He cleaned up our mess. Why? So that we could one day stand in the presence of God, clean, forgiven, and whole. His sacrifice was God's plan from the beginning. John's Gospel states it this way: "In the beginning was the Word..." (John 1:1 NASB). The Greek word "Logos," most often translated "Word," can also be translated "Answer." So "In the beginning was the Answer." God has a plan for your mess. His name is Jesus.

Prayer
Father, we praise you for your eternal plan for our redemption! Amen.

Day 733 — Isaiah 54: Endless Love

> "'For the mountains may move and the hills disappear, but even then my faithful love for you will remain. My covenant of blessing will never be broken,' says the Lord, who has mercy on you." Isaiah 54:10 (NLT)

Observation

Isaiah 54 and 55 form a brief unit. Chapter 54 speaks of God's promise of salvation for Israel, and chapter 55 invites Israel to receive it. The first aspect of God's promise of salvation is that God will enlarge and repopulate the land of Israel. The "desolate woman" (Jerusalem) will have abundant children. God calls the residents to enlarge their homes and build additions to house the growing population. The second aspect of the promise is that when the entire nation turns to the Servant for deliverance, the nation will be fully restored. The "sins of youth" (referring to a rebellious period when Israel rejected God's leadership) will be remembered no more. Israel will be as God's spouse—she will be protected, and the people will find security. God promises never to rebuke Israel again. God will establish a forever covenant of blessing. The third aspect of the promise is that when salvation comes, Israel will be renewed. Jerusalem will be rebuilt with precious stones and jewels. (This imagery is echoed in Revelation in the description of New Jerusalem.) Jerusalem will be set apart from every other city on earth.

Application

Change is inevitable. Recently I was traveling with my wife in the Cool Springs area, just south of Nashville. We have lived in the area for more than 20 years. As we drove, we talked about how many things have changed. There are shops, stores, hotels, condos, restaurants, and even entire shopping centers that didn't exist when we first arrived. Back then the area had few businesses, but now everything has changed.

In the midst of changes, it is good to know that God's love for us will never be altered, weakened, or changed. This portion of Isaiah teaches us that as history moves forward, as the ages come and go, and even if the mountains and hills should disappear, God's love will remain—constant, faithful, enduring. God promises a "covenant of blessing" to all of God's children. God promises to love us, provide for us, and bless us with good and perfect gifts. This promise will never be broken; it comes with eternal security and joy. We all have days when we feel the dizzying effect of change. Familiar neighborhoods grow old. Quaint restaurants are torn down. Small, quiet towns become bustling cities. Trusted mentors get sick and die. Nothing remains the same...or maybe I should say almost nothing remains the same. God's love for us will never change, not ever. So as the winds of change continue to disrupt your world, know that God's love remains solid.

Prayer

Father, we thank you this day for your constant and eternal love for us. Amen.

Day 734 — Isaiah 55: Clearing Your Mind

> "Let the wicked change their ways and banish the very thought of doing wrong. Let them turn to the Lord that he may have mercy on them. Yes, turn to our God, for he will forgive generously." Isaiah 55:7 (NLT)

Observation
Isaiah 55 continues the prophet's thoughts about the salvation of God, a glorious pronouncement of God's provision. We should read this chapter over and over to glean its rich harvest. It begins with an invitation to eat and drink freely from God's storehouse of blessings. These blessings are offered to all who wish to satisfy the deepest desires of their hearts. God calls on people to eat and drink what is good, not the things that offer no satisfaction. God will sustain the people by their obedience and through God's eternal covenant. Through Isaiah, God proclaims superiority: "My thoughts are not your thoughts, My ways are not your ways" (v. 8). The rain cycle, described in verses 10 and 11, is a metaphor for the ways God's word produces life. Isaiah prophesies about the "mountains and hills bursting into song and the trees clapping their hands." The joy of God's salvation will echo throughout the earth.

Application
Have you ever gotten a song stuck in your head? It keeps bouncing around in your mind all day long. The other day, a coworker brought his little daughter to work. She had an electronic device that kept playing, "The Wheels on the Bus Go Round and Round." If you know that song, it will now be stuck in your mind for the rest of the day. You're welcome. And just as a song can get stuck in our minds, so can a thought or an idea. We can get so captivated by something that it overtakes everything else. As James reminds us, "Then when lust has conceived, it gives birth to sin; and when sin is accomplished, it brings forth death" (James 1:15 NASB). To paraphrase, bad thoughts lead to bad actions. If we dwell on a bad thought, like lust, revenge, anger, deceit, etc., then our actions will soon follow. Our thought lives will lead us into sinfulness. Isaiah begs us to respond differently. If we are to change our ways, we must "banish the very thought of doing wrong." Let's be honest: all of us occasionally have a bad thought. We are human, and therefore at times an ugly thought comes to mind. The point is not to allow the thought to take root and grow. We can't control every thought that enters our brains, but we can decide which ones we will keep. When a thought enters your mind and you know it displeases God, claim it for what it is. Acknowledge that it is evil and wrong. And then banish the thought with a prayer, a distraction, or a better thought.

Prayer
Father, give us the strength to banish the evil thoughts from our minds. Amen.

Day 735 — Isaiah 56: Inclusion

> "I will also bless the foreigners who commit themselves to the Lord, who serve him and love his name, who worship him and do not desecrate the Sabbath day of rest, and who hold fast to my covenant. I will bring them to my holy mountain of Jerusalem and will fill them with joy in my house of prayer. I will accept their burnt offerings and sacrifices, because my Temple will be called a house of prayer for all nations." Isaiah 56:6-7 (NLT)

Observation

Isaiah 56-57 deal with the subject of the Gentiles' inclusion in the Messianic Kingdom of God. Chapter 56 teaches that all people, regardless of ethnicity, can receive God's blessings and eternal realm if they obey God's commands and seek God's purposes. The prophet emphasizes keeping the Sabbath. Sabbath worship is an important part of God's Kingdom requirements. The foreigner and eunuch, who are normally excluded from the promises made to Israel, will find inclusion through their obedience to God. These words fulfill the Abrahamic covenant that promised Abraham's offspring would be a blessing to all the nations. The final section of this chapter offers a word of rebuke and judgment on the "spiritually blind watchmen" of Israel who once led the nation astray.

Application

A local nonprofit in the greater Nashville area strives to get food into the hands of those who are hungry. They accept donations of both food and cash, and their trucks make daily runs to the local grocery stores to pick up food that is nearing the expiration date but still viable. Then, every weekend, they host "food giveaways" at schools, churches, or even city-owned parking lots. The process is simple: anyone who needs food can come to the location and pick up a box. (Multiple boxes are given to large families.) There is no paperwork, no forms to complete, no information exchanged. If a person needs food, they just show up and receive a box, no questions asked.

I like this approach. Everyone is included. Everyone's need can be met, regardless of qualification, registration, or address. In our focus verse, God takes a similar approach in filling the Kingdom. God will bless foreigners and others who are considered outcasts, bring them to the holy mountain to worship, and fill them with joy. There is a wideness in God's mercy, an open-door policy for God's Kingdom. All are included, embraced, and welcomed. All whose hearts long for God's heart, whose desire is to follow God, whose humility seeks dependency on God, will find a place of welcome. Certainly, all of us are like foreigners. We are not worthy…not even close. But through the sacrifice of the Messiah, we find our place.

Prayer

Father, thank you for including each person within the reach of your Kingdom. Amen.

Day 736 — Isaiah 57: Final Reward

> "For those who follow godly paths will rest in peace when they die."
> Isaiah 57:2 (NLT)

Observation
Isaiah 57 opens with another reflection on those who have acted wickedly and brought about the judgment of Israel. These "foolish leaders" were indifferent to the death of the godly, acting as though it was no big loss when the righteous perished. But the righteous will rest in peace and receive God's reward. Condemnation of the wicked continues as Isaiah speaks about the shameful acts of pagan worship, the hilltop shrines and idolatrous altars. The people have even placed pagan symbols in their homes. Many have exchanged fear of Almighty God for fear of worthless idols. God speaks harshly to the wicked, saying, "Let's see if your idols will save you!" (v. 13). The final section of the chapter ends on a more positive note, though, as God promises to dwell with those who repent and forsake false worship practices. But no peace will come to those who oppose God's ways.

Application
Have you experienced a long, exhausting day that drains every ounce of energy from your body? Imagine it's a warm Saturday and you wish to complete six different projects in your yard. You mow the grass and trim the hedges. You edge the sidewalk and clean out the gutters. You plant flowers for the summer and add mulch around the hedges. By the end of the day you fall into bed, completely exhausted from all the work. Sleep comes quickly. Not only is your body tired, but even your mind is at rest with the satisfaction of completing your tasks.

I hope that death will come in similar way for most of us. I hope that we go gently into that good night with a sense of satisfaction that we have completed the tasks outlined for our lives. I hope that others say we loved dearly, served tirelessly, shared sacrificially, extended grace abundantly, and forgave seriously. We want to die with our minds at rest, believing that all is well with our souls. I also hope that we fall into eternal rest completely exhausted from our labors of serving God. I hope that we leave nothing on the table, no gas in the tank, no energy left unspent. We often hear athletes at the end of a big game say something like, "We left it all on the field," meaning that they gave their all in the fight for victory. I hope the same will be said of us—that we gave our all. We want our lives to count. We want our lives to make a difference. How can we assure that we accomplish those goals? Perhaps by echoing the words of the psalmist in saying, "This is the day the Lord has made; I will rejoice and be glad in it." Maybe we should add, "And I will give it my all."

Prayer
God, may we exhaust ourselves in the joyful pursuit of responding to your daily call.

Day 737 — Isaiah 58: The Rumor Mill

> "Stop pointing your finger and spreading vicious rumors!"
> Isaiah 58:9b (NLT)

Observation

Isaiah 58 begins the third and final section of the book of Isaiah (chs. 58-66). This final section covers three different topics. Isaiah speaks about deliverance from Babylon, deliverance from sin, and deliverance at the end of days. These final chapters carry an eschatological theme—focusing on the end times. Chapter 58 starts with God as the speaker. God speaks to the primary sin of Israel: hypocrisy. The first type of hypocrisy is fasting with impure motives. The people are not fasting as an act of humility or penitence but as a way of furthering their selfish desires. They believe their attempts at fasting will manipulate God's actions. True fasting, declares God, will result in holy action; the oppressed will be set free, and the downtrodden will receive care. The second form of hypocrisy deals with Sabbath observance. Again, the people are self-serving. While acting as though they desire to observe the Sabbath, their actions say otherwise as they continue to maintain oppressive labor practices.

Application

A rumor can take on a life of its own. Embedded deeply within our human nature is a desire to pass along the rumors that come our way. We can't wait to share a juicy tidbit. We care little if others are potentially hurt. We don't often stop to consider the collateral damage we can cause by spreading rumors. Rumors are like wildfire. Once released, they spread with blinding speed. And rumors don't have to be true to inflict damage, doubt, or suspicion; they just have to be plausible in some way. Maybe in our selfish motivations we think that by making others look bad, we somehow make ourselves look better. The truth, however, is that when we pass along a vicious rumor, we damage our own reputations as well.

In our focus passage, God speaks to the Israelites in the context of offering instruction about genuine worship. God chastises the people for their outward attempt at looking pious while they inwardly live with evil desires. God declares, "Stop spreading vicious rumors!" One of the most damaging forces in the life of a community of faith is spreading gossip and rumors. It ruins reputations, destroys trust, and gives evil the victory. As members of the body of Christ, it is essential to be cautious when a rumor hits our ears. Will we help our church by passing it along? Will we honor God by destroying the reputation of one of God's children? Surely, we can do better. Instead of passing along a rumor, why not send up a prayer for those involved?

Prayer

Father God, take away our desire for hurtful gossip and damaging rumors. Amen.

Day 738   Isaiah 59: The Savior of the Oppressed

> "He was amazed to see that no one intervened to help the oppressed. So he himself stepped in to save them with his strong arm, and his justice sustained him." Isaiah 59:16 (NLT)

Observation
In addition to being called out for hypocritical fasting and Sabbath observances (ch. 58), Israel must also deal with the biggest problem: disobedience. The people's disobedience has alienated them from God. In both deed and word ("hands and tongue," v. 3), the Israelites have committed grievous sins before God. In a pursuit of their own self-interests, comfort, and security, many have overrun others. God calls them out for their sins. In verse 9, the narrative shifts in voice. Instead of third person pronouns, now the second person pronoun is employed. By saying "we," the attention turns to Israel's self-confession of her sins. The people admit to offering little justice to others. They admit to rebellion and perverse behavior. In response, God will bring about the nation's salvation by God's own strength. God will battle whatever plagues Israel. Even the Gentiles will praise the name of the Lord as they see God's redemptive work.

Application
Recently a young woman, just 17, was verbally assaulted by a man on a Vancouver train. She wore a hijab due to her Islamic faith. Her assailant began to scream at her, using a number of vulgar and racists words. The verbal attack went on for several minutes, with the man's voice and emotions growing ever stronger. Other passengers watched from a distance but took no action to intervene. Finally, the attacker stood over the young woman and began slapping her face. Seeing this physical abuse, a stranger who happened to play on a local rugby team raced to her aid and quickly put an end to the attack. He was later hailed as a hero. Surely the others on the train should be condemned as cowards.

Many people are oppressed in our world. Some are oppressed because of ethnicity. Others are oppressed because of race. Others are oppressed because of religion. And still others are oppressed because of things like gender, language, and poverty. As long as good people remain silent, the oppression, hostility, and violence will continue. In our focus verse, Isaiah declares that "God was amazed to see that no one intervened to help the oppressed." That verse should speak clearly and forcibly to Christians everywhere. We are made in the image of our Father. We are called to bring hope and redemption to those who are oppressed. And though we cannot solve every social ill, we must at least raise our voices.

Prayer
Father God, forgive us when we fail to stand up and act bravely. Amen.

Day 739 — Isaiah 60: Urban Renewal

> "Though you were once despised and hated, with no one traveling through you, I will make you beautiful forever, a joy to all generations."
> Isaiah 60:15 (NLT)

Observation

As the nation of Israel turns back to God in repentance, the Lord will begin redeeming the people. This chapter reveals the future glory that God will bring to the people and to the city of Jerusalem. According to verse 1, they are called to "arise and shine." The glory of the Lord will shine on them, and in turn they will be a light to the nations. Many things will happen as God brings restoration. The powers of the world will bring Israel's children back to Zion, along with great wealth. God's new Temple will be established as an eternal sanctuary that will draw all people. Verses 19-20 will become the basis for the description of Jerusalem offered in Revelation 21-22. God promises that there will be perpetual joy from generation to generation. The gates of the city will be open continually, and the presence of the Lord will illumine it both day and night. As our focus verse states, the city of Jerusalem, once despised and avoided, will be made beautiful forever.

Application

Many areas of Nashville are undergoing renewal efforts. Old houses are replaced by new and innovatively designed multi-family units. High-rise condos are built on the spot where old warehouses once stood. Old stores are transformed into bright and shiny retail spaces. There are new roads, new office buildings, and new companies. Recently, as I looked out across the Nashville skyline, I counted 13 construction cranes. Things are changing rapidly. Renewal is coming.

Old houses, buildings, and bridges are not the only things that need renewal. People need renewing as well. We tend to get worn down with age and experience. It is not that our bodies grow weak as much as our attitudes harden, our minds close, and our compassion becomes limited. We often get more "siloed" as life rolls along. We tend to cling to those who are familiar, whose viewpoints mirror our own, whose skin tone, language, and ethnicities match ours. Maybe it's time for a little renewal. Maybe it's time to ask God, in the words of David, to create a clean heart within us and renew a steadfast spirit. I believe we can form wonderful relationships, gain great perspectives, and enjoy amazing experiences if we open ourselves to the creation of new friendships, conversations, and viewpoints. Such things definitely involve some risk. They take initiative. They take courage. But the risk of renewal will produce great results in our lives. Don't grow bitter as you age. Grow better. Seek renewal in all the aspects of your life.

Prayer

Father God, open our hearts, minds, and eyes to possibilities of renewal. Amen.

Day 740 — Isaiah 61: Joy Clothes

> "I am overwhelmed with joy in the Lord my God! For he has dressed me with the clothing of salvation and draped me in a robe of righteousness."
> Isaiah 61:10a (NLT)

Observation

Isaiah 61 speaks of God's promise of deliverance through the work of the coming Messiah, specifically the Messiah's ministry to Israel. Jesus quotes these opening verses in Luke 4:18-21 as he identifies himself as the Servant Messiah: "The Spirit of the Sovereign Lord is upon me, for the Lord has anointed me to bring good news to the poor…" (Isa 61:1). With the coming of the Messiah, the time of God's favor will come as well. Deliverance will come to Israel because the Spirit of the Lord will make it happen by anointing the Servant to the special task of deliverance and redemption. God promises that Israel will once again be revived as a nation of priests, demonstrating God's message of salvation to the world. God will enter an everlasting covenant with the people.

Application

The fashion industry has many terms for various types of apparel: formal wear, semiformal wear, business casual, and casual, just to name a few. Because we care about our appearance, we want to make sure that we are wearing the right clothes for all occasions. When I was young, we used to talk about our "Sunday clothes" or, as some would say, "our Sunday-go-to-meeting" clothes. This meant a coat and tie for the boys and a dress for the girls. Certainly, those lines have blurred a little in our day. Comfort and casual have replaced "dress-up" clothes for many people. Still, we pay attention to what we wear. Our identity is often tied to our clothing.

As Isaiah describes the renewal that the Messiah is bringing forth, he claims that God's people will be dressed in "the clothing of salvation and draped in a robe of righteousness." I love this image. When God calls us to new life in Christ, we exchange the old for the new. We remove the tattered rags of sin, shame, and past mistakes that have clothed us and put on the clothing of salvation. We wear the robe of righteousness. Just as the father in the parable of the prodigal son insisted that his reclaimed son should now dress in the best robe, indicating both kinship and acceptance, God insists that we dress in robes that signal our redemption and future hope, not in the filthy, sin-stained rags of our past. Sometimes we keep a favorite old pair of pants or a soft shirt to wear around the house because we feel comfortable in them. We become blinded to how bad we look in our "lounge wear." Sometimes, we have worn our "old clothes" long enough. It's time to change.

Prayer

Father God, may we embrace the new life before us as we cast off the old. Amen.

Day 741 — Isaiah 62: The Prayers of the Watchmen

> "O Jerusalem, I have posted watchmen on your walls; they will pray day and night, continually. Take no rest, all you who pray to the Lord."
> Isaiah 62:6 (NLT)

Observation
Isaiah 62 records Isaiah's prayer for Jerusalem. It is a reminder that when the Messiah returns to Israel, he will completely transform Jerusalem and her residents. The darkness of the city will turn to glorious light as the Messiah enters. The city's salvation will be like a "burning torch" to the nations, revealing God's glory. Even the reputation of the city will change. She who was called "forsaken and desolate" will be known as God's "delight." The Lord's devotion to her will be like that of a bridegroom for his bride. Isaiah calls on key leaders to pray continually for the fulfillment of these promises. He asks for "watchmen on the walls" who continually pray over the city. The chapter ends with a call to respond. The people of God are called to prepare for the coming of the Messiah. He will bring rewards to those who remain faithful.

Application
Do you pray for the city where you live? Do you pray for the health and well-being of the people who live within its limits? Imagine the mayor of your community building a tall tower and employing you to climb to the top each day so that you can watch over the city. What would you notice? Would you see the beauty of the trees or hear the laughter of children at play? Would you spot a house fire in time to save the structure? Would you see a crime and be able to stop it? Would you see storms on the horizon or smell the sweetness of spring flowers? Of course, your mayor is not going to hire you to do any of those things. But should we, as people of faith, serve as "watchmen on the walls" for our communities? In other words, should we hear the call to pray for our city, for its protection and prosperity, for its people and its properties?

What if God expected you to watch over your neighborhood? Who is praying for its residents? Who is seeking God's protection for those who live nearby? Aren't we as believers called to shepherd all the people of God? Could you start praying for your closest neighbors? Could you pray for their health, safety, and job security?

And let's shrink the scope of our responsibility even further. Are you being a watchman over your family? Are you praying for the protection and prosperity of your spouse and your children? Certainly, part of your daily responsibilities as a God-follower is to pray faithfully, relentlessly, and specifically for your family. Don't let them down.

Prayer
God, make us faithful in our role of watching over what you entrust to us. Amen.

Day 742 — Isaiah 63: Unbreakable Kinship

> "Surely you are still our Father! Even if Abraham and Jacob would disown us, Lord, you would still be our Father. You are our Redeemer from ages past." Isaiah 63:16 (NLT)

Observation

Isaiah 63 opens with a future look at the Messiah's judgment of Edom. The Messiah will one day come to judge all the enemies of Israel. One day, the nations of the earth will pursue a bloody war against Israel, but the Messiah will conquer. He will defeat the nations by "trampling out the winepress of his wrath." The middle portion of this chapter is devoted to remembering God's faithful covenantal action. The people are called to remember how God responded to their bondage in Egypt and delivered them through the wilderness experience. In light of God's past faithfulness, the prophet pleads for God to once again act on Israel's behalf. The final part of the chapter deals with an interesting question. Isaiah seems to question why God has allowed the people to act rebelliously. The answer is not that God has caused the people to sin. God merely acts in response to their actions. The key factor is the people's willingness to rebel and grieve the Holy Spirit of God (v. 10).

Application

My father is Floyd Roebuck. There is no need to run a DNA test to prove our kinship; just look at us to see that we are undoubtably related. We look alike, think alike, and even have many of the same mannerisms. He will always be my father, and I will always be his son. Though there is always the potential for the relationship to break or splinter, there will never be a moment when the kinship is severed. That's just the way it is. Thankfully, my father and I have always enjoyed a great relationship with no brokenness through the years. But have I always been perfect? No. Have I disappointed him? Sure. There was the time when my brother and I cleaned his newly restored '54 MG with a Brillo pad…that wasn't a good day. And then there was the time when my dad and I disagreed on whether I should join a fraternity when I went off to college. He questioned my choice. I'm sure there have been other days when he questioned my judgment. But here's the point: he will never cease to be my father, and I will never cease to be his son. It's an unbreakable kinship.

That is also the kind of kinship we share with our heavenly Father. We are created in God's image. You were carefully, meticulously, and fearfully made. God's bond of love for you is unbreakable. God's affection for you is unstoppable. God's watchcare over you is unrelenting. Though you may not always please God with your actions, attitudes, and thoughts, the kinship remains. God will always listen and will always act towards you in love. You will always be God's child. The kinship is secure, even on the days when you behave poorly.

Prayer

God, we thank you for the unbreakable kinship we share with you. Amen.

Day 743   Isaiah 64: Hope for Constant Sinners

> "We are constant sinners; how can people like us be saved? We are all infected and impure with sin. When we display our righteous deeds, they are nothing but filthy rags. Like autumn leaves, we wither and fall, and our sins sweep us away like the wind." Isaiah 64:5b-6 (NLT)

Observation

Isaiah 64 opens with the prophet asking God to come down and work in the lives of the people as God has done in the past. Throughout the history of the Israelites, God's power and presence was demonstrated in powerful ways like the exodus experience, the Sinai moment, the crossing of the Jordan River, and the tumbling walls of Jericho. Isaiah pleads for God to act on behalf of Israel again. God does so, fully aware of the people's disobedience. Despite their shortcomings and sins, Isaiah pleads for God to temper God's anger and forget the sins of the people (v. 9). As Isaiah considers the destruction of the Temple and the city of Jerusalem, he asks if God will act and relent from further punishment.

Application

Most mornings when I am at work, I park in a below-ground parking deck situated beneath one of the main academic buildings on Belmont's campus. On each level of the parking deck, exhaust fans are strategically placed in order to keep fresh air moving in and around the structure. Over the past few months, I've noticed that on level 3, one of the continually running fans has developed a loud squeak, probably a bearing going out on the electric motor (that's my "expert" diagnosis). It will continue to squeak loudly, constantly making that awful noise, until someone with the ability to repair the problem is alerted and takes the initiative to fix it.

Isaiah confesses that we are constant sinners and ponders how people like us will be saved. He's right. We are constant sinners. We were rebellious yesterday, we are rebellious today, and we will be rebellious tomorrow. Claiming the name of Jesus doesn't make us immune from our sinful disobedience. We hope that each day we will continue to conform to the image of Christ, but that process is far from complete. We will struggle with our sins until we are made whole when Christ returns or chooses to call us home. We live in the meantime with the acknowledgment that we are constant sinners. How, indeed, will we be saved? Here's how: in response to our constant sins, God offers us constant grace through Jesus. Though our sins never please God, God is always pleased to forgive us and cleanse us. God acts out of unchangeable love for each of us. Live this day knowing that you are loved and that yes, once again, God will forgive.

Prayer

God, thank you for your willingness to match our sinfulness with your constant grace. Amen.

Day 744 — Isaiah 65: The Salvation of the Nation

> "'But I will not destroy them all,' says the Lord. 'For just as good grapes are found among a cluster of bad ones (and someone will say, "Don't throw them all away—some of those grapes are good"), so I will not destroy all Israel. For I still have true servants there. I will preserve a remnant of the people of Israel and of Judah to possess my land.'" Isaiah 65:8-9a (NLT)

Observation

Isaiah 65 describes the judgment and final salvation of God for the nation of Israel. The opening verses speak of the way God will descend to judge those who have engaged in idolatry, false worship, unclean practices, and selfish pride. They will fall under God's wrath. But not all people will suffer. God will spare a remnant of the righteous. The middle verses describe God's transformation of the land. From the plain of Sharon in the west to the Valley of Achan in the east, the land will be redeemed and produce abundant quantities of fruits and vegetables. As the glory of God descends, not only will the land be transformed but people will be transformed as well. God promises that people will live long and joy-filled lives. They will not be considered old even at the age of 100. The final verses describe how God will restore the original state of creation when all animals will live in peace and harmony.

Application

One of the more interesting conversations in scripture occurs between Abraham and God. Abraham bargains with God about the destruction of Sodom (Gen 18). He gets God to agree that if God is able to find 50 righteous people, the city will not be destroyed. And then Abraham asks, "But what if there are only 40?" God agrees not to bring destruction if there are 40 righteous people. Then Abraham pushes God to agree to 30, 20, and finally just 10. If 10 righteous men are found, God will preserve the city.

I am reminded of that conversation as I read Isaiah's account of God's final judgment of Israel. Because there is a faithful remnant, the nation will not be destroyed but redeemed. This indicates the enormous value of just a few righteous people who live in an evil culture. Through the faith of those few, the culture can be redeemed, evil can be overcome, and righteousness can rule the day. Jesus later told his disciples that they were to be the salt of the earth and the light of the world. Here's my point: a few righteous people who carefully and purposefully live out their faith can have a massive impact on both culture and community. Will you be counted as one of those people?

Prayer

Father God, call us to righteous living so that we might transform our world. Amen.

Day 745 — Isaiah 66: The Key to Blessing

> "I will bless those who have humble and contrite hearts, who tremble at my word." Isaiah 66:2b (NLT)

Observation

This final chapter of Isaiah describes the judgment of the wicked that will come when the Messiah returns. It begins with a declaration followed by a rhetorical question: "Heaven is my throne, earth is my footstool. Could you build me a temple as good as that?" The emphasis is not that God doesn't want the people to build places of worship. The emphasis is on God's superiority over all humanity. God reminds the people, through the words of Isaiah, that attempts at worship with false motivations and impure hearts do not impress the Lord. God longs for those who are humble and contrite in spirit, those who recognize and respect the distance between a Holy God and sinful humanity. For many, religious rituals are empty and devoid of meaning because those who worship are tainted by sin. The wicked will be punished, but God will comfort those who practice righteousness, like a mother comforting her child. The righteous will be sent out into all the world as witnesses of God's glory before the nations. God will gather the people. When the Messiah comes, all creation will be cleansed, sin will be removed, and God's order will be restored.

Application

One of the saddest moments in scripture is recorded in Genesis 27:38, when Esau realizes that his father Isaac has given his blessing to the younger son, Jacob, instead of to Esau. When Esau realizes that his brother deceived their father and stole his blessing, he cries out, "Do you only have one blessing? Oh my father, bless me, too!" (NLT). It is a gut-wrenching moment. Fortunately for all of us, our Heavenly Father has an unlimited number of blessings to share. But our focus verse says that those who qualify for God's blessings must have "humble and contrite" hearts. In the Hebrew language, the word humble means "poor" or "one who is in need of help." Contrite means "crippled" or "wounded." Put those ideas together. God longs to bless people who recognize their need for God's help—those who understand the difference between God-dependency and self-sufficiency. God also longs to bless those whose life experiences have wounded or crippled them. God will bless people who have no expectation of such grace in their lives. Let's readily confess that we are impoverished in spirit. We are wounded by the circumstances of our lives. And yet God longs to bless us immeasurably. This is not because of who we are but because of who God is. Do you need a blessing? God has many to give.

Prayer

Father God, we seek your blessing this day, even amid our difficulties. Amen.

# Day 746 — Jeremiah 1: No Excuses

> "'O Sovereign Lord,' I said, 'I can't speak for you! I'm too young!' The Lord replied, 'Don't say, "I'm too young," for you must go wherever I send you and say whatever I tell you. And don't be afraid of the people, for I will be with you and will protect you. I, the Lord, have spoken!'"
> Jeremiah 1:6-8 (NLT)

Observation

The book of Jeremiah offers a prophetic word to the southern kingdom of Judah as Babylonian captivity looms on the horizon. It is a revealing look at the inner struggle of a prophet who is at times overwhelmed by his prophetic calling and by the message of judgment and destruction he is called to deliver. Jeremiah, a contemporary of the prophets Zephaniah, Ezekiel, and Habakkuk, is from the town of Anathoth just three miles northeast of Jerusalem. His words will echo some of the same themes as those of Isaiah as he speaks boldly concerning the people's idolatry. Chapter 1 is devoted to Jeremiah's call to ministry. He will speak on the Lord's initiative and not his own. In fact, according to this chapter, God placed this call on Jeremiah's life even before his birth. Jeremiah is fearful of the prophetic task, especially at a relatively young age, but God promises to deliver him as he speaks to rulers and kings. His calling is confirmed within this chapter by two visions, one of an almond tree and the other of a boiling pot.

Application

Most of us are pretty good at making excuses, especially when we want to shirk a time-consuming or awkward responsibility. Imagine that you are invited to a Saturday afternoon bridal shower for a friend, but it's during the big game on television. Going to the bridal shower is the last thing you want to do, so you create excuses. "I would love to come, but I have another appointment." "I'm a little under the weather and I don't want to share my cold with others." "I'm waiting on an important phone call and I need to be home with my meeting notes." You've done something similar, right? We all create excuses to avoid something we don't want to do.

Jeremiah had excuses for God when he was called to prophetic ministry. He tried to excuse himself with his young age and inexperience. In response, God promised to go before him and tell him exactly what he needed to say. Any excuses were nullified. Sometimes God calls us to a task. It may be to a ministry position, to a leadership role in the church, or to a new relationship. If it scares us to hear this call, we too may offer excuses. But the old adage is true: "Where God guides, God provides." Make up excuses all you want, but God can answer each one. Listen for the call and be obedient.

Prayer

Father, may we be faithful to whatever claims you make on our lives. Amen.

Day 747 — Jeremiah 2: Trading Faces

> "Has any nation ever traded its gods for new ones, even though they are not gods at all? Yet my people have exchanged their glorious God for worthless idols!" Jeremiah 2:11 (NLT)

Observation
Jeremiah 2:1-3:5 contains God's indictment against the people. In the time of Jeremiah, the people of Israel no longer remembered the earlier days when their ancestors worshipped and obeyed God. Somewhere along the way, they turned to foolish and worthless idols. Those who should have known God best no longer seemed to know God at all. According to 2:13, they abandoned the God who could offer them unlimited living water and chose instead to serve gods of their own creation—gods that Jeremiah compared to cracked cisterns that could hold no water at all. After the Assyrians overran the land, the Israelites turned to an alliance with Egypt, creating a vassal relationship. Now God accuses the people of turning in every direction for help except to the Lord. Judah, once planted by God as "a vine from the purest stock" (v. 21), has become an alien vine fertilized by foreign gods.

Application
Many years ago, while pastoring a church in Middle Kentucky, a local radio show host invited me to broadcast a weekly 30-minute devotional thought. As I drove to the studio each week, I listened to the station, interested in what aired just before my devotion. The station ran a local "swap shop" show. Callers could offer various items for sale or trade. People often called with an item to swap for the item being sold. People sold or traded everything from washing machines to livestock to comic book collections. The goal was always to "trade up." In a good deal, people were able to swap for something of seemingly greater value. We understand that concept. We long to trade up to something better, more useful, and more valuable. Apparently, the ancient Israelites were willing to trade their relationship with Holy God for the worship of false idols. They traded their allegiance to the Living God for a passion for false idols created by human beings. God rebuked their behavior and promised destruction because of their foolish worship practices. I wonder if we are any better. Don't we tend to trade in our God for the next big distraction that comes along? We may not call them idols, but in fact they become just that. We give our time, attention, and even wealth to sustain things that have no control or power over human life. A favorite singer/songwriter of mine, Dan Fogleberg, once offered this lyric: "Changing horses in the middle of the stream gets you wet and sometimes cold." Changing gods in the middle of our lives does much more than that. Be certain that you give your allegiance only to the Lord God.

Prayer
Father, forgive our foolish pursuit of things that distract us from you. Amen.

Day 748   Jeremiah 3: The Abuse of Grace

> "'Surely you won't be angry forever! Surely you can forget about it!' So you talk, but you keep on doing all the evil you can." Jeremiah 3:5 (NLT)

Observation
Jeremiah 3 depicts the continual shame of Israel, who refuses to practice full repentance. The opening verses draw from the words of Deuteronomy 24:1-4, where God's law forbids a man to remarry his divorced wife if she has already remarried in the meantime. She would be considered "defiled" by her second marriage. In like fashion, after severing the relationship with God, Israel entered into many other relationships and chased after many other foreign gods. She defiled herself in relationship to God and yet, according to Jeremiah, God makes the offer of mercy and longs to reclaim these people if they will heed the call to repentance. Judah (southern kingdom) had witnessed Israel's (northern kingdom) refusal to repent but learned little from the experience. If Judah is willing to repent now, then God's full anger will not come upon them. Repentance will become the key to healing the relationship. In the closing verses of the chapter, the people acknowledge the shame they have brought upon themselves.

Application
"Forgive me, O God…again." Have you ever said those words? We all have. You would think that being forgiven and having our sins erased would lead us never to commit the same sin again. The joy of shame lifting from our shoulders should make us determined not to sin again. But then it happens. We find ourselves asking God once again to forgive us for committing the same sins. Look again at our focus verse. The first portion is the Israelites' cry. They beg and plead for God's mercy: "Surely you can forget about it!" The second portion is God's response. The people can talk a good game, but their actions prove otherwise. They commit the same sins again and again, expecting God to forgive them over and over. We need to remember that repentance is a call for renewal, not continuation. It is an abuse of grace to ask for God's forgiveness while harboring the intent to continue our sinful ways. To repent is to change direction. It is to alter the course and redirect our behavior. We don't go through the cycle of sin, regret, confession, and repentance just to keep walking the same path, never altering our actions. Genuine repentance carries the commitment to make radical changes in our lives, changes that place us on a new path and a new course. Let's be ecstatically grateful for God's forgiving grace. But let's also be deeply committed to radical steps of change so we don't continue to make the same bad choices.

Prayer
Father, forgive us again and we will do better next time…maybe. Amen.

Day 749 — Jeremiah 4: Bird-Watching

> "I looked at the earth, and it was empty and formless. I looked at the heavens, and there was no light. I looked at the mountains and hills, and they trembled and shook. I looked, and all the people were gone. All the birds of the sky had flown away. I looked, and the fertile fields had become a wilderness. The towns lay in ruins, crushed by the Lord's fierce anger."
> Jeremiah 4:23-26 (NLT)

Observation

Jeremiah 4 continues the prophet's vision of the destruction of Jerusalem. We can hear his sense of anguish at having to describe the city's terrible fate because of the people's continued idolatry. Jeremiah suggests that if the people would put away their false idols, they would no longer "drift" from God. Faithfulness to God would bless not only Israel but all the nations of the earth. In verse 3 the people are challenged to sow seeds of righteousness in the fallow (unused) soil of their lives. In describing the coming days of wrath and judgment, Jeremiah tells the people that the destruction will be swift and decisive. Like the scorching heat of a sirocco wind from the deserts of the east, the enemy, Babylon, will quickly overcome the land. The final verses express the horror of the moment, depicting Jerusalem as the daughter of God who cries out for help while she is being murdered.

Application

For the past decade or so, my wife and I have become amateur bird-watchers. The birdfeeder on our back deck attracts a wide variety of birds: cardinals, chickadees, wrens, and the occasional blue jay. We enjoy listening to their songs and watching them flit about the feeder. From time to time, however, they seem to disappear. If we look closely, we notice that the neighbor's cat is close by. Aware of the danger, the birds stay away until the cat moves along to some other distraction.

In Jeremiah's prophecy, he mentions that the birds will fly away during the destruction of the land. The lack of birds indicates that the enemy is close. There is no more singing, chirping, or joyful sounds filling the air. Take a look at your life for a moment and consider your level of joy, your level of gladness, or even your level of song. If it seems as though the things that bring you peace have flown away, perhaps you have allowed the destructive forces of evil to invade your life. Whenever your fellowship with God is neglected and the relationship gets out of sync, joy seems to flee from your heart. The solution is faithfulness. Guard your heart and seek God's face, and the "things of earth will grow strangely dim." Do you need a little joy today? Refresh your heart by seeking God's presence.

Prayer

Father, may we know the joy of your presence this day. Amen.

Day 750   Jeremiah 5: Self-Inflicted Wounds

> "Your wickedness has deprived you of these wonderful blessings. Your sin has robbed you of all these good things." Jeremiah 5:25 (NLT)

Observation
As they read the opening lines of Jeremiah 5, students of the Old Testament may remember Abraham's bargaining with God concerning the destruction of Sodom (Gen 18:16-33). God tells Jeremiah that if he can find one "just and righteous" person, God will offer mercy. Though many people would invoke the saying, "As the Lord lives," in swearing an oath, God knew that in reality they were making false promises that belied a relationship with the Lord. Despite the dire warnings of Jeremiah and other prophets, the people continued down a rebellious path of self-destruction. Jeremiah uses an illustration of an oxen breaking free of his yoke and wandering aimlessly in the wilderness only to be attacked by wild animals. In like fashion, in her wandering from God Judah would be attacked by foreign nations. False prophets had talked of peace and of God's unwillingness to punish the people. But the true prophet, Jeremiah, announces the coming of a warrior nation that will accomplish God's divine and destructive purpose.

Application
Have you ever done something dumb with no one to blame but yourself? Several years ago, I was shopping with my wife in a Bed, Bath, and Beyond store. She was looking at china place settings for a friend about to wed. I was lazily browsing some of the items only a few feet from her. I reached up to a shelf to grab a glass paperweight that I thought might look nice on my desk. When I did, I accidently bumped a crystal candle holder. It fell from the shelf and landed on a hand-blown glass Lenox bowl, which shattered into a thousand pieces. The bowl was on sale for $740. I stood there like a deer in the headlights with everyone in the store staring at me. It was not my best day. The phrase "like a bull in a china shop" came to my mind as a nervous and distraught salesman headed my way. I was banned from the store for an entire year. (Just kidding.) Jeremiah reminds his hearers that their own sins, their own wickedness, and their own transgressions deprived them of the blessings of God. They had no one to blame but themselves. Their poor decisions kept them from knowing the "good things" of God. Understand that God never moves away from us. God never creates distance in the relationship. The separation we sometimes feel is caused by our own foolishness. When we choose to sin, when we choose the path of disobedience, we begin to drive a wedge between ourselves and our Holy God. So don't blame God if the relationship is a little fragile, but do seek God's forgiveness. God will heal and restore.

Prayer
Father, forgive our foolish ways that separate and destroy. Heal us and redeem us. Amen.

Day 751   Jeremiah 6: Stick to the Path

> "This is what the Lord says: 'Stop at the crossroads and look around. Ask for the old, godly way, and walk in it. Travel its path, and you will find rest for your souls. But you reply, 'No, that's not the road we want!'"
> Jeremiah 6:16 (NLT)

Observation
This chapter gives a vivid look at the destruction of Jerusalem that Jeremiah prophesied. Warnings to the people (though later ignored), were to take two forms. First, a trumpet would sound an alarm, warning the people as far away as Tekoa (11 miles away.) Second, signal fires were to be lit in places like Beth Hakkerem. The army of Babylon was on the march, and the people were to "make themselves ready." God also gave instructions to the Babylonians. There were to build siege ramps and use battering rams as instruments of God's punishment. The leaders within the city of Jerusalem had abused their power. They abused the poor, widows, and orphans. Verse 11 indicates that even Jeremiah was angry and weary with the nation. Religious leaders had falsely spoken of peace while continuing to rebel against God. In our focus verse, Jeremiah pleads for the people to walk the "old path." He is referring to the Torah laws of God that include the Ten Commandments. But the people continue to make other choices.

Application
Sometimes the old ways are the best ways. Sometimes the well-worn paths of relationship with God continue to be the most vital ways of drawing close to the Lord. In our modern culture, many aspects of the faith fall under scrutiny, including key doctrines and traditions. Many opt for more "progressive attitudes," insisting that those who cling to the old values and interpretations have yet to be "enlightened." Some people argue that present-day interpretations of certain texts, which completely dismiss 2,000 years of church history, are to become the "true path" for believers to follow. Can we admit that not all evolution of thought and doctrine is healthy and right? Just because cultural opinion may lean one way or the other doesn't mean we should ignore God's instruction, claiming that it's outdated and out of touch. Did you ever play the game of "Gossip" as a child? The leader would whisper a secret to the first player in line, who would then whisper it to the second player, and so forth. It was fun to hear how distorted the secret became once it traveled through all the people standing in line. But unlike our game, God's word has not been distorted through the ages. The voice of the Spirit has continued to offer correction all along the way. We should weigh our thoughts against the timeless claims of scripture and live our lives accordingly. Sometimes it is best to follow the old path.

Prayer
Father, may we never confuse cultural opinion with biblical truth. Amen.

Day 752   Jeremiah 7: Game Over

> "Pray no more for these people, Jeremiah. Do not weep or pray for them, and don't beg me to help them, for I will not listen to you."
> Jeremiah 7:16 (NLT)

Observation
Jeremiah 7 leaves no doubt about God's anger over the idolatry of the people. As the chapter opens, God directs Jeremiah to stand in the Temple and proclaim the Lord's words of judgment. According to verse 3, God is still willing to relent from wrath if the people will truly repent or "amend" their ways. God is calling for a complete transformation of their behaviors, lifestyles, and beliefs. Foolishly, the rebellious people believe that simply because the Temple is in their city, God will not bring destruction. They treat the Temple not as a place of true worship but more like a "good luck charm" that will trump their disobedience. Verse 11 describes the Temple as a "den of thieves." Jesus quotes this verse in Matthew 21:13 when he cleanses the Temple and drives out the money-changers. The hard lesson is that God's love will not prevent God from chastising the people. God's people, more than all others, should understand the call to righteousness.

Application
Does our focus verse make you feel uncomfortable? It does for me. God tells Jeremiah not to pray for the rebellious Israelites any longer. It is a waste of time. It is a futile effort. There is no need even to weep for them. Their determined disobedience has led to their downfall. This story raises difficult questions: "Is there ever a time when we should cease praying for a wayward soul, giving up hope of their redemption, acknowledging that it is a waste to time to do otherwise? Can someone's heart be so hardened and their propensity for disobedience so engrained that we should no longer waste our breath or time in praying for them?" I would answer "No," with one exception. I believe that we should pray for the lost, broken, and wayward till the very end—unless God directs us to do otherwise. In the case of Jeremiah, notice that God is the One who calls for prayers to cease. It is not Jeremiah's place to make that judgment call, nor is it ours. Let's admit that it is difficult to pray for some people. We grow weary of the discipline of lifting them up to God. But our opinion of someone's worthiness (or lack thereof) should never determine whether they are worthy of prayer. We are called to pray for saint and sinner alike, for friends and for enemies, because Christ has told us to do so. Unfortunately, we don't get to take a break from praying for a difficult person—unless God reveals that we are to cease.

Prayer
God, may we be faithful in offering our prayers each day, regardless of our opinions. Amen.

Day 753   Jeremiah 8: Sinners in the Hands of an Angry God

> "And the people of this evil nation who survive will wish to die rather than live where I will send them. I, the Lord of Heaven's Armies, have spoken!"
> Jeremiah 8:3 (NLT)

Observation
Jeremiah 8 continues the prophet's description of the terrible fate that awaits Jerusalem when God's judgment at the hands of Israel's enemies is complete. Jeremiah mentions that the bones of both leaders and common people will be desecrated, removed from their graves and scattered across the ground, never to be buried again. Unlike the birds of the air, which understand the various seasons and appointed times and migrate to avoid winter, the people of Israel have refused to acknowledge God's promptings to repent. Even the scribes of the people write with "false pens" and attempt to justify idolatry and errant beliefs. With vivid language, Jeremiah describes the sound of the "snorting of enemy horses" as the impending invasion approaches. Jeremiah is so distraught by the weight of his sorrow for Jerusalem that he confesses that his spirit is "shattered." He asks rhetorically, "Is there no balm in Gilead?" (v. 22). The answer is no. Judgment will be swift and final.

Application
In the period of history known as "The Great Awakening," Jonathan Edwards offered a sermon on July 8, 1741, in the city of Enfield, Connecticut. It was titled "Sinners in the Hands of an Angry God." His powerful message stated that God will judge sinners harshly. The sermon promised forgiveness for those who repent, but it also suggested that the time of God's mercy was drawing to a close. Edwards's powerful message won many new converts to the faith.

As I read the words of Jeremiah about Jerusalem's impending destruction, I am reminded of the phrase "sinners in the hands of an angry God." The warnings were harsh and clear. Because of rebellion, idolatry, and false worship, the people of Israel would suffer greatly. In fact, as Jeremiah suggests in our focus verse, the people who survived the initial wave of wrath would rather die than face the coming days of exile. There is an important takeaway from the story of Jeremiah: God is serious about the relationship with God's people, and we must be serious about our relationship with God. It is not to be taken lightly. It requires attention, trust, faithfulness, and time. We are foolish to think that God and God's ways don't matter. We are foolish to think that God will overlook our rebellion and disobedience. We can certainly find forgiveness through the redemptive work of Christ, but our receipt of mercy should never excuse us from a life of obedience.

Prayer
God, forgive us when we fail to commit all that we are to you. Amen.

Day 754   Jeremiah 9: The Cascading River of Deceit

> "'They pile lie upon lie and utterly refuse to acknowledge me,' says the Lord." Jeremiah 9:6 (NLT)

Observation
Jeremiah is sometimes referred to as "the Weeping Prophet" because of the tears he cries over the sins and fate of his people. As chapter 9 opens, he wishes his eyes could become "a fountain of tears" so he could weep continually because of his broken heart. He desires a wilderness refuge to escape the agony, sorrow, and bitter destruction of his people. He proclaims that all ethical standards have collapsed. The people are filled with deceit and slander. They have "worn themselves out" with sinfulness (v. 5). Using a metallurgy image, Jeremiah suggests that God will refine the people to see if any are found faithful. He insists that Jerusalem will soon become a den of jackals unfit for human habitation. He calls for women who are skilled at mourning and wailing to come quickly into the city to lament its destruction.

Application
Years ago, my parents owned a cabin on Walnut Mountain in North Georgia. For more than two decades it served as a retreat and place of respite and enjoyment. On occasion, my wife and I would visit the cabin, usually with family or friends. On one such trip, we entered the cabin after no one had visited for several weeks. Everything seemed fine as we arrived. But as we unpacked our things in one of the lower bedrooms, suddenly the ceiling above us collapsed as gallons of water poured from above. We discovered that the water line to the icemaker in the kitchen had slowly leaked for many days until our movements caused enough vibrations for the pooling water to burst through the ceiling.

    I have discovered that deceit often acts in much the same way. When we choose to tell a small lie, another lie soon follows, and then another. We lie in our attempt to get out of an unpleasant moment, and the lies begin to build up. One falsehood is stacked upon another. Suddenly our "house of cards" collapses and the ruin is great. Notice that Jeremiah describes this "piling up of lies" in our focus verse. Deception is indeed a slippery slope. It is said that to be a good liar, you'd better have a good memory, for the lies will pile up. Rest assured that deception always has a way of catching up with us. How can we escape the "lie trap"? It's simple: practice honesty in all things. Realize that the uncomfortable truth is always better than living with a comfortable lie. Start with yourself. Quit lying about your life, your actions, and your sins. Claim them, confess them, and find the freedom of honesty.

Prayer
Father, may we guard our integrity with every act and word. Amen.

Day 755   Jeremiah 10: A Plea for Mercy

> "So correct me, Lord, but please be gentle. Do not correct me in anger, for I would die." Jeremiah 10:24 (NLT)

Observation
As the destruction of Judah draws near, Jeremiah once again points to the people's foolish idolatry. They have crafted idols of wood and metal and bow down to them as though these objects have power. Rather than worship handmade re-creations of the sun, moon, and stars, the people are to worship the God who created the heavenly bodies. Jeremiah reminds them that idol worship is vanity; it is worthless. How foolish to give allegiance to that which is dumb and motionless. There is nothing to fear about such objects. These helpless, so-called gods will be destroyed. In verse 18, the people are told to "pack their bags and prepare to leave." Some of the Assyrian stone reliefs of Shalmaneser depict captives transporting household goods on their heads as they travel east into exile. Beginning with verse 19, the anguish and pain of the destruction gets personal again with Jeremiah. "Woe is me," he declares, feeling the anguish of his people whose lives will become so disrupted.

Application
The story is told of a preacher's young son who was acting badly during a worship service. Several times, as his father offered the sermon, he would give his son one of those "you're-gonna-get-it-when-church-is-over" looks. And yet the child continued to behave poorly. The father reached the breaking point. He stopped his sermon, walked down into the congregation, and grabbed his son, carrying him out of the service under his arm. The little boy looked at the congregation and said, "Y'all pray for me! I'm about to get a whipping!"

Jeremiah knows that his nation is about to receive payment for her idolatry and disobedience. Even though he is called as a prophet to proclaim the Lord's warning, Jeremiah understands that his own behavior needs correction too. He accepts the correction of God but asks God to be gentle in the punishment. He knows that neither he nor anyone else could survive the full force of God's wrath. I wonder if his words should fill our mouths as we say our morning prayer. Surely, we are old enough and discerning enough to know that our lives are far from perfect. We deserve God's punishment. And so we plead for God's mercy: "Be gentle in your wrath." The good news is that God's wrath is always tempered by mercy. Because of God's unchanging love for us, even amid our mess, God extends mercy instead of wrath. God extends grace instead of rebuke. Let's acknowledge our brokenness as we begin this day, and let's ask again for gentle mercy.

Prayer
Father, help us to understand both our sinfulness and your patience this day. Amen.

Day 756 — Jeremiah 11: Don't Mess with a Prophet

> "This is what the Lord says about the men of Anathoth who wanted me dead. They had said, 'We will kill you if you do not stop prophesying in the Lord's name.' So this is what the Lord of Heaven's Armies says about them: 'I will punish them! Their young men will die in battle, and their boys and girls will starve to death.'" Jeremiah 11:21-22 (NLT)

Observation

Jeremiah 11 opens as God gives the prophet another challenging word to share with Israel. God speaks in terms of a covenant. From the beginning, God's covenant had been clear. If the people obeyed God, then blessings would flow. On the other hand, disobedience would result in punishment. And yet it seems as though the people have forgotten. They have turned away from a loyal pursuit of God and prayed to false idols like their ancestors did. Because the people's hearts are evil, God will bring calamity. God's justice is inescapable whenever sin is intrinsic to a person's character. God tells Jeremiah that God will no longer even listen to the people's prayers when they cry out in distress (v. 14). So unpopular is Jeremiah's preaching that the people of Anathoth want to end his life. They think that by killing the prophet they will silence the wrathful words of God. But as our focus verse reveals, the people of Anathoth will be destroyed because of their threats against Jeremiah.

Application

You may have heard the old joke about a golfer who visits his priest, longing to know if there are, in fact, golf courses in heaven. The priest promises to pray about the matter and get back to him. When the two meet the following week for confession, the priest says, "I've got good news and bad news. The good news is that, yes, there are golf courses in heaven. The bad news is that you have a tee time next Monday."

Sometimes prophets, priests, and preachers are called to deliver bad news. Sometimes the message is not popular. Words of conviction and judgment are always hard to hear, but a true word from the Lord must be delivered. According to the text, Jeremiah's words were so enraging to hear that people wanted to kill him. They did not like the uncomfortable truth the prophet was called to deliver. Perhaps Jeremiah held up his hands and said, "Don't shoot me; I'm only the messenger!" Sometimes we have the awkward role of speaking truth into someone else's life. There are moments when, with godly insight, we can see something in a person's life that they cannot see for themselves. It may be a spouse, a coworker, or a child, but if God gives us a word of insight to share with someone, then we are bound to share it, even if it is an unpopular word.

Prayer

Father, may we have the courage to speak truth when prompted to do so. Amen.

Day 757 — Jeremiah 12: False Piety

> "Your name is on their lips, but you are far from their hearts."
> Jeremiah 12:2b (NLT)

Observation

Jeremiah 12 opens with the prophet "pleading" with God like a petitioner bringing a legal grievance before a judge. He questions God about the difficult topic of why the wicked prosper. Jeremiah tries to make sense of his world and the impending destruction of his nation. In his conversation with God, he begs God to bring judgment upon the nations that have assaulted Israel. One of the key problems for Israel was belief; even though they were warned repeatedly about God's judgment, they still refused to believe that God would actually bring about destruction. Later in this chapter, God tells Jeremiah that he will face increasing turmoil as he proclaims God's judgment. God also promises that the land will become desolate. The land that had once known overwhelming blessing would experience devastating judgment. The chapter ends, however, with a glimmer of hope as God promises to eventually have compassion on the people. They will one day return to the land, in spite of the days of judgment that are upon them.

Application

I was recently walking across campus and encountered a group of students making their way to class. One student wore an Alabama cap, so naturally I said, "Roll Tide!" He looked startled and asked, "Did you say something to me?" "Yes," I replied. "I saw your Alabama hat and thought I'd give you an Alabama greeting." "Oh," the student replied, "I don't really keep up with college sports. This hat belongs to my roommate and I just borrowed it for the day." I'm glad that kid is in college; he has a lot to learn.

Sometimes what we display on the outside is inconsistent with what is happening on the inside. For many, there is a disconnect between proclaiming to have faith and actually living an active, genuine faith resulting from a heart changed by the love of Christ. I see it all the time: people adorn their cars with an ichthus (a fish symbol representing Christianity), wear a Christian t-shirt, or even get a religious tattoo, but their hearts are closed to the transformative love of Christ. The name of Jesus may be on their lips, but their hearts are far from God. If you dare, get on Twitter or Facebook and read through some comments. You will discover that some of the most bigoted, angry, and judgmental posts are written by self-proclaimed Jesus followers. I am certainly not the judge of anyone. It is not my place to pass a sentence on the core beliefs in someone else's life. But I do think that darkness and light cannot inhabit the same life. Blessing and cursing should not come from the same mouth. If we claim to follow Christ, let's choose to live fully under his lordship.

Prayer

Father God, give us a consistent, transformative faith. Amen.

Day 758 — Jeremiah 13: Set in Our Ways

> "Can an Ethiopian change the color of his skin? Can a leopard take away its spots? Neither can you start doing good, for you have always done evil."
> Jeremiah 13:23 (NLT)

Observation

God often commands prophets to "act out" their words of prophecy. In this chapter, God tells Jeremiah to act out his message using a linen loincloth. This cloth was like kilts worn by men. Jeremiah is told to hide his linen cloth in the dirt and rocks of the Euphrates River. This is not an easy request. The Euphrates was over 700 miles away, a two- to three-month journey each way. (Some translations suggest a different reading, perhaps reflecting a location in Palestine at the headwaters of the Wadi Farah.) Once exposed to the elements, the linen cloth was ruined, profitable for nothing. So, too, Judah's pride and arrogance reduced the nation to ruins. What was once unspoiled and useful had now become worthless. Rather than embracing a close relationship with God, like a linen loincloth would provide on one's body, Judah's allegiances with the pagan gods of Assyria and Babylon destroyed the people's relationship with God. Using additional imagery of a wine bottle, God promises to fill the bottle with the sinful people of the land and then smash the bottle, leaving utter destruction. Verse 17 indicates Jeremiah's continual lament for his people.

Application

Though most of us would never dare to admit it, we become set in our ways, even at an early age. Psychologists suggest that most men become set in their ways by the age of 24. By that age, most men have set their value systems, their political affiliations, their moral values, and more. Most women do the same by the age of 26. It's sad to think that most of us will spend the bulk of our adult lives rather stubbornly set in our ways. It may pain us to think that we are no longer pliable or able to see with new perspectives or insights. In fact, as Jeremiah suggests in our focus verse, some things, like a leopard's spots or the color of our skin, will never change. And yet there are thoughts, attitudes, and beliefs that we need to alter. In our own strength, it is impossible to make the change from human nature to godly perspective. Such a change is the slow work of God alone. With people such things are impossible, but with God all things can change. If you are like me, you are probably living in a deep rut. You are set in your ways and tend to like the comfortable place that you have built over the course of your lifetime. But the gospel calls us to transformation. God longs to craft us more into the image of God's Son and less into the image of self. It takes honesty and self-reflection to change. What about your life needs a little work? What perspective needs to change? What attitude needs adjustment? Open your heart to the slow work of God and see what happens.

Prayer

Father God, we are stubborn, foolish, and self-righteous. Change us…please. Amen.

Day 759   Jeremiah 14: Deceptive Words

> "Then the Lord said, 'These prophets are telling lies in my name. I did not send them or tell them to speak. I did not give them any messages. They prophesy of visions and revelations they have never seen or heard. They speak foolishness made up in their own lying hearts.'"
> Jeremiah 14:14 (NLT)

Observation

As Jeremiah 14 opens, a terrible drought has come upon the land of Judah. It is the direct result of God's punishment for the people's disobedience. Various segments of the nation begin to mourn the destructive nature of the drought as it affects people, livestock, and crops. The wealthy send out servants to find water in the usual places, but no water is found. Farmlands are devastated. Wild animals search in vain for water. Because the people have continually practiced no restraint in terms of sin, judgment becomes inevitable. God instructs Jeremiah not to pray for the nation or offer any fasts or burnt offerings. All such attempts to thwart God's judgment will be in vain. The false prophets in the land insist that God will relent and deliver the people. As our focus verse indicates, they are telling lies. They offer messages that do not come from God. The last several verses describe the eventual pleas for mercy on the part of the people. Yet it is too little, too late.

Application

Recently, an email was sent to all Belmont employees that appeared to come from the university president, Dr. Bob Fisher. It was not a carefully worded email, and it also encouraged the reader to click on various "links" within the body of the message. It seemed suspicious. Within minutes, an alert was sent out by the IT Department asking people to quickly delete the email from Dr. Fisher. It was a fake message attempting to put a "virus" on the university email network.

    Sometimes we are inundated with distortions, lies, and deceptive advice…even at church. Not everyone who claims to speak "a word from the Lord" actually has an authentic message to convey. If a preacher/teacher insists that "God has told me to say this or that," be careful. Sometimes false prophets invoke the name of the Lord in a manipulative way. There are ways to test the words of a prophet. Do they reflect the heart and Spirit of the Lord? Do they offer grace and kindness? Do they lift up rather than tear down? Do their words match both the attitude and truth of holy scripture? Regrettably, there are people who long to distort, twist, and manipulate the words of God for personal profit or power-grabbing reasons. Don't just listen to the words of a "religious leader." Look at the fruit of his or her ministry. Look at their attitudes. Look at the fruit of their labors.

Prayer

Father God, give us discernment that will separate preachers from charlatans. Amen.

Day 760 — Jeremiah 15: Controlling the Flow

> "If you return to me, I will restore you so you can continue to serve me. If you speak good words rather than worthless ones, you will be my spokesman. You must influence them; do not let them influence you!"
> Jeremiah 15:19 (NLT)

Observation

Jeremiah 15 offers a definitive word from God concerning the destruction of Judah. God refuses to relent. God states that even if Moses and Samuel pleaded for God to relent, God would still not be persuaded. It is clear that judgment must come upon the nation for her rebellion. The complete judgment will be seen in four ways: death, sword, famine, and captivity. Jerusalem is defiled by the idol worship and child sacrifice that have taken place in the Temple courts during Manasseh's reign. Complete devastation must follow. According to verse 6, God is "weary of relenting." The time for judgment has come. Like wheat chaff scattered by a winnowing fork, the people of God will be scattered to distant lands. In verse 10, Jeremiah pleads his own case before God. He is suffering persecution and strife because of his faithful preaching. God promises to protect him from harm and rescue him from danger.

Application

Are you familiar with a "backflow" valve? You should be. Hopefully there is one installed in your house. It can protect your home from a huge sewage problem. Basically, this valve prevents sewage in an overloaded main sewer line from backing up into your basement or another area of your home. In other words, it controls the direction of sewage water from your house to the main sewage line on your street. It prevents a "backflow." A good friend had the unfortunate experience of this valve failing. You don't want to know the damage and disruption this caused. What a mess.

In our focus passage, God warns Jeremiah about a backflow issue. God is talking in terms of influence. Jeremiah is instructed to make sure that he influences the evildoers rather than the evildoers influencing him. It's a word of warning that all of us should hear. Culture throws a thousand darts of influence our way each day. We are influenced about how we think, what we should buy, and whom we should hate. And yet we are called to be the "salt and light" of the world that constantly beckons the world into a transformative relationship with Christ. It is our responsibility to influence those around us, not to be influenced by them. We have to control the flow. As you faithfully live within your culture this day, I pray that you will be carefully aware of the surrounding voices that seek to influence your life. Stay strong and focused. Be the influencer Christ needs you to be.

Prayer

Father God, may we turn a deaf ear to the destructive voices of our culture. Amen.

Day 761 — Jeremiah 16: A Land without Laughter

> "For this is what the Lord of Heaven's Armies, the God of Israel, says: In your own lifetime, before your very eyes, I will put an end to the happy singing and laughter in this land. The joyful voices of bridegrooms and brides will no longer be heard." Jeremiah 16:9 (NLT)

Observation

As chapter 16 opens, Jeremiah is called once again to act out his prophetic preaching. God tells him not to marry nor have children "in this land." This will be a sign to the nation of destruction so terrible that children will die of terrible diseases with no one left to mourn them or bury them. This prophecy was also detrimental to Jeremiah's good name. In that culture, celibacy was abnormal. Large families were a sign of God's blessing, and yet Jeremiah was told not to seek a large family. God alone was Jeremiah's sole source of comfort and support. He was not even to participate in the normal grief processes for those who die or join in any family celebrations. These symbolic acts will communicate that his listeners are no longer the people of God because of their rebellion. And yet, after this blistering word of judgment, the chapter ends on a hopeful note as God promises to one day restore Israel. It will not happen in the lifetime of this current generation, but God promises that it will surely come.

Application

Can you imagine a land without laughter? I can't. For me, laughter truly is good medicine. It gladdens the heart, it lifts the spirits, and it even heals the wounds of difficult moments. We need to laugh each day. We need the release, the comfort, and the joy that it brings. At the grocery store where I shop, I have begun to build a relationship with an old, grizzled employee. He's past retirement age but has to work in order to make ends meet. He seldom looks up when he scans a cartful of groceries. It's all tedious and mundane from his perspective. I decided about six months ago to begin a simple conversation with him. I deliberately choose his checkout line. I speak to him and ask about his day, his life, etc. And then one day, out of the clear blue, he asked me, "Do you have a joke for me today?" I told him one of the corny jokes my granddaughter had recently told me. "What kind of pants do ghosts wear?" The answer—"Boo jeans!" He nearly doubled over with laughter. Now I go into the store armed with both cost-saving coupons and a silly joke. And it seems to help. Something about laughter and joy is contagious. I hope you get to laugh a little today and maybe help someone else to do the same.

Prayer

Father God, may we live a life with both joy and laughter today. Amen.

Day 762   Jeremiah 17: A Firmly Planted Life

> "But blessed are those who trust in the Lord and have made the Lord their hope and confidence. They are like trees planted along a riverbank, with roots that reach deep into the water. Such trees are not bothered by the heat or worried by long months of drought. Their leaves stay green, and they never stop producing fruit." Jeremiah 17:7-8 (NLT)

Observation
As chapter 17 begins, Jeremiah states that the sins of Israel are deeply engraved in the hearts of the people; they cannot be removed. The people's lives are inextricably entangled with rebellion, so judgment must come. Because of rebellion and idolatry, the Babylonians will carry away all of Jerusalem and the treasures of the Temple. The heart of the problem is a lack of trust in God. Those who trust only in human wisdom will never be firmly planted and bear fruit like those who trust solely in God. Jeremiah uses the image of a partridge sitting on another bird's nest as a metaphor for the foolish pursuits of those who trust in wealth and not in God. When the eggs hatch beneath the partridge, the young birds will not recognize her as their mother. They will flee. In like fashion, those who gain wealth unjustly will soon be abandoned by their wealth. In the final section of this passage, God tells Jeremiah to proclaim his message in all the gates of the city so that both kings and peasants will hear his voice. In particular, Jeremiah is to warn the people about their abuse of Sabbath practices.

Application
Remember the old metal swing sets from childhood? Constructed of cheap metal, most sets had a place for two swings, maybe a glider, and maybe a slide on the end. What I remember most is that when several people were swinging at the same time, the legs of the swing set would pull out of the ground. Sometimes the swing set would actually move away from its resting place. The solution for this problem was to anchor the swing set legs in concrete. When the legs were firmly planted, the set remained stable.

It's important to raise the question, "Where is your life planted?" Notice that Jeremiah suggests that a life planted in the rich and well-watered soil of God's provision will know blessing and peace. When times of drought and turmoil come, such a life will endure. Where have you anchored your life? Are you dependent on your wealth, your position, or your relationships to get by? All of those will one day fail. The wise person anchors his/her life in the Eternal. God's provision for our lives will give us lasting security, joy, and contentment. Let your roots grow deeply in God.

Prayer
Father God, teach us to place our trust, our allegiance, and our faith in you alone. Amen.

Day 763   Jeremiah 18: Deaf Ears

> "But the people replied, 'Don't waste your breath. We will continue to live as we want to, stubbornly following our own evil desires.'"
> Jeremiah 18:12 (NLT)

Observation

In chapter 18, God directs Jeremiah to go to the local potter's shop and observe his work. The potter was working the clay into a certain kind of vessel, but it did not turn out as intended, so he remade it into an acceptable vessel. Similarly, God will reform Israel into a nation that will serve God's purpose. Even at this point in the narrative, God is willing to relent of the promised destruction, but the people are unwilling to forego their stubborn rebellion. Like the work of the potter, God has fashioned a disaster for Judah (v. 11). The people continually turn away from the commandments of God. Jeremiah mentions an east wind that will come upon the land with destructive force. The people will not see God's face in the destruction but only God's back; this means God has turned away from the people (v. 12). They are so upset by Jeremiah's preaching that they dig a pit intending to get rid of him. They look to other prophets to give them a more favorable word.

Application

My neighbor down the street owns four cats...or more precisely, they own him. These cats, which are about 10 years old, are all from the same litter. They are named Louie, Gigi, Zeus, and Leo. They like to lurk in the front yard of his house. If you drive up the street late at night, you might think you are in a Stephen King movie with all those eyes peering at you. My grandchildren are fascinated by the cats and always want to visit them when they come to our house. But like typical cats, my neighbor's pets remain aloof and disinterested. And if I dare try to call one of them to come over, the cat will look at me as only a cat can, with noncommittal indifference. I am truly wasting my breath when I call their names.

In his prophetic role, God told Jeremiah no longer to waste his breath on preaching to the people. They would forever be rebellious. I wonder how many sermons have fallen on deaf ears...including my own. How many times do we hear a word of truth but ignore it? How often do we allow the proclamations of the Lord to go in one ear and out the other without taking root? Are the people sent to speak truth in our lives wasting their breath? I hope not. It is my prayer that all of us would listen carefully to the messengers of God as they faithfully share with us each week. God has many things to say.

Prayer

Father God, give us open hearts, minds, and ears to receive your message. Amen.

Day 764 — Jeremiah 19: As the People Watch...

> "As these men watch you, Jeremiah, smash the jar you brought. Then say to them, 'This is what the Lord of Heaven's Armies says: As this jar lies shattered, so I will shatter the people of Judah and Jerusalem beyond all hope of repair. They will bury the bodies here in Topheth, the garbage dump, until there is no more room for them.'" Jeremiah 19:10-11 (NLT)

Observation
Jeremiah will once again "act out" his prophetic words. God instructs him to buy a small flask. This small, narrow-necked jar made of clay was probably 6-10 inches tall. He is to summon the elders of Israel and lead them to the Valley of Hinnom, which served as the town's dump area. God says Jeremiah's words will make the people's ears "ring" with the harsh, resounding judgment of God. Jerusalem is no longer the city where God chooses to dwell. It has become a place to worship alien gods and goddesses. The people have even practiced child sacrifice like the vile Phoenicians, Moabites, and Canaanites. Their practice of pagan worship voids the counsel God has offered to the elders. The siege and destruction of the city will be so devastating that the people will revert to cannibalism as the final days wear on. Jeremiah breaks the small flask in the presence of the elders as a symbol of the way God's judgment will soon shatter the city.

Application
We live in an age when most of our movements are recorded. From the time we leave our homes in the morning until we return home at night, our steps are constantly monitored. Security cameras and cell phones make us visible. From time to time, there are even reports of individuals being watched in the privacy of their homes or in a rented vacation spot. We have to assume that someone is always watching. I say this not to make you paranoid but to make you accountable. I'm not worried that someone has seen you shop at Kroger or run a red light at the intersection. I'm more concerned about those who watch your life, eager to learn more about the ways of Christ. People are looking for role models. They need the example of individuals who will do and say the right thing amid distracting cultural and societal influences. They look at you to see if you are authentic, consistent, and real.

As you walk through the routines of your life today, be aware of the fact that people really are watching. Your actions, your words, and your attitudes are being scrutinized. Does the unspoken testimony of your life bear witness to the lordship of Christ, or does it reveal an alarming inconsistency?

Prayer
Father God, as people watch, may we be faithful to honor you in all things. Amen.

Day 765   Jeremiah 20: A Fire in My Bones

> "But if I say I'll never mention the Lord or speak in his name, his word burns in my heart like a fire. It's like a fire in my bones! I am worn out trying to hold it in! I can't do it!" Jeremiah 20:9 (NLT)

Observation

It's not always easy to be God's prophet. When the prophetic words become too uncomfortable, God's enemies sometimes have difficulty separating the message from the messenger. According to the narrative of Jeremiah 20, a man named Pashhur was the chief governor and priest in Jerusalem. He was in charge of the Temple, the Temple guards, entry into the various courts, and more. Jeremiah's voice was a great threat to his position and power, so he tried to silence the prophet's message by having Jeremiah beaten and put into stocks. He was held in a spot typically reserved for those who behaved badly or defiled the Temple courts. When released the following day, Jeremiah declared that the enemies of God would terrorize Pashhur. When the Babylonians plundered Jerusalem, Pashhur and his family would be carried off to Babylon and die in that place. (Part of the judgment pronounced on Pashhur was due to his earlier false declarations concerning the safety of Jerusalem.) Because of his persecution, Jeremiah was both devastated and demoralized. But he confirmed that he still trusted in God's promise and protection.

Application

My friend Logan is a rabid University of Tennessee fan. He lives and breathes the "Big Orange." Most of his wardrobe is composed of bright orange apparel. Even when the team is not playing well, he continues to boast and brag. There is an eternal optimism to his loyalty. Recently, he even made an appearance as a contestant on The Price is Right television show. When he spun a perfect $1.00 on the big wheel, he let out a loud, "Go Vols!" His adoration is a fire in his bones that he can't deny.

Most of us have some "fire" in our bones that we can't deny. We have loyalty, love, or passion within us that we can't silence. Yes, it can be for a sports team, a hobby, or an organization about which we feel strongly. But notice what caused Jeremiah's burning heart. It was a desire to proclaim God's message to the people. If only we could be taken with such passion. What if God's word was so forceful, so important, and so meaningful in our lives that we couldn't stop proclaiming the Good News of the Kingdom? What if the words of life offered to us through Christ were so impactful that we couldn't help sharing our story with everyone? May we know that fire.

Prayer

Father God, stir our hearts so that we might enthusiastically proclaim your Word. Amen.

Day 766   Jeremiah 21: Cause and Effect

> "For I have decided to bring disaster and not good upon this city, says the Lord. It will be handed over to the king of Babylon, and he will reduce it to ashes." Jeremiah 21:10 (NLT)

Observation
Jeremiah 21 begins yet another section devoted to judgment. Chapters 21-23 focus on the kings of Judah. Jeremiah states that the Babylonians have no escape; Jerusalem's fate is sealed. King Zedekiah pleads for Jeremiah to petition God on behalf of the nation so that King Nebuchadnezzar of Babylon will stop his siege of the city. Zedekiah hopes for God's deliverance, remembering a similar siege when Sennacherib of Assyria attacked the city in 701 BC. Through Jeremiah, God offers a devastating response. Rather than provide relief, God will take away even the few resources the people of Jerusalem can muster. Because of their rebellious ways, the people have made themselves the enemy of God. God will not spare them or have pity on them. The only option for saving their lives is to surrender to the Babylonians.

Application
I have a busy week with two somewhat unpleasant appointments: my annual physical and a teeth cleaning. Both doctors will evaluate my overall health and give me instructions as I move forward. My doctor will want me to stop eating like a teenager, cut out sugary drinks, and get more exercise. My dentist will tell me to floss, brush regularly, and get on a more regular schedule of checkups. Of course, I already know to do these things. But here's the point: there is a cause and effect when it comes to healthcare. When I do the right things, I enjoy a healthier lifestyle. When I pay little attention to healthy habits, my body suffers.

    In our focus verse, God has chosen to bring disaster on the city of Jerusalem. The people will soon begin to experience God's wrath firsthand. Who is to blame? Not God but themselves. God's nature is one of mercy, loving-kindness, and grace. It is not that God suddenly desires to break off the relationship with the people. Rather, God's people have made the choice to break off their relationship with God, completely ignoring the laws, instructions, and commands given through the prophets. There is a cause and effect. Rebellion still brings judgment. To be clear, God is probably not going to send the king of Babylon to destroy and plunder your city. But whenever we choose rebellion, we affect the relationship that God longs to have with us. Whenever we step outside the boundaries God has established for our good, we set ourselves up for ruin. God does not choose to abandon us…we choose to ignore God's ways, and the result is never good.

Prayer
God, forgive our foolish rebellion this day. May we live according to your purpose. Amen.

Day 767   Jeremiah 22: A Regrettable Legacy

> "People from many nations will pass by the ruins of this city and say to one another, 'Why did the Lord destroy such a great city?' And the answer will be, 'Because they violated their covenant with the Lord their God by worshiping other gods.'" Jeremiah 22:8-9 (NLT)

Observation
Jeremiah 22 offers prophetic words of judgment against three specific kings of Judah. God instructs Jeremiah to go to the royal palace just south of the Temple courts and speak words for three groups to hear: the kings, the kings' servants and royal officials, and the people of the city. Righteous kings should care for strangers, orphans, and widows. Such leadership would result in a never-ending Davidic dynasty on Judah's throne. If righteousness is nonexistent, the house of David will become desolate. In addition to prophetic words concerning the king's palace, three kings are called out for their wicked behavior. Jehoahaz has exploited his people rather than defend them. Jehoiakim's acts are so vile before the Lord that God says no one is to lament his death as he is dragged out of the city and dumped like a dead donkey. Jehoachim will serve only three months and then be taken captive to Babylon. None of his sons will inherit the Davidic line.

Application
Preachers often talk about the importance of leaving a legacy. I've preached that message many times in my own ministry. I have spoken about honesty, integrity, and the careful practice of faith disciplines. We long to model the faith expectations that we want our children to inherit. In the story of the ancient Israelites, God reveals the negative side of a regrettable legacy. Because of the idolatry of the people, God's wrath will come upon the Israelites, including the destruction of the king's palace. As the people from other nations pass by, they would ask about the destruction and why it occurred. The answer would be, "Because they violated the covenant with the Lord their God."

    I hope not to leave a regrettable legacy to those who later look on my life. I don't want people to say, "Look at all the destruction. What was the cause?" How do we live without the threat of leaving such a negative impression concerning our lives? We walk honestly. We speak truthfully. When wronged, we forgive. When we injure, we apologize. We encourage. We share. We listen. We support. We connect faith to the everyday decisions and testimonies of our lives. We give careful attention to each spoken word and every decision. A legacy matters. Leave the right kind.

Prayer
God, grant us this day the discipline to live a holy and virtuous life. Amen.

Day 768 — Jeremiah 23: Testing the Prophets

> "I have not sent these prophets, yet they run around claiming to speak for me. I have given them no message, yet they go on prophesying."
> Jeremiah 23:2 (NLT)

Observation

Amid discouraging words of destruction and judgment, Jeremiah 23 opens on a hopeful note as God promises the return of a faithful remnant to the land of Israel. Jeremiah continues to offer judgment concerning false prophets who have not proclaimed the word of the Lord but rather their own thoughts and opinions. He also speaks words against the kings of Israel. The kings should have protected and nurtured the "flock of Israel." Instead, they have destroyed and scattered the people by their poor leadership. In describing the work of the new generation of kings that will rule the land when God restores Israel, Jeremiah declares that these kings will place the people's welfare and God's will above all other considerations. The remaining portion of the chapter contains a harsh word of rebuke against the false prophets who have misled the nation. They have allowed the people to stray morally, mentally, and spiritually. They have made up their own visions and offered false words of prophecy. In comparison, a true prophet is sent by God with a word from God.

Application

Many people claim to speak on behalf of the Lord—people who don't know God and have never heard from God. Whenever someone says, "The Lord told me...," watch out! Most likely their words reflect a selfish opinion or a cause they long to push forward. I'm not suggesting that the Lord doesn't still speak; the Lord certainly does. But not everyone who claims to have a word from God truly has one to share. It is important to test the words of a prophet. New Testament writer John offers a litmus test to help us with discernment: "Dear friends, do not believe everyone who claims to speak by the Spirit. You must test them to see if the spirit they have comes from God. For there are many false prophets in the world. This is how we know if they have the Spirit of God: If a person claiming to be a prophet acknowledges that Jesus Christ came in a real body, that person has the Spirit of God" (1 John 4:1-2 NLT). I have discovered that those who truly speak on behalf of God tend to offer more grace than condemnation, more mercy than judgment, more unity than divisiveness, more peace than anger, more acceptance than arbitrary barriers. The true prophets speak with civility and respect. Even if their message is hard to hear because of its convicting nature, it is still offered in the hope of redemption and reconciliation. Test out what you hear from each modern-day preacher. The message should be evident.

Prayer

God, may we have discernment this day as we listen to the voices around us. Amen.

Day 769　　　　　　　　　　　　　Jeremiah 24: Fig Preserves

> "I will watch over and care for them, and I will bring them back here again. I will build them up and not tear them down. I will plant them and not uproot them." Jeremiah 24:6 (NLT)

Observation
This short chapter tells of a vision Jeremiah received from the Lord, much like the visions God gave to Amos and Joel. In verse 1 Jeremiah states, "The Lord gave me this vision." The vision is of two baskets of figs set before the Temple of the Lord. Such a scene was familiar during the annual fall Festival of First Fruits, when people presented baskets of luscious fruit at the Temple (Deut 26:1-11). In Jeremiah's vision, one basket contains good, ripe figs while the other contains rotten figs. The good figs represent the deported exiles whom God set apart for later redemption. God would one day bring them back to the land, multiply their crops, and give them a heart for the Lord. The bad figs represent the individuals who had neglected God's way and attempted to escape God's wrath by fleeing to Egypt. Not only would King Nebuchadnezzar of Babylon defeat Israel; Egypt and Assyria would as well. In other words, the punishment of the wicked was certain.

Application
For many years, my in-laws had a fig tree growing in the side yard of their home. Each year when the figs were in season, my father-in-law found joy in picking the fruit and sharing it with family and friends. My mother-in-law made fig preserves and canned as many jars as she could. Spreading a little of those fig preserves on a hot buttered biscuit was about as good as it gets—at least according to my father-in-law. He passed away nearly three decades ago, and the fig tree is long gone, but still I remember the joy "fig season" brought to his life.

In Jeremiah's vision of the basket of figs, one basket contains figs representing those who will be "preserved." Though in exile and separated from their homes, their traditions, and their place of worship, God promises the hope of a return. The time will come when God will set the captives free and reestablish the covenant. This story should serve us well when we find ourselves amid a difficult season in our lives. We face moments when we feel defeated, troubled, and maybe even abandoned. We have little hope in the future and wonder when and if God will ever make things right again. In such a moment, we need to remember that the gospel story always faces forward. There is hope up ahead. There is light up ahead. There is joy up ahead. The ancient Israelites are not the only ones who lived with the promise of future redemption and restoration. We, too, look to that better and brighter day when God's will shall come on earth as it is in heaven. So take heart. The Kingdom will surely come and we will be "preserved."

Prayer
God, let us revel in the joy of our hope in the Coming Kingdom. Amen.

Day 770 — Jeremiah 25: The Danger of a Deaf Ear

> "For the past twenty-three years—from the thirteenth year of the reign of Josiah son of Amon, king of Judah, until now—the Lord has been giving me his messages. I have faithfully passed them on to you, but you have not listened." Jeremiah 25:3 (NLT)

Observation
Jeremiah 25 focuses on the prophetic word that came to Jeremiah during the first year of King Nebuchadnezzar's rule in Babylon. According to our focus verse, Jeremiah had faithfully proclaimed the word of the Lord for 23 years. He was diligent and persistent in his task. Other prophets like Habakkuk and Zephaniah had also warned the nation to repent so that they might inherit the land. But the problem of idol worship remained and the people failed to repent. Babylon would become the chosen agent of God's judgment. The anger of God would bring harsh realities as Nebuchadnezzar destroyed Israel and a number of other nations including Egypt, Edom, and Moab. Verse 11 reveals that God would force the Israelites into exile for a period of 70 years. The final section of the chapter speaks of an image that God gives to Jeremiah for his preaching. God tells Jeremiah to take "a cup of judgment" to the people. They are to drink from it until they get drunk and eventually vomit. God's judgment would indeed be difficult for the people to experience.

Application
We are often inundated with warnings concerning potential dangers. Some of them are important to understand and to heed. Others hardly register in our minds. For example, I recently received a cordless vacuum from my wife as a birthday gift. As I opened the package and prepared it for use, I didn't take a minute to read the warning flyer that came with the packaging. I figured I know enough about electricity to charge a cordless vac, so I paid little attention to the warning. However, on the same day, I went to my doctor for my annual physical. He ordered a blood profile to check my vital numbers. Fortunately, things looked good, but he did give me this piece of warning: "How well you live your fifties will determine to a great extent how well you will live your eighties, so take care of your health." This is a good warning to heed, right? I would be foolish to ignore the words of a trained physician.

For at least 23 years, God had used Jeremiah to speak to the Israelites about their sinful rebellion. Had they listened, they could have changed both their hearts and their rebellious ways and avoided much suffering. Instead, they chose to turn a deaf ear to God's warnings. There is danger in turning a deaf ear to the warnings in our lives, especially those that come from the Almighty. God gives us guidelines for successful living. God gives us the ability to confess sins and find forgiveness. God offers salvation through Christ. Why would you not listen?

Prayer
God, give us the wisdom needed to heed the important warnings in our lives. Amen.

Day 771 — Jeremiah 26: The Whole Nine Yards

> "This is what the Lord says: Stand in the courtyard in front of the Temple of the Lord, and make an announcement to the people who have come there to worship from all over Judah. Give them my entire message; include every word." Jeremiah 26:2 (NLT)

Observation

It is never easy being a prophet with an unpleasant word. Chapter 26 tells the story of the death threat Jeremiah experienced because of his faithful proclamation. Early in the reign of King Jehoiakim of Judah, God sent a message to Jeremiah to stand in front of the Temple and preach the words God would give him. Most likely while standing in one of the inner courts, Jeremiah speaks with heavy boldness to the pilgrims who have traveled to worship. He offers a word of conditional judgment. If the people will repent from their evil ways, God will still relent in bringing the promised calamity. The people are angry because Jeremiah speaks about the potential destruction of the Temple. This was considered a word of blasphemy, and the crowds wanted to kill him. The city leaders call for an official inquiry, and one of the elders speaks of a precedent for this moment. King Hezekiah once spared the life of Micah, who preached a similar word of judgment. In this angry moment, a man named Ahikam steps in to save Jeremiah's life.

Application

You have probably heard the expression, "Give 'em the whole nine yards!" But you may not know its origin. It goes back to the Second World War. Many American combat planes were equipped with machine guns. The bullets were linked together in a chain so people could quickly load them into the guns while rapidly firing at enemy planes, tanks, etc. These chains of bullets were 27 feet, or 9 yards, long. To bring about the most possible devastation, the gunner would fire the entire chain of bullets—the whole nine yards. In other words, the gunner would give the enemy the most lethal firepower possible.

In our focus verse, God tells Jeremiah to speak God's "entire message." He is to include every word without leaving any portion of God's instruction out. I wonder if we are sometimes negligent in how we handle the word of God, especially when we are offering words of instruction to a group or audience. The temptation might be to speak only of pleasant promises and wonderful grace. We might be tempted to leave out the words of instruction that seem unpleasant to our audience. And yet we are called to preach the word, both in season and out, when it is popular to do so and when it is not. It takes courage.

Prayer

God, as you give us words to share, may we have the courage to share all of them.

Day 772   Jeremiah 27: Why Do You Insist on Dying?

> "Why do you insist on dying—you and your people? Why should you choose war, famine, and disease, which the Lord will bring against every nation that refuses to submit to Babylon's king?" Jeremiah 27:13 (NLT)

Observation

In chapter 17, Jeremiah once again acts out his prophetic words. God tells him to make a yoke and wear it on his shoulders. A yoke was a wooden beam attached to a pair of oxen by leather straps, literally binding them to each other. Used in this preaching context, the yoke symbolizes bondage, restraint, and enslavement. Jeremiah is told to give his message not only to the king of Judah but also to foreign ambassadors who will relay it to their leaders. The people must realize that the God of Israel is sovereign over all human affairs. God's reign is over all the earth, and God alone will give power to nations and kings. The yoke also symbolizes an alliance God commands the nations to form with Babylon. God will use Babylon as an instrument of judgment. Those who will not submit to becoming vassals of Babylon will be punished. Submitting to Babylon means submitting to the will and purpose of God.

Application

"Why do you insist on dying?" I have often asked that question when watching videos of daredevils around the world attempting the most foolish things. I used to cringe when I watched the Valendas do their tightrope walk routine. And I can hardly watch as climbers scale steep cliffs with no ropes. I don't understand why people hang off the side of tall skyscrapers or jump out of planes with no parachute, hoping to land in a big net on the ground. What about the guys who climb tall television antennas to replace light bulbs? Surely, they have a death wish.

Jeremiah asked the people of his day why they insisted on dying. God told them that the only path to survival was submission to Babylon—God's chosen instrument of judgment. It seems foolish that when a clear path is established, people choose to defy the proclamations of Almighty God. And yet many make that choice. The word of God is absolutely, profoundly, abundantly, and jarringly clear: there is salvation only in Christ. As 1 John 5:12 states, "He who has the Son has life; he who does not have the Son of God does not have life" (NASB). God offers every person the opportunity to claim eternal life by accepting Jesus as Lord and Savior. That is the plan. There is no other option. Why do people insist on dying when God offers them a path to life? Maybe no one has bothered to let them know about this path.

Prayer

Father God, make us accountable with the gospel story that is ours to share. Amen.

Day 773 — Jeremiah 28: Fake News

> "Then Jeremiah the prophet said to Hananiah, Listen, Hananiah! The Lord has not sent you, but the people believe your lies. Therefore, this is what the Lord says: 'You must die. Your life will end this very year because you have rebelled against the Lord.'" Jeremiah 28:15-16 (NLT)

Observation
Soon after Jeremiah places the wooden yoke on his shoulders and proclaims judgment against Judah (ch. 27), another prophet named Hananiah appears on the scene. He is from nearby Gibeon and claims to speak in the name of the Lord, but he proclaims a message contradicting everything Jeremiah has said. He indicates that God will bring imminent deliverance from the Babylonians in just two years! He also proclaims that the sacred items Nebuchadnezzar took from the Temple will be returned to Jerusalem. This "popular" message is not at all what God has said through Jeremiah. Hananiah goes so far as to break the wooden yoke Jeremiah wears symbolically around his neck. Jeremiah declares that Hananiah has led the people astray with a lie, and as a result he will die in two months.

Application
We live in an amazing age of technology. One of the most astounding advances over the past couple of decades is the Global Positioning System (GPS.) Now incorporated into our cell phones and even into our watches, a GPS receiver can plot our position at any place on the planet and give us directions from Point A to Point B. It really is amazing. No longer do we get out an atlas or road map and plot our next journey. We simply type in our destination and the GPS provides turn-by-turn directions...at least most of the time. Every once in a while, the GPS gets it wrong. Sometimes it may attempt to lead us across a field where there is no road or even send us to the wrong address. Granted, it isn't wrong often, but incorrect directions can disrupt our journey.

In the time of Jeremiah, two prophets came before the people speaking "a word from the Lord." One was a true prophet, but the other was a charlatan. Those who listened to the false words soon discovered that he was a fraud. The story reminds us how important it is to carefully discern the messages we receive. In our attempt to align ourselves with the will and purpose of God, we need to assess the messengers who speak to us. Have they spent time with the Father? Do they listen to the leadership of the Spirit? Has their wisdom been tested as true? God speaks with clarity and consistency. Be careful of those whose messages seem to distort God's voice.

Prayer
Father, may we possess the discernment needed today to identify and listen to your voice. Amen.

Day 774   Jeremiah 29: The Length of a Promise

> "This is what the Lord says: 'You will be in Babylon for seventy years. But then I will come and do for you all the good things I have promised, and I will bring you home again.'" Jeremiah 29:10 (NLT)

Observation
Jeremiah 29 tells of the key message the prophet sends to the exiles in Babylon. He writes a letter that is sent from Jerusalem to Babylon. The king and government officials have already been exiled. What remains in Jerusalem is mostly a peasant population. In his letter, Jeremiah reminds the people that God has brought about the exile and not the king of Babylon, and thus the exilic period will end in God's timing. Jeremiah tells them that the exile will last 70 years. During that time the people are to move on with their lives. They are to settle in and carry out normal life routines. They are to build, plant, and multiply. In fact, God declares that they should expand in population and not be diminished. They should seek the peace of the city in which they live. They should live in peace as a benefit of God's sovereignty over their situation. Though the promise will span 70 years before its ultimate fulfillment, this is a hopeful word as God promises to remember the covenant of restoration.

Application
God keeps promises. God always has and always will. In this situation, God promised the full restoration of the people. God promised this even though the exile would last 70 years. That's a long time. Many people would die during that time, clinging to a hope that God would keep the promise. Many were also born during those days who had never lived in Israel and had to be told what it once was and would one day become. The hope contained in the promise sustained the people across several generations.

We live with the promises of God that were made long ago and are yet to be fulfilled. God has promised our salvation. God has promised a new heaven and earth. God has promised a day when joy shall never end, when sickness is forever banished, and when death is no more. God promises a day when every tear caused by the pains of life will be wiped dry. And like the ancient Israelites, we are called to wait…to wait with hope, with expectancy, and with longing. Just because a promise spans many years and lifetimes, it is in no way diminished or less valid. God is at work and will remember God's promises.

Prayer
Father, we joyfully, triumphantly, and patiently wait on the fulfillment of your promises. Amen.

Day 775   Jeremiah 30: The Golden Ticket

> "They will have their own ruler again, and he will come from their own people. I will invite him to approach me, says the Lord, for who would dare to come unless invited?" Jeremiah 30:21 (NLT)

Observation
Jeremiah 30 begins a section filled with messages of hope and deliverance. Chapters 30-33 are sometimes referred to as "The Book of Consolation," for they speak of ultimate restoration and blessing. (These chapters certainly look beyond the present age to the coming Messianic Age.) God instructs Jeremiah to record, or write down, all of God's words on a scroll. God promises that the people of Israel will once more possess the land. Those who have felt defenseless, hopeless, and distraught will find hope again. God promises to break the yoke of Babylon's oppression. Israel will no longer serve foreign people. They will once again find peace and rest. These words offer careful reminders of the great affliction of God's punishment, yet they are coupled with assurance that God will heal the wounds of the nation. God also promises to bring judgment on Israel's oppressors.

Application
In the 1971 film Willy Wonka and the Chocolate Factory, Charlie Bucket longs to win a rare golden ticket that will allow him to tour Wonka's mystical, magic chocolate factory. He does find the one remaining ticket and joins the other winners for the once-in-a-lifetime experience. Only those invited are allowed to enter the factory.

In Jeremiah's prophetic pronouncement, he declares that God will once again raise up a ruler from the nation of Israel—specifically from David's lineage. The King (Messiah) will be invited to approach the presence of Almighty God. And then God adds, "for who would dare to come unless invited?" Who among us would dare to enter into the presence of Almighty God? Who is worthy? Who is clean enough? Righteous enough? Holy enough? The answer, of course, is that none of us fit the criteria. Sinful humans have no right to stand in the presence of Holy God…unless we are invited to do so. And we are. Jesus Christ ushers us into his Father's presence. He declares that we are worthy, that we are joined to him. In fact, because we know Jesus, God both invites and welcomes us to come. The moment Jesus died on the cross, the huge Temple veil that once kept sinful people away from God's presence was torn in two. Access to God was made possible through the atoning death of Christ in which he bore our sins so that we could stand forgiven in God's presence. You're invited… welcome in.

Prayer
Father, we thank you that we are found to be acceptable in your sight. Amen.

Day 776 — Jeremiah 31: Godly Forgetfulness

> "And they will not need to teach their neighbors, nor will they need to teach their relatives, saying, 'You should know the Lord.' For everyone, from the least to the greatest, will know me already, says the Lord. And I will forgive their wickedness, and I will never again remember their sins."
> Jeremiah 31:34 (NLT)

Observation

Continuing the theme of restoration, Jeremiah 31 speaks of hope and promise for the people of Israel. The restoration of the nation to its land would coincide with the fulfillment of God's covenant with the people. In the early verses of this chapter, Jeremiah uses language that harkens back to the Egyptian deliverance. Out of "covenant loyalty," God will deliver the people and reestablish them in the land. Village life will be restored. Crops will be bountiful. Vineyards will be productive. Jeremiah refers to the nation as "Virgin Israel." This implies a return to her former glory, long before corruption became rampant. God will make Israel pure and holy once again. Watchmen, who once warned the people of potential danger from the towers, will now call people to joyful worship. Verse 33 mentions God's establishment of a new covenant, later to be fulfilled in Christ, which will be written in the hearts and minds of the people.

Application

Whenever we list the attributes of God, we include qualities like majesty, glory, power, knowledge, love, and creativity. I doubt any of us would list "forgetfulness" as one of God's virtues, but we should. Forgetfulness is not something we want to embrace as individuals. If we forget where we placed our keys, where we left our phones, or the name of a neighbor, we recoil and think, "I must be losing it." We want to remember names, dates, numbers, conversations, etc. But like our Heavenly Father, perhaps there are some things that we would do well to forget. Jeremiah insists that God remembers to forget our sins. After offering forgiveness, God is self-disciplined no longer to remember our sinful ways, never holding them against us again. To "forget" makes God's forgiveness possible.

If I choose to forgive someone and yet fail to forget the transgression, have I really offered forgiveness? If I choose not to forget, then each time I bring the infraction to mind, I must practice the discipline of forgiveness all over again. My lack of forgetting will continue to create distance between myself and the person who has wronged me. If I want to be like my Heavenly Father, then I must be willing to practice forgetfulness. That's hard. We all want to cling to injury and to thoughts of revenge. But the grace that will save us and others is the discipline of forgetting.

Prayer

Father, may we learn to forget the sins that others have committed against us. Amen.

Day 777   Jeremiah 32: The Purchase of Land

> "So I bought the field at Anathoth, paying Hanamel seventeen pieces of silver for it. I signed and sealed the deed of purchase before witnesses, weighed out the silver, and paid him." Jeremiah 32:9-10 (NLT)

Observation

Jeremiah 32 opens with references that speak to the time when these events took place. All that occurs in this chapter happened in 587 BC, the year when Jerusalem fell to the Babylonians after a difficult siege. In this chapter, King Zedekiah, angered by Jeremiah's continual prophecy of doom and gloom, has imprisoned the prophet in the palace courtyard. The Lord tells the prisoner Jeremiah to buy his cousin's field, located in Anathoth (Jeremiah's hometown). This later proves to be a prophetic act of hope through which Jeremiah reminds the people that one day they will return to the land, owning property and planting crops. Jeremiah and his cousin meet, the money is paid, and everything is carefully recorded. Following that story, Jeremiah returns to his theme of pronouncing Jerusalem's destruction. God will give the city over to the Babylonians, who will set fire to it. The destruction is the direct result of the people's refusal to listen to God's instruction and obey. The final section of the chapter reminds the people of God's promise of restoration that will eventually come to those who are soon to be exiled.

Application

It sometimes worries me that I don't own any land. Sure, I own the ¼ acre that my house rests on, but beyond that I can make no claim on any piece of land. I always thought it would be nice to own a little piece of property, maybe a wooded area or a field with a small fishing pond. Even some oceanfront property at the beach would suit me fine. In my mind, there is assurance in having some land to call my own. It's the feeling of having an inheritance to pass down to future generations. It's the feeling of having the security of an investment to cash in if needed. It's the feeling of permanence in the knowledge that I own something no one can legally take from me. Some of these emotions must be in Jeremiah's heart as he speaks a word of hope to his generation. When God eventually restores the people, the land will produce crops. The owning of land will demonstrate God's message of restoration. Maybe for us believers, the key is not so much owning land as claiming land. What if we claimed our neighborhood, our city, even our country as belonging to God's Kingdom? What if our claim meant that we would share freely, love abundantly, forgive graciously, treat respectfully, and proclaim Christ fervently?

Prayer

Father, may our concern this day be that of "claiming" this land for Christ. Amen.

Day 778   Jeremiah 33: Unlocking the Mysteries of God

"Call to Me and I will answer you, and I will tell you great and mighty things, which you do not know." Jeremiah 33:3 (NASB)

Observation
Still held captive in the courtyard of the king's palace, Jeremiah receives another word from the Lord. Even though destruction is imminent, God promises to show the people great and mighty things that they cannot even imagine. In vain, they have attempted to keep the Babylonian army out of their city. They have torn down homes and buildings in an attempt to fortify Jerusalem's walls. Yet God has already declared destruction. In the midst of the punishment, God promises to cleanse and forgive the people. In verse 8, God uses the word "pardon" in relationship to sin. In the Old Testament, God is always the only One who can offer pardon. (This is why the Pharisees of Jesus' day bristled at his statement claiming that he could pardon sin in Mark 2:7.) In talking about restoration, God speaks of the flocks (and people) that will once again fill the regions of Israel.

Application
Have you ever been captivated by a discovery? I once read a book about the hidden biases that most of us have without even knowing it. It was a fascinating look at how our minds make judgments about people based on all kinds of input. Sometimes I am captivated by the stories people tell of faraway places and unique experiences. I recently watched a special on television about the Apollo 11 astronauts and their steps on the moon. Though it happened half a century ago, the story still boggles the mind. It's fascinating and enlightening when the mysteries of the mind, universe, and heart are revealed.

In our humanity, none of us can even begin to understand the vast mysteries of God. God's thoughts and ways are certainly higher than our ability to comprehend. That's one of the reasons the ancient Israelites used the name "Elohim" for God. This plural name attempts to encapsulate all that God is. If you and I were asked to describe God, we might say…God is love. God is great. God is Father. God is Savior. God is redeemer. Just as no single concept can fully describe the nature of God, no single name can fully embrace all that God is. Thus, Elohim describes the God who is all things without attempting to list every attribute. Maybe the name is best translated as "The God who is beyond description." And yet, in speaking to Jeremiah, God tells the people to call out to God and they will hear of great and mighty things. That's God's nature. God longs to be revealed to us. And though we cannot begin to hold all of the mysteries in our minds, God lovingly offers to teach us all things as we ask for guidance.

Prayer
Father, even this day, show us the great and mighty works of your Kingdom. Amen.

Day 779   Jeremiah 34: Good Intentions...

"The officials and all the people had obeyed the king's command, but later they changed their minds. They took back the men and women they had freed, forcing them to be slaves again." Jeremiah 34:10-11 (NLT)

Observation
After he speaks words of hope and restoration to the people, Jeremiah 34-45 depicts the prophet once again taking up words of judgment against the Israelites. God will bring the army of Babylon, along with the armies of all the captured nations, to defeat Jerusalem. Jeremiah tells King Zedekiah that he will not escape but will meet King Nebuchadnezzar face to face. However, he will not die by the sword but will die in peace in Babylon. (The end of his life is still harrowing. Second Kings 25:6-7 tells of Zedekiah watching as his sons are killed before his eyes, and then his own eyes are gouged out as he is led away to Babylon.) The rest of Jeremiah 34 speaks of a covenant the people made with the king to release all Hebrew slaves in Jerusalem. The slaves were freed, but then as the siege of Jerusalem wore on, their former owners enslaved them again. The breach of the covenant defamed the name of God because it was originally made in God's name. Thus, the fate of the city was sealed.

Application
Do you remember taking multiple-choice tests in school? Teachers always suggested that when you weren't sure of the answer, you should go with your first inclination. The first choice is often the right choice. In my own test-taking, I noticed that whenever I debated an answer or even changed an answer, I usually made a poor decision. Sometimes it is best to go with your first thought. In Jeremiah's story, the Israelites made a good choice: they set their slaves free under the guidance of God, who had established this practice in the Levitical Law. But then they changed their minds...

We can learn from their experience. Whenever we willfully, obediently, and deliberately plan a course that helps us pursue the things of God, it is best not to change our minds. Certainly, we have all redirected ourselves; we get caught up in a moment and make a promise to God that we later refuse to keep. One moment's resolve is sometimes defeated when the pressures of life take over. We simply change our minds. In terms of Kingdom pursuits, this practice can be dangerous. Jesus said, "Anyone who puts a hand to the plow and then looks back is not fit for the Kingdom of God" (Luke 9:62 NLT). In most circumstances, it is important to finish what we start. When we make the commitment of discipleship, the option for turning back is forever gone. We can't change our minds. Christ calls us to a faithful, lifelong pursuit of the Kingdom. Don't look back, even for a second.

Prayer
Father God, give us faithfulness in our pursuit of you. Amen.

Day 780 — Jeremiah 35: "Lips that Touch Wine…"

> "But they refused. 'No,' they said, 'we don't drink wine, because our ancestor Jehonadab son of Recab gave us this command: You and your descendants must never drink wine. And do not build houses or plant crops or vineyards, but always live in tents. If you follow these commands, you will live long, good lives in the land." Jeremiah 35:6-7 (NLT)

Observation

Jeremiah 35 continues the theme of impending judgment, offering a reminder of why God will judge the Israelites. The story focuses on a group of people named the Recabites, founded by Jehonadab, son of Recab. This tribe descended from the Kennites and were likely metalsmiths. (According to 2 Kings 10:15-28, Jehonadab once assisted Jehu in purging the prophets of Baal from the land of Samaria.) The Recabites were nomadic, living in tents. Their leader Jehonadab instructed them to build no houses, sow no crops, plant no vineyards, and drink no wine. As a demonstration to the Israelites concerning faithfulness, Jeremiah brought some of the Recabites into the Temple and set before them cups and pitchers of wine. They refused to drink, citing their obedience to the covenant and promises made by their leader Jehonadab. Jeremiah used their faithful example as a teaching opportunity for unfaithful Jews who refused to practice obedience.

Application

An expression from an earlier time and generation says, "Lips that touch wine shall never touch mine!" Obviously, this was said by someone who viewed alcohol as the root of many sins and refused to associate with people who drank. It seems outdated and quaint in today's culture, but it illustrates someone's resolve about a matter important to them. My goal is not to argue for or against the use of alcohol. Instead, I want to focus on identity. The ancient Recabites knew who they were and what they believed. They lived within the boundaries of their belief system. All of us should try to understand "identity." We must recognize who we are, what we believe, and what standards we will raise. Of all the ways we might choose to identify ourselves, the defining principles are governed by the words "Christ follower." If our identity is truly centered in that confession of faith, then our actions must match it. Being Christ-like is the standard. Loving people is the watchword. Living a life of discipline because of his lordship is the day-to-day practice. Because we belong to Christ and choose to bear his name, we must act in ways that honor all that he is. And so we must extend grace to those who have fallen, mercy to those who have injured, love to those who are enemies, and faithfulness to our identity.

Prayer

Father God, may we find our identity in Christ and live out that allegiance. Amen.

Day 781 — Jeremiah 36: A Book Burning

> "Each time Jehudi finished reading three or four columns, the king took a knife and cut off that section of the scroll. He then threw it into the fire, section by section, until the whole scroll was burned up."
> Jeremiah 36:23 (NLT)

Observation
The incidents in Jeremiah 36 occurred during the fourth year of King Jehoiakim's reign. God tells Jeremiah to write down all the words of preaching and prophecy that he has declared through the years. (This represents nearly 22 years of Jeremiah's ministry.) Jeremiah painstakingly dictates his words to Baruch, a trained scribe and close friend of Jeremiah. Because Jeremiah is still held captive in the courtyard of the king's palace, Baruch is told to go to the Temple and read the scroll to the people assembled for worship. In this bold and daring move, he continues to proclaim the impending destruction of Jerusalem because of disobedience. A bit later, the king tells his servants that he wants to hear the scroll for himself. Jehudi reads it to the king. The king offers no signs of fear or lament and tosses the scroll into a fire as if he can silence its message. The Lord then tells Jeremiah to write a second scroll, which he does, adding even more material.

Application
History is full of stories of book burnings. The Romans did it in the first century. Nazis did it during World War II. The Mayan codices were once burned. Burning a book is an attempt at censorship. It is typically done to gain control culturally, religiously, or politically. Book burning has been described as cultural genocide because it can cripple thought, expression, science, and even religion. In Jeremiah's story, the king attempts to silence the message God wants to reveal to the Israelites. Of course, the burning of the scroll does not keep God from commissioning a second scroll, just as the destroyed stone tablets from Sinai, broken as Moses angrily threw them at the feet of disobedient worshippers, were quickly replaced by God according to Exodus 34:1. The point is that God's message is more powerful than anyone's attempt to silence it. To ensure that God's word prevails, God states in Hebrews 10:16, "This is the new covenant I will make with my people on that day, says the LORD: I will put my laws in their hearts, and I will write them on their minds" (NLT). Our technological advances (from stone to paper to digital files) do not preserve the word of God throughout the ages. It is preserved when the faithful read it, obey it, memorize it, and apply it. So the question is, "How well are you preserving the word of God today?" Is it in your heart, in your mind, and reflected in your words?

Prayer
Father God, preserve your word through each of us this day. Amen.

Day 782 — Jeremiah 37: A Call to Vigilance

> "This is what the Lord says: 'Do not fool yourselves into thinking that the Babylonians are gone for good. They aren't!'" Jeremiah 37:9 (NLT)

Observation

Chapters 37-39 are arranged in chronological order to describe the final days before the fall of Jerusalem. They carefully trace the life and ministry of Jeremiah during the last siege and destruction of the city. King Zedekiah has rejected the word of God and the warnings from God's messengers concerning Jerusalem's destruction. In this narrative, the king sends an envoy to Jeremiah to seek a word from the Lord. Around this time (588 BC), the Egyptians invaded southern Judah, hoping to defend the Israelites against the Babylonians. The Babylonians withdrew their siege of Jerusalem in order to battle the Egyptians. Zedekiah hoped that the Babylonians would be defeated, but it was not to be. Jeremiah told the king that nothing had changed; the Babylonians would return and destroy the city. During the time when the siege was lifted, many residents took the opportunity to move outside the city. Jeremiah had hoped to travel to the east and claim his property in the land of Benjamin. As he left the city, however, he was arrested and accused of defection. He was beaten and placed in prison. Finally, the king requested another audience with him, which allowed him to remain in the king's custody and not return to prison.

Application

We hope certain enemies will never return…and yet they do. Take the weeds in your lawn. No matter how well you kill them off this season, they will surely return next year. Have you ever battled black ants in your kitchen? You can spray a little RAID and solve the problem, but only temporarily. Or go to the dentist and have your teeth cleaned and the plaque removed. It feels great, right? But you'd better go back again in six months. Certain enemies continue to return.

Jeremiah desperately tried to warn the king of Judah that the Babylonians were returning. It was not a time to relax. They needed to prepare. Like the king, we are occasionally lulled into sleep, thinking that we can defeat and hold off the enemy of temptation. Nothing could be further from the truth. Jesus himself was tempted in the wilderness by the devil. Once Jesus defeated him, the scriptures simply state that the devil departed until "an opportune time" (Luke 4:13 NASB). We will never defeat our temptations for good during this life. We may win today, but there is a battle waiting to be fought tomorrow. Even so, take courage; we do not fight the battle alone. Christ promises to be with us always, and if we lean into his lordship, we can become more than conquerors.

Prayer

Father, help us to win our battles over temptation this day. Amen.

Day 783   Jeremiah 38: The Power to Influence with Words

> "So these officials went to the king and said, 'Sir, this man must die! That kind of talk will undermine the morale of the few fighting men we have left, as well as that of all the people. This man is a traitor!'"
> Jeremiah 38:4 (NLT)

Observation

As Jeremiah 38 opens, several princes who served under King Zedekiah overhear Jeremiah describe the impending destruction Jerusalem is about to face. They go to the king, demanding that Jeremiah be put to death. His treasonous words will destroy morale…or so they claim. The king, who continues to display weak leadership, is somewhat powerless before this alliance of princes. He tells them to do whatever they want to Jeremiah. They put him down a cistern in the courtyard of Malachiah, one of the king's sons. No water remains in the cistern due to the long siege of the city and the shut off water supply. The bottom of the cistern contains thick, damp mud. Jeremiah sinks into the mud. It seems likely that he will die a slow, unpleasant death. Another servant of the king, Ebed-Melech, secretly goes to the king, tells him what has happened, and asks for permission to remove Jeremiah from the muddy cistern. Jeremiah is rescued, and in a secret meeting with the king he reminds Zedekiah that his best hope is to surrender to the Babylonians.

Application

Our voices have the power to encourage, inspire, and motivate others to action. The great leaders of history had voices that led nations and movements. My generation will remember the words of President Kennedy, who spoke of the challenges of reaching the moon and how America must lead the way: "We choose to go to the moon in this decade and do the other things, not because they are easy, but because they are hard…." The nation rallied behind his words. Others of us will never forget President Obama's speech about the Charleston murders when he sang "Amazing Grace." It was a healing word in a fractured moment.

During Jeremiah's ministry, he was chastised for his words. He spoke unpopular truths that were hard to hear. He was accused of destroying morale and spreading discontent. Sometimes we, too, proclaim an uncomfortable truth. There are moments when the word of God stands in stark contrast to the whims of culture. Those who speak only what others want to hear instead of what they need to hear will never influence their generation. May God help us to speak truth, grace, and honest words even if doing so puts us at odds with others.

Prayer

Father, may our words be seasoned with grace, love, and truth. Amen.

Day 784 — Jeremiah 39: The Problems of Poverty

> "But Nebuzaradan left a few of the poorest people in Judah, and he assigned them vineyards and fields to care for." Jeremiah 39:10 (NLT)

Observation
Jeremiah 39 describes the events of July 18, 586 BC. According to Babylonian records, this is the day when the prophecy concerning Jerusalem and the fall of King Zedekiah came to pass. The army of Babylon finally breached the wall of Jerusalem (probably the north wall) and poured into the city. The princes of Babylon sat in the city gate to assert authority. Zedekiah attempted to escape using the gate on the south side of the city. He fled into the plains of the Jordan Valley but was soon captured and taken to the city of Riblah. There he met King Nebuchadnezzar of Babylon face to face, just as Jeremiah had prophesied. Nebuchadnezzar pronounced judgment upon him. Zedekiah was forced to watch his sons being slaughtered. Then his own eyes were gouged out. He was led away to Babylon in bronze fetters. The city of Jerusalem was burned and the buildings destroyed. Nebuchadnezzar spared the life of Jeremiah, along with the lives of the poorest people.

Application
Let's be clear: there is no positive side to poverty. Living in perpetual poverty is a difficult existence. No one would choose to live without the basic needs of food, clothing, and shelter. But many in this world are forced to live in the depths of poverty. I have visited people in some of the poorest regions in the world. (It is ironic, perhaps, that my affluence is what allows me to see the poverty of others. In fact, once on a trip to Haiti to work with the poor, because of an overbooked flight I was given a seat in first class...such a strange contrast.) I have seen the poor of Brazil, Ecuador, Haiti, the Dominican Republic, and the mountains of Honduras. On a recent trip to Honduras to teach a group of bi-vocational pastors, our group stayed in a bunkhouse with multiple beds. One of the pastors, who lives on very little, kept falling out of his bed at night. I discovered that he lacks any kind of bedding in his dwelling at home and typically sleeps in a hammock. No, there is no plus side to poverty. It is interesting that as the Babylonians destroyed the city of Jerusalem and took the residents into exile, they spared the poor. The poor were left behind to manage the fields and the crops. People like them, so abused and mistreated by the circumstances of life, are listed among the most blessed in the life to come. Jesus said, "Blessed are the poor, for theirs is the Kingdom of Heaven." Though we would never desire to live the life they live, may we exhaust ourselves in helping them to live the life we enjoy.

Prayer
Father, remind us that those who are blessed are called to help those who are not. Amen.

Day 785 — Jeremiah 40: The Dangers of Not Listening

> "They said to him, 'Did you know that Baalis, king of Ammon, has sent Ishmael son of Nethaniah to assassinate you?' But Gedaliah refused to believe them." Jeremiah 40:14 (NLT)

Observation

Jeremiah 40-45 describes the aftermath following the destruction of Jerusalem. The city of Ramah, about five miles north of Jerusalem, was a staging area for those being exiled to Babylon. Jeremiah is among the group, led in chains to Babylon. Nebuzaradan, captain of Nebuchadnezzar's guard, releases Jeremiah from bondage with three options: First, he can go to Babylon and receive special protection and treatment. Second, he can stay in Judah under the care of Gedaliah, the Babylonian-appointed governor of Judah. Third, he can go anywhere he desires. He receives food and provisions and chooses to live under Gedaliah's care. A group of Jewish army captains, who fled to the rugged hills during the siege of Jerusalem, conspire against the governor's leadership. A man named Johanan goes to Gedaliah to warn him about the assassination plot led by Ishmael. But Gedaliah is far too trusting of Ishmael and foolishly refuses to heed the warning. Chapter 41 will tell the story of Gedaliah's assassination.

Application

Words of warning are important to hear…and to obey. How many times have you heard warnings against drinking and driving? How many times have you heard warnings against operating a motorcycle without a helmet? What if you ignored those warnings? Earlier this week, a coworker told me the story of her cousin who drank too heavily at a party and then chose to ride his motorcycle without a helmet. He didn't get far down the street before he wrecked his bike and injured his body, including a huge concussion from his head hitting the pavement. He is lucky to be alive. Warnings are given for a reason. They tell of impending danger or the consequences of poor actions. But sometimes we don't listen. The story of Gedaliah is an example. He was warned of an assassination plot but chose to ignore it, and the results were devastating. If you turn through the pages of scripture, you will see many words of warning, words given not to limit our lives or curb our enjoyment but to protect our relationships, our families, and even our health. Remember, we are told not to create any gods or to place anything in prominence over God. God is to be the priority. God's purposes are to become our passions. And yet we don't always heed that instruction. Sometimes we go our own way, ignoring the safe protocols God longs to build into our lives. Do you want the best life possible? Stay in the lanes that God outlines for your life. You will find joy, safety, and contentment.

Prayer

Father God, teach us to carefully follow your ways each day. Amen.

Day 786 — Jeremiah 41: The Joy of Liberation

> "The people Ishmael had captured shouted for joy when they saw Johanan and the other guerrilla leaders." Jeremiah 41:13 (NLT)

Observation
The story told in Jeremiah 41 begins with the assassination of Gedaliah, the Babylonian-appointed governor of Judah. This assassination may have happened as early as three months after Jerusalem's fall. Ishmael killed the governor, just as Johanan had warned. First, Ishmael and his men took a number of people captive and led them away. Two days later, a group of faithful pilgrims made their way towards Jerusalem to worship, and Ishmael tricked them into entering the city of Mizpah, where they were massacred. Their bodies were thrown into a cistern. Ishmael and his followers then fled to the land of Ammon to join forces with some of his allies. When Johanan heard about the attack on the worshippers, he and his men pursued the rebels into the wilderness of Ammon. During the ensuing skirmish, most of the rebels were killed, but Ishmael and several of his men escaped. Fearing further trouble with the Babylonians, Johanan and his group, which included Jeremiah, began a journey of escape towards Egypt.

Application
Sometimes when we receive good, rewarding, and satisfying news, we shout with joy. When we hear about a pregnancy, we rejoice. When we hear that our team has won, we let out a yell. When we discover that we got a raise at work, we shout with glee. Whenever we get excited enough about good news, we respond with verbal affirmation. This happens in the narrative recorded in Jeremiah 41. When a group of people taken captive by an evil man were released, they shouted for joy.

Though we may never be held captive in a prison cell by an angry dictator, or by some oppressive regime, we have likely felt the oppression of our past sins and mistakes. We feel the burden of sin. We know the guilt of shame. We feel the oppressive weight of disappointing others. Our past is shackled to our souls, and there seems no way of escape. We feel as though we will live forever with the weight of our poor choices and missteps. And yet the gospel offers us liberation. The story of Jesus tells us repeatedly that God forgives, grace heals, and guilt is erased. When that message finally sinks in, we should shout with joy at the news of our liberation. John 8:36 reminds us, "So if the Son makes you free, you will be free indeed!" You may have started your day laboring under the terrible strain of your mistakes and poor choices. But it doesn't have to stay that way. In Christ, grace abounds and freedom is offered. Shout with joy!

Prayer
Father, may we walk with joy this day, knowing that grace has covered our sins. Amen.

Day 787 — Jeremiah 42: An Unpopular Word

> "Whether we like it or not, we will obey the Lord our God to whom we are sending you with our plea. For if we obey him, everything will turn out well for us." Jeremiah 42:6 (NLT)

Observation
Under Johanan's leadership, the people struggle with whether or not to flee to Egypt. They seek Jeremiah's counsel, asking him to petition the Lord on their behalf. They pledge that they will accept whatever the Lord reveals. Jeremiah agrees to pray on behalf of the people. Ten days later he hears from the Lord. The message is clear: "do not go to Egypt." God promises the remnant of people from Judah, "I will be with you, I will save you, and I will deliver you." God says they will not face war or hunger if they remain in Judah. But if they refuse to obey, they will suffer consequences. They will die in Egypt as a result of sword, famine, and pestilence. So the people are once again left with the decision to obey God or to choose what seems best in their own minds.

Application
When we were young, our parents established parameters to govern our behavior: what words we could say and not say, what places we could go and not go, what TV shows we could watch and not watch, what clothes we could wear and not wear. If we dared to test the limits of those parameters, we suffered the consequences. It was never a question of whether we liked the rules; it was whether we would choose to obey them.

The ancient Israelites made a declaration to Jeremiah: "Whether we like it or not, we will obey the Lord our God." They were wise enough to understand that God's purpose for their lives might not be pleasant or easy to follow. They said the right thing, but as the story continues, we will discover that they did the wrong thing. They promised faithful obedience but refused to listen when God's direction didn't coincide with their wishes. Are we any better in our practice of faith? Sometimes we make the same declarations: "Whether we like it or not, we will do whatever God says." But when obedience becomes hard, when choices become unpopular, and when God dependency battles human nature, what choices will we make? Can we admit that sometimes God has a difficult word for us? God makes demands of us as our Father—demands not punitive in nature but instructional. God longs to give us what is best. God longs to create a life for each of us that is "good, acceptable, and perfect." Sometimes God's ways are not our ways, and God's thoughts are not our thoughts. When those moments come, whether we like it or not, we must obey...consistently, faithfully, and humbly.

Prayer
Father, teach us obedience even when it makes demands of us. Amen.

Day 788 — Jeremiah 43: Picked Clean

> "He will set fire to the temples of Egypt's gods; he will burn the temples and carry the idols away as plunder. He will pick clean the land of Egypt as a shepherd picks fleas from his cloak." Jeremiah 43:12 (NLT)

Observation
Chapter 43 tells of the prophetic words of Jeremiah to the Israelites who have foolishly chosen to flee to Egypt to escape the perceived dangers of Babylon. Azariah and Johanan spoke out against Jeremiah, who had told them not to take this perilous journey. Now Johanan leads the migration of people all the way to the city of Tahpanhes on the eastern side of the Nile delta. Jeremiah prophesies that once again God will use King Nebuchadnezzar of Babylon to bring judgment upon the rebellious people of Israel and Egypt. Jeremiah is told to embed some stones under the courtyard of Pharaoh's house as a sign to the people. He prophesies that one day Nebuchadnezzar will place his royal pavilion on this spot, symbolizing his power over Egypt. The chapter closes with words of judgment against both the remnant of Israel and the rulers of Egypt.

Application
My wife and I placed a birdfeeder on a post at the end of our back deck. Several times a week, we fill the feeder with safflower seeds. (We learned that some of the larger birds and squirrels don't like the taste of these seeds, but the smaller songbirds, like chickadees and wrens, love them.) Within moments after we fill the feeder, the birds begin their relentless assault on the seeds. Over the course of just one day, they can completely empty the feeder. Any seeds that fall below the feeder are also quickly scavenged away. The birds literally "pick clean" the feeder.

In describing the destruction of Egypt, Jeremiah indicates that Nebuchadnezzar will pick clean the land of Egypt like a shepherd picking fleas from his cloak. We get the image of someone carefully, patiently, and meticulously removing every tiny insect from his garment. Think of the countless sins, transgressions, and mistakes we commit, even on a daily basis, that threaten to disrupt our relationship with our Holy God. Image them as fleas on shepherd's cloak. And then imagine the meticulous work of the Great Shepherd removing each one from our lives so that we can stand faultless before the throne of God. Every sin, every mistake, every transgression...carefully and loving picked clean from our lives. What love God has for us that we should be called God's children. As you begin your trek through another day in which you will inevitably collect a few more fleas, consider the atoning work of Christ who meticulously removes each one.

Prayer
God, we praise you again this day for the grace and forgiveness we have in Christ. Amen.

Day 789 — Jeremiah 44: Willful Defiance

> "We will not listen to your messages from the Lord! We will do whatever we want. We will burn incense and pour out liquid offerings to the Queen of Heaven just as much as we like." Jeremiah 44:16-17 (NLT)

Observation
As the fleeing Israelites settled into the land of Egypt in places like Memphis and Pathros, they adopted the pagan worship practices of the Egyptians. In particular, many began to worship the goddess Ishtar, "Queen of Egypt." Jeremiah once again spoke out in judgment concerning their rebellious acts. Just as God destroyed the city of Jerusalem because the people broke the covenant, God would once again destroy the idolaters in Egypt who practiced willful disobedience. Rather than learn from past mistakes, the people grew even more stubborn. They became angered at Jeremiah's words and rejected all that God was saying through him. In chapter 44, harsh words are directed at the women because they led worship in the cult of Ishtar. After declaring complete destruction of the wayward Israelites, Jeremiah indicated that only a small group would survive and return to Israel one day in order to bear testimony to Jeremiah's prophecy.

Application
In the news this week, another tragic story emerged about a foolish visitor at a zoo. This time, the incident occurred at the lion exhibition in a zoo located in India. A man was mauled to death by lions after he scaled a 20-foot barrier and climbed into the enclosure. Apparently, he wanted to take a couple of pictures, maybe even a selfie, with the lions standing just behind him. We read such a story and wonder about a person's common sense. If you ignore warning signs and place yourself in a dangerous situation, how can you expect anything but bad results? Unfortunately, the man's foolish choices cost him his life.

Notice the words the Israelites spoke defiantly to Jeremiah: "We will not listen to your messages from the Lord! We will do whatever we want." Does that sound familiar? It should, because most of us have said it. Whether we spoke them aloud or not, we have surely voiced them in our minds. At times we stubbornly say, "I will do whatever I want to do. No one can tell me what to do." We boast in our fierce independence, and then we suffer the consequences. We don't talk much these days about "fearing" the Lord. We talk a lot about God's grace, love, and compassion, but rarely do we think in terms of fearing God's wrath. Maybe a little fear can be a helpful voice in our minds. If we willfully, consciously, and defiantly disobey God's words and ways, we should expect to suffer the consequences. The choice is ours—obedience or defiance.

Prayer
Father, forgive our foolish ways whenever we choose to ignore your directions. Amen.

Day 790   Jeremiah 45: A Pledge of Protection

> "Are you seeking great things for yourself? Don't do it! I will bring great disaster upon all these people; but I will give you your life as a reward wherever you go. I, the Lord, have spoken!" Jeremiah 45:5 (NLT)

Observation
This short chapter is out of place chronologically. It refers back to events that unfolded in chapter 36. (According to the text, the date of this message is 604 BC.) Perhaps Jeremiah places it here as a word of encouragement to the exiled readers already living in Babylon. It would remind them of God's salvation of the faithful even amid their current circumstances. Remember that the scribe Baruch assisted and encouraged Jeremiah while he was imprisoned. Baruch carefully recorded the words of God given to Jeremiah. Baruch was told to read the scroll he had written before a crowd gathered at the Temple. King Jehoiakim obtained the scroll and burned it, so Baruch faithfully recorded a second scroll. In Jeremiah 45, Baruch is filled with sorrow as he anticipates the destruction of Jerusalem and the trials that will befall the people. He suffers both mental anguish and personal rejection. Though he once hoped for position, honor, and distinction, God promises that because of his faithfulness, God will protect him from the impending destruction and will continue to protect him wherever he goes.

Application
Sometimes we are protected in ways we can't even imagine. A coworker at Belmont recently told me about his brother's line of work. His brother is an FBI agent whose department is responsible for security details at all major sporting events, such as NFL games and major college games. The stadiums are filled to capacity with excited fans, all waiting to cheer on their teams. What fans don't know is that while they enjoy the game, undercover FBI teams constantly monitor every section of the stadium for possible threats, scanning the crowds for suspicious activity or danger. This happens every week at every major stadium. Does that surprise you? Does that encourage you? I have to admit that I was glad to hear about the work of these FBI teams. I attend a lot of games, and it helps to know about this layer of protection.

    God promises Baruch an even greater level of protection. God will protect him wherever he goes. It should encourage us to know that the God who once made that promise of protection offers us the same promise. "The Lord keeps watch over you as you come and go, both now and forever" (Ps 121:8 NLT).

Prayer
Father, may we be reminded this day of your watch care and protection. Amen.

Day 791   Jeremiah 46: Panic at the Delta

> "The nations have heard of your shame. The earth is filled with your cries of despair. Your mightiest warriors will run into each other and fall down together." Jeremiah 46:12 (NLT)

Observation

Jeremiah 46 begins a series of oracles against Israel's enemies. These pronouncements of judgment will cover the nations from west to east—from Egypt to Babylon. The text includes brief messages concerning the restoration of Israel. The first oracle describes the events in 605 BC when King Nebuchadnezzar of Babylon began his southern campaign against King Neco of Egypt. Clearly, Babylon would overpower Egypt. During this period (lasting about 300 years), Egypt had a fairly weak defense even though she produced and exported superior chariots across the known world. In this oracle, God punishes Egypt for Josiah's death. God would use Babylon as the instrument of judgment. Jeremiah declares that Babylon will mow down the forces of Egypt like "lumberjacks cutting down a forest."

Application

Our focus verse speaks of the panic that will set in among the warriors of Egypt. They will literally "run into each other" in the confused fray of battle. When the Babylonians arrive, the Egyptians will scatter in all different directions.

I play a fun little game with my grandkids called "I'm a dinosaur!" I use a beach towel to make silly disguises. Sometimes I wrap it around my shoulders and pretend to be an old woman with a shawl. Sometimes I cover my head like a shepherd. The children come close to me as I use funny voices. Suddenly, I throw off the towel and shout, "I'm a dinosaur!" and I chase them around the yard. They scream and run in all directions. We play this game for hours in the backyard. It never seems to get old.

But unlike in that silly game for children, sometimes more serious foes pursue us. We let the monsters of worry, anxiety, and fear put us into a panic. We scatter in all directions with little sense of hope or direction. We lose sleep, we sacrifice our health, and we cast aside our better selves in a mad attempt to escape such foes. We would do well to remember the image of the Lord as "our Shepherd." If we remember that God is with us, for us, and defending us, how foolish our fear would seem. God has not created us to cower in fear and anxiety. Over and over again, God tells us to place our burdens on God's shoulders with the promise to cast out our fear. If you are in a bit of a panic today, take a moment to name and claim your fears and the sources of your worry and anxiety. Carefully and intentionally place them at the feet of the Great Shepherd, where you will find peace.

Prayer

Father, help us to exchange our panic for peace. Amen.

Day 792 — Jeremiah 47: The Sound of Terror

> "Hear the clatter of stallions' hooves and the rumble of wheels as the chariots rush by. Terrified fathers run madly, without a backward glance at their helpless children." Jeremiah 47:3 (NLT)

Observation
Jeremiah 47 describes God's oracle against Philistia. Using the metaphor of "rising waters," Jeremiah describes the coming invasion of the Babylonians as a river that overflows its banks. Just as the water will run across the land, the armies of Babylon will spill out across the region. With such swift and powerful devastation, parents will be caught up in the paralyzing terror and will abandon their children as they attempt to flee. The oracle mentions cities in Philistia (Southern Palestine) and the cities of Tyre and Sidon in the north. These two people groups, the Philistines and the Phoenicians, are associated with the Northern Mediterranean and Aegean islands. They came to the Palestinian coast around 1500 BC. Once powerful, these people will fall to the power of Babylon, and their mourning will be "great." God's patience has been exhausted, and the time of judgment has now come.

Application
Because of my seminary experiences in Louisville, I have an interest in the Kentucky Derby that many folks don't share. Admittedly, I am not a rabid fan, but I do tend to look in on that first Saturday of May as the "fastest two minutes in sports" take place. While most people focus on the end of the race, I enjoy the start when the bell sounds and the gates open and the horses rush forward. The sound of all those thoroughbreds beginning their way down the track is impressive. It's almost like a caged thunder that suddenly explodes as the horses are released.

As Jeremiah describes the scene of destruction coming to the Philistines, he mentions the clatter of the stallions' hooves and the rumble of the chariot wheels. What a terrible and awesome sound that must have been…one that surely struck fear in the hearts of those who heard it. A loud sound can have an interesting effect on our bodies. Sound can strike fear, slow our steps, and cause us to cower in paralyzing anxiety. But sound is usually caused by something powerful, and sometimes the noise helps us recognize God at work. When the ancient Israelites heard the sound of God in the tops of the poplar trees (2 Samuel 8), they knew God would lead their battle. When the sound of a rushing wind filled the ears of the faithful at Pentecost, they felt the presence of God. And yes, when we one day hear the sound of the great trumpet call of God, we will know that God has come to make all things right.

Prayer
Father, teach us to listen for your voice in both the small and great sounds around us.

Day 793 — Jeremiah 48: No Escape

> "'Those who flee in terror will fall into a trap, and those who escape the trap will step into a snare. I will see to it that you do not get away, for the time of your judgment has come,' says the Lord." Jeremiah 48:44 (NLT)

Observation

Chapter 48 records Jeremiah's proclamation of God's judgment upon the nation of Moab. Moab had long trusted in the pagan deity Chemosh, god of fertility and storms. In ancient Middle Eastern culture, taking a pagan deity captive would render that god powerless to help its people. Capturing the national statue of such a deity would devastate the nation. Jeremiah states that Chemosh will go forth into captivity. Moab, as a nation, will be taken captive and her cities destroyed. The great pagan god will stand powerless before the Lord Almighty. Even the mighty fortress at Dibon will be destroyed and shame will fall upon the nation. Crops and vineyards will fail, and there will be utter lamentation.

Application

We have a number of young grandchildren, all of whom are mobile. On a recent family vacation to Gatlinburg, we took a portable playpen that can be configured into multiple shapes. When fully extended, it creates an enclosure six or seven feet in diameter. It's big enough to take up most of a small room. During key moments of the trip, we found it helpful to place all of the kids in the playpen. We nicknamed it "Baby Jail." The kids actually loved playing in that space, and we loved having the ability to keep them all contained, at least for a little while!

God had given an important word of warning to the sinful Moabites through Jeremiah's preaching. God told them that they would not escape, for the time of judgment had come. Speaking of no escape, let's consider the scope of God's grace. There is no limit to God's mercy and forgiveness. There is no boundary to God's love. You and I have been captured by it. We cannot escape. We claim God's attention. We are seen by God's eyes. Our pleas are heard by God's ears. We are loved by God's heart. There is no escape. To be sure, we can shun God's affection and blatantly disregard the offer of grace. But that's on us, not on God. As far as God is concerned, we are of great worth, redeemable, loveable, and fully acceptable. This is not a trap; it's the tender embrace of our Father who loves us beyond what we can even imagine. If you are feeling a little down today, maybe feeling a little left out, take heart. You are held today in the inescapable arms of your Father.

Prayer

Father, may each of us feel the warm embrace of your love this day. Amen.

Day 794 — Jeremiah 49: True Religion

> "But I will protect the orphans who remain among you. Your widows, too, can depend on me for help." Jeremiah 49:11 (NLT)

Observation

In chapter 49, Jeremiah continues his oracles of judgment—in this case against five nations or cities. First in verses 1-6 he offers prophetic words against Ammon, a nation formed from the descendants of Lot. Historically, these people were frequent enemies and poor allies of Israel. Their patron deity Milcom would be taken during the destruction of the region. Next, Jeremiah pronounces judgment upon Edom in verses 7-22. Located south of Moab and southeast of the Dead Sea, this region contained the descendants of Esau. They had a long history of trouble with Judah. While they were known for wisdom and strong fortresses, God promises to destroy both. Next, Jeremiah will speak against Damascus in verses 23-27, promising that God will consume its strongholds and palaces. Then, Jeremiah will describe the judgment against Kedar and Hazor in verses 28-33. This important Arab tribal group consisted of sheep herders and merchants from northern Arabia. Finally, in verses 34-39, Jeremiah will speak against Elam, a region known for skilled archers who were part of the Persian army under Cyrus. God will "break the bow" of their forces.

Application

Tucked away in his oracle against Edom, Jeremiah offers an interesting word about the plight of widows and orphans who are left behind. God promises to protect them and to provide for their needs. God has always defended the marginalized and vulnerable. In fact, New Testament writer James echoes the same sentiment: "Pure and undefiled religion in the sight of our God and Father is this: to visit orphans and widows in their distress, and to keep oneself unstained by the world" (James 1:27 NASB). It seems that if God singles out these two specific groups for protection, watch care, and attention, then they should be important to us as well. I once served a church in Birmingham where a retired schoolteacher, who was a widow, attended faithfully. She lived on a limited income and rarely splurged on anything remotely extravagant. Imagine my shock one day when I was called to offer a prayer of dedication for a new building at a local children's home named in her honor. I discovered that she and her late husband had lived a life of sacrifice in order to provide for the needs of these children. Their lifetime gifts amounted to over 2 million dollars! Out of their meager income they had provided extravagantly. I bet there are widows and orphans in your town who could use a little support. Why not offer a gift to help these people of whom God is especially fond? Remember that your time is often as valuable as your income. Give generously.

Prayer

Father, may we have a heart of generosity and give freely. Amen.

Day 795 — Jeremiah 50: American Idols

> "The sword will even strike her water supply, causing it to dry up. And why? Because the whole land is filled with idols, and the people are madly in love with them." Jeremiah 50:38 (NLT)

Observation
Chapters 50 and 51 form a unit describing Jeremiah's prophetic word against Babylon. The nation that was once God's instrument of judgment upon Judah will now suffer destruction for her treatment of God's chosen people in captivity. According to Jeremiah's words, Israel will be gathered and restored from the countries to which God has banished them. There is some debate in interpretation. Some argue that these words describe what will occur in 539 BC when the Persians overtake Babylon and release the Israelites. Others argue that the passage is more eschatological in nature, meaning that the described events will occur at the "end of days" when the Messiah returns to make all things new. Either way, Jeremiah is commanded to declare and proclaim the public destruction and humiliation of Babylon. Historically, Babylon declined steadily as a nation after the death of Nebuchadnezzar. Apparently, Cyrus of Persia was able to conquer the land with little effort. The pagan gods of Babylon were destroyed and the nation was plundered. The once-captive Israelites were freed and began the migration back to the Promised Land.

Application
Jeremiah describes the destruction of Babylon caused by their pursuit of pagan and worthless idols. The people were "madly in love with them." We may wonder why people in ancient cultures were gullible enough to pursue manmade idols as if they had power or the ability to give aid. But are we not as foolish in our pursuit of the idols we create? We tend to worship, bow down, and give both allegiance and attention to a lot of powerless gods. Some have been around for a long time; we worship power, success, wealth, greed, and lust. We crave such things and will do almost anything to attain them. Other idols are newer but were created by the same cravings that have plagued human nature from the beginning. Think in terms of the screens we worship. How many hours a day do we stare at a television, computer, or phone screen as though any of them contain the answers to life's biggest questions or can solve humanity's biggest needs? We create idols of our hobbies and leisure pursuits. We create idols of our politicians and celebrities. We bow down to the idols of status, wealth, and fame. Many have even worshipped at the altar of nationalism. Here's the problem with idols: we fall madly in love with them to the point that we love them more than we love our Heavenly Father. Idol worship always leads to ruin…even now.

Prayer
Father, forgive our foolish pursuit of things that don't matter. Forgive our false worship. Amen.

Day 796 — Jeremiah 51: No Fight Left in Them

> "Her mightiest warriors no longer fight. They stay in their barracks, their courage gone." Jeremiah 51:30 (NLT)

Observation
Jeremiah 51 continues the words of judgment against Babylon begun in chapter 50. Jeremiah states that destruction will come upon the land like a scorching wind. He reminds God's faithful that even though Israel and Judah have forsaken the lordship of God, God has not forsaken them. At this point, Babylon is beyond healing; the nation will be destroyed. Jeremiah uses the image of a plague of locusts to describe the swarm of enemy soldiers who will pour across the land (v. 14). According to verses 29-32, the mighty soldiers of Babylon will cease fighting in the face of utter and complete defeat. The Nabonidus Chronicles, which describe the fall of Babylon, state that "Cyrus entered Babylon without a battle." As our focus verse indicates, the mighty warriors did not even come out of their barracks—"their courage gone." Jeremiah promises that the nations will sing joyfully at Babylon's fall. The chapter ends with Jeremiah instructing Seraiah, who would be taken captive to Babylon, to read this scroll of prophecy within the walls of Babylon and proclaim the future judgment of God.

Application
My senior year of high school football was a lot of fun. My team played well and reached the playoffs at the end of the season. We won a nail-biter victory in the first round and then faced a powerful team in the second round. That's when the fun went out of the season. We played horribly during the first half. We went to the locker room losing by four touchdowns. (And it never got better, by the way.) Our coaches tried everything they could to rally our courage and spirits. They even tried a little reverse psychology; one coach suggested that maybe we should stay in the locker room and not return to the field if we weren't going to play any better.

Notice that the ancient Babylonians never even left the barracks when the Persian army walked into the city. They were totally defeated and demoralized. This passage makes me consider the plight of many modern-day Christians in America. It seems that many have abandoned the fight for the salvation of our nation, choosing to stay within the safe confines of the church sanctuary, cursing the darkness without a thought of actually taking the light of the gospel into that darkness. Let me remind you that the world is not impressed, nor will it be changed by our private devotions. The evil around us will only be defeated when we boldly and deliberately take the hope of the gospel beyond the walls of our barracks.

Prayer
Father, give each of us a zeal to proclaim your Kingdom and live out your will. Amen.

Day 797 — Jeremiah 52: The Remnant

> "In Nebuchadnezzar's twenty-third year he sent Nebuzaradan, the captain of the guard, who took 745 more—a total of 4,600 captives in all."
> Jeremiah 52:30 (NLT)

Observation
This final chapter of Jeremiah is a historical appendix to the book that vindicates the prophet and encourages the remnant still in captivity. Much of the material is contained both in previous chapters of Jeremiah and in the book of 2 Kings. Zedekiah is listed as the last king of Judah, reigning from 598-586 BC. God finally casts him away from God's presence because of the evil he has committed. By this time, Jerusalem has been under siege for two years. Finally, in July 586 BC, the food supply was exhausted and the walls were breached. The Babylonian army poured into the city. All of the city was burned and the Temple was destroyed. The sacred objects, furniture, and implements used in the Temple were taken as booty. The city's leaders were rounded up and chosen for execution. Chapter 52 offers a numerical listing of those taken into exile. Over several deportations, a total of 4,600 people were taken to Babylon…a surprisingly small number.

Application
I have a friend who pastors a large church in Birmingham, Alabama. In fact, it is one of the leading congregations in the city. But it hasn't always been that way. For many years, the church was located in a deteriorating area of west Birmingham. Numbers declined for decades. Finally, a catalytic moment occurred. Church membership, which had been close to a thousand members in the 1950s, dropped to just 75. At that moment, the church decided that something had to happen. They sold the property and moved to the south side of town, and suddenly the old church sprang to life again. Sometimes we get surprised by the renewal of life that only God's Spirit can call into being. The ancient Israelites diminished down to less than 5,000 people who lived in exile. And yet God did not forget them or abandon them; God actually brought them back to life. The people returned to reclaim the land, and the nation still stands today. Renewal happens not only to old congregations and wayward nations…it also happens to us. God's Spirit at work in us continually forgives, transforms, and renews us. Though we may feel cast aside, forgotten, and maybe too marred by poor choices to be of any value to God, the Spirit residing in us continually calls us to life again and again. The small spark becomes a raging flame. The tiny hope becomes a bright future. God is in the business of new beginnings. Take heart if you have stumbled and lost your way. You are not abandoned, never forgotten, and soon to be renewed.

Prayer
Father God, take the small hope within us and transform us into life again. Amen.

Day 798   Lamentations 1: A Time to Grieve

> "Jerusalem, once so full of people, is now deserted. She who was once great among the nations now sits alone like a widow. Once the queen of all the earth, she is now a slave." Lamentations 1:1 (NLT)

Observation
The book of Lamentations reveals Jeremiah's broken heart as he grieves over the national tragedy that has unfolded before his eyes. Jerusalem has fallen to the Babylonians. The Temple has been destroyed. The people have been either slaughtered or taken into captivity. There are five chapters in this book. The first two build up to the climax affirmation in chapter 3, "Great is Thy faithfulness." The last two chapters are a decrescendo from chapter 3's pinnacle. In the Hebrew text, the book begins with the word "How," as in "How lonely sits the city…." This type of beginning is typical of laments and funeral songs. It expresses an astonishing, sorrowful dismay over all that has happened. (This opening chapter focuses specifically on Jerusalem.) The residents of Jerusalem turned their backs against God and now suffer as a result. Both in the sanctuary of their hearts and in the Temple itself, the things of God have been desecrated. Jeremiah laments that "no longer will there be throngs of pilgrims traveling the roads of Jerusalem in order to come and worship."

Application
Grief is a difficult foe. At times, we grieve over the loss of someone or something that we greatly loved and now miss. For example, we grieve over family members who have died, over once great institutions or churches that no longer exist, or over simple, innocent times that are forever gone. Yet sometimes our grief bubbles to the surface over our horrible mistakes or poor decisions. We live with the painful regret of bad choices and errant ways. The grief in such cases is self-inflicted. We have acted poorly and now we lament our actions. Such was the case with the residents of ancient Jerusalem. Their willful disobedience before God caused their downfall, and Jeremiah is right to grieve over the loss of innocence, purity, and fidelity that the people once knew. Most people who read this devotional have likely buried, deep down inside of them, the painful grief of some wayward step or poorly made decision. We mourn the loss of our innocence, our purity, and our feelings of acceptance with God. Because we see ourselves as broken people, we carry the baggage of remorse for years and years. It doesn't have to be that way. God has sent the Son the be the Savior of the world… not the judge of our past mistakes. If you will ask, God will forgive you and cleanse you from all unrighteousness.

Prayer
Father, may we experience the lifting of heart that forgiveness brings. Amen.

Day 799 — Lamentations 2: Enough Is Enough

> "I have cried until the tears no longer come; my heart is broken. My spirit is poured out in agony as I see the desperate plight of my people. Little children and tiny babies are fainting and dying in the streets."
> Lamentations 2:11 (NLT)

Observation
Lamentations 2 reveals God's intense anger at sin. Because of the unrelenting committing of sin, idolatry, and disobedience, even in the face of God's repeated warnings through the prophets, God brings the full force of wrath upon the people of Jerusalem. God shows no mercy even towards the Temple (v. 10). God has destroyed all of Jerusalem with righteous judgment. Twenty-five times in this chapter, Jeremiah uses the words "he" or "his" to indicate God's participation in the destruction. Verse 3 indicates that God has "drawn back his right hand," indicating that God will no longer offer protection over the people or the city. Thus, the people are "swallowed up" (v. 5).

Application
In our focus verse, Jeremiah indicates that he has cried so much in anguish over his city and his people that he is all cried out. He has no tears left to weep. If you read the words of this chapter carefully, you will begin to appreciate all that his eyes have seen and all that his heart has endured. Jeremiah has seen firsthand the wrath of Almighty God, and it is not a pretty sight. We are forced to ask, "Why has such destruction come to Jerusalem at the hands of God?" Simply stated, God's patience was exhausted. For generations, God spoke about the sins of the people. God sent messengers, prophets, and priests to challenge the people to turn from their wicked ways. But the time came when in essence God said, "Enough is enough! Something has to change." That line of thinking may make us a bit uncomfortable. We like to rest securely in the thought of God's grace, patience, and compassion. But we must consider God's corrective intent as well. God continually calls us into transformation. God longs to conform us into the image of God's Son. God wants to draw us out of the darkness of sin and into glorious light. And yet, despite God's offer of grace and forgiveness, we sometime fail to even consider our own repentance. God doesn't forgive us simply to enable us to continue down wrong paths. God's work is redemptive. If we find forgiveness and mercy and then continue in our sinful ways, have we not abused God's grace? Let us not labor under the false assumption that God will always look the other way as we continue our sinful pursuits. There is a point where enough is enough. We may exhaust God's patience and force God to correct us with difficult circumstances. In such moments, we have only our stubborn selves to blame.

Prayer
Father, forgive our abuse of grace and lead us into transformation. Amen.

Day 800   Lamentations 3: Bedrock Confessions

> "I will never forget this awful time, as I grieve over my loss. Yet I still dare to hope when I remember this: The faithful love of the Lord never ends! His mercies never cease. Great is his faithfulness; his mercies begin afresh each morning." Lamentations 3:20-23 (NLT)

Observation
Lamentations 3 takes on a different tone as it speaks of the hope of God's faithfulness and loyal love. It is Jeremiah's response to Jerusalem's desolation. Unlike the previous two chapters, this one is 66 verses long, containing three verses for each letter of the Hebrew alphabet. The chapter opens with Jeremiah's reaction to the suffering he has experienced. He mentions in verse 4 that his "flesh has aged." As a product of his calling, his experiences have taken a toll on his life, both physically and emotionally. He describes moments when God forbade him even to pray for Judah's deliverance. Yet his words contain hopeful signs. As our focus verses indicate, the fact that the prophet is still alive to record these words and that the remnant is still around to hear them is a reminder that God remembers to be faithful to the righteous. The chapter ends with a prayer asking God to deliver, restore, and vindicate the people.

Application
All of us cling to "bedrock confessions." Certain passages, words, or lyrics resonate in our minds, waiting to be called to the forefront when we need assurance, strength, and hope. For example, I continually cling to these promises: "Greater is he that is in me than he who is in the world," "I will never leave you nor forsake you," "If you confess your sins, he is faithful and just to forgive you and to cleanse you from all unrighteousness," and "The Lord is my Shepherd." Along with scripture, sometimes the words of an inspired hymn bring comfort: "O to grace how great a debtor, Daily I'm constrained to be! Let Thy goodness, like a fetter, Bind my wandering heart to Thee. Prone to wander, Lord, I feel it, Prone to leave the God I love; Here's my heart, O take and seal it, Seal it for Thy courts above" ("Come Thy Fount," Robert Robinson, 1757). If given a quiet moment, all of us could bring to mind words that sustain, give comfort, and provide hope. We need the power and promises of such words. Amid life's ordeals, we need solid rocks on which to anchor our lives and emotions. Jeremiah found strength in remembering that God's faithful love never ends. He claimed the mercies of God with each coming day. I can't protect you from the potential adversity that will come your way today, but I can remind you to stubbornly cling to the God who offers assurances. May God help you as you claim the hope of your bedrock confessions.

Prayer
Father, help our unbelief. Give us strength amid each trial. Amen.

Day 801 — Lamentations 4: The Loss of Respect

> "The Lord himself has scattered them, and he no longer helps them. People show no respect for the priests and no longer honor the leaders."
> Lamentations 4:16 (NLT)

Observation

In this narrative, Jeremiah continues to tell of the degradation of Jerusalem following the Babylonian siege. The opening verses describe the destruction of the Temple. The beautiful, huge, precious stones that once made its walls are now scattered in the streets. The children of the city, more precious than jewels, have been discarded. The chapter emphasizes thirsty and starving children. The people are so desperate for food that they grovel among the various trash heaps looking for something to eat. Jeremiah suggests that it would have been better to die violently during the siege of the city than to die a long, slow death by starvation. Even those who attempted to flee to other lands were not welcomed. Jeremiah offers an especially harsh indictment of the priests and prophets who misled the people. God's wrath was severe towards them, and the people certainly lost all respect for them.

Application

At one time, preachers and pastors were among the most respected people in any city or community. They were among the esteemed leading citizens of the town. Why? Because they were people of integrity who modeled honesty, respect, and dignity. They lived a life of servanthood, offering compassion for even the least among the citizens. But now that has changed. Once listed as the most trusted members of the community, pastors now rank about 27th on the list of the most trusted, wedged between used car salesmen and lawyers. I have certainly seen this shift in my ministry career. When I fly on a plane and the person next to me asks, "What do you do for a living?" if I say, "I'm a Baptist minister," the invisible wall goes up and the conversation soon ends. But if I say, "I direct a leadership center at a major university," then the fellow traveler longs to engage in meaningful dialogue. What has happened along the way? Why are ministers no longer trusted as they once were? Could it be that our thoughts and sermons are too opinionated and less Bible centered? Have we traded kindness and decency for a vain popularity on social media because we like the attention given to crazy rants? Have we perhaps bought into a prosperity gospel that has removed us from a servant mentality? Or could it be that we have failed to hold ourselves to the high standards expected of a minister in both personal and professional life? If you are a minister, take your calling very seriously. If you are a parishioner, pray daily for those who lead you.

Prayer

Father, may all ministers be people of integrity, respect, and dignity. Amen.

Day 802 — Lamentations 5: The Unimaginable

> "We have to pay for water to drink, and even firewood is expensive."
> Lamentations 5:4 (NLT)

Observation
This final chapter of Lamentations shares many themes with the earlier chapters. These lines contain much about the terrible fate of those who remain in and around Jerusalem after the Babylonian destruction. The "Promised Land," once offered as an inheritance to Abraham and his descendants, now seems to be in the hands of strangers and aliens. Things are so bad in the land that even those who plant meager crops must collect the harvest with the threat of attack from nomadic bandits. Jeremiah describes the "hot skin" of the people, a reference to various diseases and illnesses that have broken out across the land. Judah has clearly lost her place of honor among the nations. And yet the chapter ends with a prayer for deliverance: "Turn us back to You, O Lord, and we will be restored."

Application
Who would have imagined that people would pay for water beyond their tap supply? People go to the store every week and buy bottles of water. At a convenience store, it's not unusual to pay a couple of bucks for a bottle. It's also unimaginable that people pay $4 for a cup of coffee, $200 for cable service, or hundreds of dollars a year for a cell phone. Some things are hard to imagine, but they are true nonetheless.

As Jeremiah writes his words of prophecy, he is amazed at how desperate the situation has become. The land is so barren and unproductive that people pay for water to drink, and even the firewood, once collected freely in the woods, is now offered at a price. He could never have dreamed of a moment when the glorious city of Jerusalem would fall into such a state of desolation and desperation. He begs for God to remember the people once again and restore what is broken and lost.

Have you ever looked at your own life and thought, "How did things get to this point? How did I let relationships fail, how did I neglect my health, how did I lose sight of my better self? When did I become this person that I no longer recognize?" It happens. Slowly but steadily, we begin to move away from our values, our morals, and our anchor points. We don't mean to walk away from God. We don't wake up one day and choose to be rebellious. It just happens with a single poor choice or bad decision. We let the lure of temptation get a foot in the door. We play with possibilities. We begin our slide down a slippery slope until we find ourselves living far away from the Father's intention for our lives. The key is daily attention to our faith disciplines. Pray. Read the word. Seek the wisdom of God.

Prayer
Father, may we have the wisdom to avoid the slippery slope. Amen.

Day 803　　　　　　　　　　　Ezekiel 1: What's in a Name?

> "The Lord gave this message to Ezekiel son of Buzi, a priest, beside the Kebar River in the land of the Babylonians, and he felt the hand of the Lord take hold of him." Ezekiel 1:3 (NLT)

Observation

Much like the call of Moses, Jeremiah, and Isaiah, Ezekiel's call to ministry comes through a supernatural encounter with the holiness of God. This call comes to him on July 31, 597 BC. Ezekiel is 30 years old, the age when he should begin his service in the Temple as a priest. Instead, he lives with the exiles of Judah in the land of Babylon. Verse 4 begins a series of visions. God's glory will be revealed to Ezekiel from the center of a great storm cloud. Four creatures emerge from the storm. These are likely angels who join other celestial beings to celebrate the glory and holiness of God. As in other biblical accounts, God appears in the fire and lightning of the storm. This passage also speaks of the well-known "wheel in a wheel imagery" of Ezekiel. Though many suggest a wide range of interpretations, the image is probably of the chariot of God's Spirit that has the ability to move quickly, forcibly, and powerfully in any direction.

Application

It is plausible that Ezekiel's name was a nickname describing his role as a prophet. The name is drawn from two Hebrew words. The first part means "to hold fast." The second part refers to God. Thus, Ezekiel literally means "one who is held fast by God" or "the man whom God has seized." God had certainly taken hold of this young priest and commissioned him to prophesy in a special way.

Names are important. Sometimes nicknames become even more important. Think of Jacob, the father of the 12 sons whose descendants would become the 12 tribes of Israel. His name literally meant "heel holder" or "supplanter" because of how he exited his mother's womb. Every time someone said his name, he would remember his trickery and deceit that continued to follow him during his young life. And then, at the Jabbock River, God gave him a new name: Israel. This name meant "one who has faithfully wrestled with God and found victory in the struggle." The new name redefined his whole life and self-esteem. God has a name for each of us. It may not be the name we receive at birth but a name that reflects God's love for us. Maybe God calls us "faithful one," "beloved," or "child." Rejoice today knowing that God has given you a name to remind God not of your past or frail nature but of God's joy in creating you.

Prayer

God, thank you for calling us your beloved children, reminding us of who we are. Amen.

Day 804 — Ezekiel 2: Stand Up, Speak Out

> "And whether they listen or refuse to listen—for remember, they are rebels—at least they will know they have had a prophet among them."
> Ezekiel 2:5 (NLT)

Observation
This short chapter begins by outlining Ezekiel's task. God explains and empowers his mission. Ezekiel will be challenged to stand fearless in the face of adversity. The Spirit will indwell his life, giving him supernatural power to carry God's message to a reluctant audience—the rebellious sons of Israel. He is told to deliver this message whether they listen to him or not. Twelve times in the book, Ezekiel refers to Israel as a "rebellious house." God tells him not to fear them or their harsh words. As chapter 2 closes, Ezekiel is handed a scroll containing funeral songs, words of sorrow, and pronouncements of doom on both sides. As chapter 3 opens, Ezekiel will be instructed to eat the scroll and thereby internalize the word of the Lord.

Application
My wife is a political junkie. She is knowledgeable, insightful, and relentless in her quest to parse out truth from various politicians. As she scrutinizes the news feeds and social media accounts, she always has an idea of what is going on and who speaks boldly as opposed to who speaks with partisan prejudice. Sometimes she texts or calls me to make sure I am paying attention to things that matter. She can always tell when a politician is speaking with truth or falsehood.

In the Old Testament world, prophets like Ezekiel had two tasks. One to foretell events in the future. The other was to "forth-tell" the word of God. For situations to change or for hearts to repent, someone must be brave and bold in speaking the truth. In fact, for change to happen in our culture, someone has to stand counter to the culture and proclaim truth even when it is uncomfortable for both proclaimer and audience. Many 21st century Christians have adopted a universalism that prevents us from taking on any challengers and waters down our evangelistic zeal. Though we may still believe that Christ is the only way to the Father, we seem reluctant to ask nonbelievers to confront that reality. In our lack of faith sharing, we reduce the gospel's worldwide reach and weaken the truth of God's message. Conversion is not our responsibility. Conversion only happens through the mysterious work of the Spirit. Our responsibility is gospel proclamation. We must stand and speak truth, in season and out of season, when it is popular to do so and when it is not. It must be said of us that the people knew a prophet had stood among them.

Prayer
God, give us boldness in our witness and faithfulness in our missionary zeal. Amen.

Day 805 — Ezekiel 3: Tongue-tied

> "And I will make your tongue stick to the roof of your mouth so that you will be speechless and unable to rebuke them, for they are rebels. But when I give you a message, I will loosen your tongue and let you speak. Then you will say to them, 'This is what the Sovereign Lord says!' Those who choose to listen will listen, but those who refuse will refuse, for they are rebels."
> Ezekiel 3:26-27 (NLT)

Observation
Ezekiel 3 outlines Ezekiel's calling in great detail. He is to eat the scroll that contains God's instruction. This symbolic act of eating the scroll demonstrates Ezekiel's internalization of God's word into his life. God reminds him that even though the Israelites share the same language and culture, many of them will not pay attention to Ezekiel's message because they are hard-hearted rebels. God promises to give Ezekiel strength for his task, telling him to speak boldly regardless of his audience's response or actions. He travels to Tel Abib to sit for seven days among the exiles. Seven days was the normal amount of time for a priest's consecration. Once he is fully commissioned, God tells him that he will be as a "watchman" over Israel, whose responsibility is to carefully warn the rebellious people. If Ezekiel fails to give a warning, their sins will be his responsibility. But if he carefully warns the people and they fail to respond, they will have only themselves to blame.

Application
Have you ever been tongue-tied? Have you ever experienced a moment when you were at a loss for words? Being "tongue-tied" can result from confusion, bewilderment, or nervousness. Some moments simply render us speechless. I recently experienced a funny moment when a gentleman told me about an event in his life earlier in the week. He had seen the "Moments that Matter" commercial that my program at Belmont runs every week on CBS Sunday Morning. (It's a minute-long devotional thought that appears during the first commercial break each Sunday.) "I didn't get to watch your commercial this week," he said, "because I was stuck on the toilet. But I heard your voice and it was so inspiring!" I had no idea how to take that comment! I was tongue-tied and could offer no response.

In our focus passage, God tells Ezekiel that he will be unable to speak until the moment God wants him to share a message. God will loosen his tongue in order for him to boldly proclaim God's words. I pray that you are not tongue-tied the next time God presents you with a moment to speak on God's behalf. Let the Spirit direct your thoughts and actions so that you will become a useful servant doing God's work.

Prayer
God, loosen our tongues so that we can proclaim your word this day. Amen.

Day 806 — Ezekiel 4: A Side Show

> "Now lie on your left side and place the sins of Israel on yourself. You are to bear their sins for the number of days you lie there on your side. I am requiring you to bear Israel's sins for 390 days—one day for each year of their sin." Ezekiel 4:4-5 (NLT)

Observation
It was not easy to live the life of a prophet. Ezekiel 4 is a vivid display of what God calls him to do in order to demonstrate his prophetic words. (Chapters 4-24 are oracles of doom. Specifically, chapters 4-7 proclaim the terror against Jerusalem and the land.) As the chapter opens, God tells Ezekiel to take a soft clay tablet, often used for writing, and draw an image of the city of Jerusalem under siege. He is to draw a wall around it, indicating that the city will be starved into submission. Next, God tells Ezekiel to go to the center of town and lie on his left side for 390 days…one day for each year of Israel's rebellion. At the end of that period, God tells him to turn over to his right side and remain for 40 additional days to indicate the years of Judah's sinfulness. The text indicates that God will bind him with ropes so that he can't turn over while prophetically modeling his message. God tells him to make a mixture of dough. He is to eat only eight ounces of bread each day and drink one jar of water for the entire time he remains on his side. The scarcity of his food will symbolize the terrible scarcity that will happen in the city as it remains under siege.

Application
If I were to write a book about the life of Ezekiel, I would have to title it The Great Side Show. He lies on his side for hundreds of days to show God's message to the people. Sometimes delivering a message takes a little more than the spoken word. Sometimes we need to demonstrate the instruction we teach in more creative ways. For a number of years, I coached Little League baseball. I loved working with the players and helping them learn how to become better players. But often it was not enough for me to say, "Throw the ball, steal the base, or catch the fly ball." It took a lot of hands-on coaching and demonstration. I had to model the skills that I wanted them to learn.

The same attention is needed in terms of teaching faith disciplines to each generation. It is not enough to say to a child or teenager, "You need to follow Christ. You need to read your Bible. You need to serve in a ministry setting." Our actions speak volumes. If we are to communicate our faith well, we must model it consistently. People are always watching and listening. How you live out your faith each day in their presence is vitally important. It's not easy to live the life of a prophet, or even the life of a parent. May God bless your effort.

Prayer
God, may we live out our faith carefully and deliberately this day. Amen.

Day 807 — Ezekiel 5: Making an Example

> "You will be a warning to all the nations around you. They will see what happens when the Lord punishes a nation in anger and rebukes it, says the Lord." Ezekiel 5:15 (NLT)

Observation

The difficult work of the prophet continues in chapter 5. God tells Ezekiel to take a sword and shave his head and beard. (A sword symbolized God's sword of wrath that would come against Israel.) A shaved head was a sign of disgrace in the Hebrew culture. It was also a sign of defilement. Ezekiel would be defiled and unable to carry out his priestly duties. His actions would demonstrate the people's upcoming humiliation and defilement. Next, God tells Ezekiel to divide the shaved hair into three piles. He is to burn one pile after placing it on his homemade clay model of the city. He is to chop up the second pile with the clay tablet. And he is to scatter the third pile to the wind. These symbolic actions depict the three fates awaiting the rebellious Israelites who remain in Jerusalem. Some will be burned to death during the siege of the city. Others will be killed by the sword. And the others will be scattered into exile. Ezekiel warns of unparalleled devastation coming to Jerusalem. In the covenant with Israel, God had promised to meet disobedience and rebellion with severe judgment (Deuteronomy 28).

Application

Sometimes punishment is used as an example to others in hopes that even the threat of punishment will convey a lesson. For example, when I was a kid, grade-school teachers were allowed to paddle students for poor behavior. Typically, that happened in the front of the classroom as a deterrent to the other students. It was an effective deterrent, especially in my fifth-grade class when our teacher used a leather strap on a wayward student. Sometimes she even said, "I am going to make an example out of this student." Message conveyed.

God told ancient Israel that God's actions towards the wayward nation would be an example to other nations. "They will see what happens when the Lord punishes a nation." Surely no other nation would want to bear such wrath. What if God wants to use us as an example today? Not as the recipients of horrible wrath but as the recipients of glorious grace. Our story of sin, redemption, and recovery can be used to God's glory. Whenever we offer testimony of our "before and after" life status, we can affect others in positive ways. I challenge all of you who have felt the forgiving grace and unending love of God to share your story. Be an example. Let God use you to help others see and discover the story of grace waiting to unfold in their lives.

Prayer

Father, use our stories to your glory and purposes this day. Amen.

Day 808 — Ezekiel 6: A Not So Gentle Reminder

> "But I will let a few of my people escape destruction, and they will be scattered among the nations of the world. Then when they are exiled among the nations, they will remember me. They will recognize how hurt I am by their unfaithful hearts and lustful eyes that long for their idols. Then at last they will hate themselves for all their detestable sins." Ezekiel 6:8-9 (NLT)

Observation
In chapters 6 and 7, Ezekiel offers two sermons. The first conveys the coming judgment of Israel. In particular, Ezekiel focuses on the cause of Israel's judgment: her rampant idolatry. God tells Ezekiel to face the mountains and hills of Israel and prophesy against them. The mountains and hills are synonymous with the "high places" on which the people built pagan altars. God will bring a sword against Israel, smashing the pagan shrines, temples, and altars and obliterating the pagan objects of worship. The slaughter of the unfaithful will be so great that the slain, unburied bodies will defile the land. But according to our focus verse, a few will be scattered around the world and will remember God. In their remembrance of a Holy God, they will hate their detestable deeds that have brought God's wrath. This remnant exists so that God can create a repentant and fully restored people who seek God's heart.

Application
All of us can be a forgetful at times. To keep our lives and schedules on track, we create reminders for ourselves. Maybe we place an event on our calendar or set an alarm on our phones. Maybe a well-placed sticky note reminds us of something we dare not forget. Every Monday morning, I write a "To Do" list of what I need to address during the week so I can stay on track and remember what I must accomplish. I even create reminders in my car to help me remember what I need to pick up on the way home from work. Sometimes I leave the sun visor down or open the glove box door until I stop to get the things I am supposed to remember. Reminders are important. There are things we cannot allow ourselves to forget.

God offered the ancient Israelites a not-so-gentle reminder. God stated that the people living in the discomfort and anguish of exile would remember the demands of Holy God, and as they remembered they would repent of their actions and seek a renewed relationship with God. I hope none of us needs a "not-so-gentle" reminder from God about some wayward action. As we find falsehood, deceit, and sin in our lives, let us be careful to expose it early and offer a truly repentant heart, lest we get a God-sized reminder.

Prayer
Father, we need both your correction and grace. Teach us even this day. Amen.

Day 809   Ezekiel 7: Some Things Never Change

> "For what God has said applies to everyone—it will not be changed!"
> Ezekiel 7:13 (NLT)

Observation
Ezekiel 7 begins with repetition of the word "end." It stresses the fulfillment of prophecy: the destruction of Jerusalem is at hand, and there is no more time for repentance. God's wrath will affect all "four corners" of the land. None will escape. A sense of great doom comes upon the people. The land's destruction is used to cultivate in the people a better understanding of God. When God declares that the people are not to worship false idols, this word is forceful and unrelenting. Even buyers and sellers in the city will feel the economic impact of Babylon's destruction. Their riches and wealth will be powerless to help. Those left behind will flee to the hills. They will mourn and dress in sackcloth, displaying their humiliation for all to see. God declares that the "worst of the Gentiles" will possess their houses, defile the Temple, and bring violence to the land.

Application
I recently had breakfast with an old friend. Years ago, we were coworkers who served the same church for over a dozen years. It was great to see him and catch up with each other's lives. There was reassurance in the conversation, friendship in the meal, and laughter in the remembrance of shared memories. I walked away from the meal saying to myself, "Some things never change." And I was grateful for the comfortable "sameness" of that relationship.

You and I know that change is a real part of modern life. Nothing seems to stay the same for long. How we do business changes. How we communicate changes. How we spend our time changes. How we experience worship changes. How we think about key issues changes. We are caught in a constantly swirling vortex of new ideas, new thoughts, new devices, and new standards. It is reassuring and comfortable, however, to reconnect with an old friend and find that the relationship hasn't changed…that conversations can resume after being on hold for years.

As Ezekiel preaches to the Israelites, he forcibly reminds them of God's instructions and commandments. The word applies to all: "it will not be changed." They had brought this difficult word of judgment on themselves. Not only does God's word never change nor its meaning diminish, but God's love for us also doesn't change. God loves you this very moment and always has. You can do nothing to deflect God's love in any way. You are not the enemy; you are God's beloved child. Sometimes it's good to know that some things never change.

Prayer
Father, thank you this day for your unending and unchanging love for each of us. Amen.

Day 810   Ezekiel 8: Vices That Become Habits

> "'Have you seen this, son of man?' he asked. 'Is it nothing to the people of Judah that they commit these detestable sins, leading the whole nation into violence, thumbing their noses at me, and provoking my anger?'"
> Ezekiel 8:17 (NLT)

Observation
Chapter 8 opens with the description of a vision Ezekiel experiences while in his home. He is met by a man-like creature who appears to have fire below his waist and metal as his torso. This being transports him to the Temple so that he can see firsthand the detestable acts committed by the Israelites. They have placed idols in the sacred spots, foolishly believing that the presence of the Temple guarantees God's protection. What they fail to realize is that God has chosen to leave God's dwelling place. From the vantage point of a hole in the Temple wall, Ezekiel is able to see even more heinous acts of idolatry. Later, Ezekiel is shown 25 Levites who, having literally turned their backs on the Temple, are facing east and bowing down to the sun.

Application
Sometimes we lose sight of our better selves. A bad habit becomes acceptable behavior. Poor actions become an ordinary occurrence. We allow the constant erosion of temptation and poor choices to slowly eat away at our best intentions and noblest pursuits. We hardly notice what we once considered to be bad behavior.

My wife and I often talk about the lack of civility and simple respect that we notice in day-to-day life. People have forgotten how to say, "Excuse me," when they break in line. People never hold the door open for others like they once did. People seldom say, "Thank you," for a kind deed. Surely you have seen it…this slow spiral into poor behavior and bad habits. The story of the ancient Israelites is an example. In earlier years, they would have never considered worshipping a false idol or allowing a pagan deity to reside anywhere near the Temple of Holy God. But their inattention to what matters to God slowly allowed a compromise of their morality and behavior. One person's lazy morality led others to follow suit. Here's the problem: we are either consciously, willingly, and courageously battling the influence of culture, or we are being conformed to it. We begin to accept the unacceptable. We erase the lines separating right from wrong. We compromise and conform. If we lose our distinctiveness, our character, and our reverence for the things of God, how will we be made salty again (see Matt 5:13-16)? May we live out our convictions and refuse easy compromise.

Prayer
Father, may we never lose sight of our calling to be your image bearers. Amen.

Day 811 — Ezekiel 9: Inclusion

> "He said to him, 'Walk through the streets of Jerusalem and put a mark on the foreheads of all who weep and sigh because of the detestable sins being committed in their city.'" Ezekiel 9:4 (NLT)

Observation

The context for chapter 9 is Ezekiel's vision of the destruction of Jerusalem (which began in the previous chapter). This chapter focuses on the wicked who are to be slain. In the vision, six men are appointed to punish the city in a vengeful visit. Another man, dressed differently, also appears in the vision. His task is to mark with a pen the righteous people of the city—those who mourn and are devastated by the sins of others. They will become the remnant whom God will spare. All those not marked by the writer's pen will be slain. In verse 3, Ezekiel describes God's glory departing from the Temple. Jerusalem will be no more. The Temple itself will be defiled with the bodies of the dead.

Application

Years ago, while participating in a mission experience to Haiti, I was given a difficult task. My role was to hand out sacks of beans to needy families. But not to everyone. Our medical clinic provided care to a large number of individuals. Depending on the severity of need as assessed by the doctors, each person received a small card as they left the clinic. Some cards had a small red sticker while the others did not. The families with a sticker got a sack of beans because their needs were deemed critical. Those without a sticker did not receive a sack. It was heartbreaking to tell many families that they would not receive food while others would. I wished the sponsoring ministry agency had sufficient funding to give food to everyone, but the need was too great and the resources too little.

It can be a difficult experience when some are chosen and others left out. In the case of the ancient Israelites, the people chosen for a saving "mark" had lived with a greater awareness of God's holiness and detested the sins of those who worshipped false idols. In terms of our faith experience and promise, there will be a day of judgment when some will find inclusion in God's eternal Kingdom and others will be left out. The tragedy for those not included is that they could have made choices that led to salvation. God's offer of grace and mercy is extended to all. There is room for every person in God's presence. The determining factor for inclusion is simple: faith in Jesus Christ. Salvation is in the Son. I pray you have claimed that promise.

Prayer

Father, we are thankful for the inclusion we have through Jesus Christ. Amen.

Day 812 — Ezekiel 10: When the Glory Departs

> "Then the glory of the Lord moved out from the door of the Temple and hovered above the cherubim." Ezekiel 10:18 (NLT)

Observation
Continuing the narrative of his vision, Ezekiel describes the glory of the Lord departing the Temple. God is too holy to share a dwelling place with idolatry. Because the people corrupted the Temple's sacred nature, God, along with the cherubim, leave the Temple. In this process, the glory of the Lord, depicted by a thick cloud, fills the Temple, hesitates, and then departs. During the process, the four cherubim are instructed to give flaming coals to the man dressed in linen (see earlier chapters) so that he can scatter the flaming coals throughout Jerusalem. The coals will represent God's chastising judgment and cleansing. What a powerful and frightening image for Ezekiel to witness!

Application
In moments of worship, participants sometimes feel the presence of God in the room. Over the course of my life, I have had many moments when I felt God's presence moving, convicting, healing, and empowering worshippers to action. It is powerful to sense the Lord's presence during worship or in the life and work of a church. It is also powerful and disarming to sense God's departure.

Years ago, I served a church in Birmingham that struggled with how to be the presence of Christ in its contextual setting. The church was primarily a white congregation. Through the years, the surrounding neighborhoods had transitioned from mostly white households into African American households. In an attempt to reach these neighbors, the church implemented and successfully carried out several community-based programs (sports, mentoring, and parenting skills). However, several key leaders in the church did not feel comfortable welcoming Black families into congregational life. I began to sense a deep-seated racism that would not be easily addressed. For the first time in my ministry, I also began to sense the Spirit of the Lord departing that congregation because of its short-sighted and Spirit-limiting attitude. In God's grace, new doors of opportunity opened for my family and me, and we soon moved to a new place of service. The church continued to decline over the next two decades and eventually closed its doors. (I am glad to report that in recent years, a vibrant and inclusive congregation has come to inhabit the facility.) It is indeed a frightful moment when the Glory of the Lord departs. I pray that you will always be sensitive to God's leadership and will respond obediently to God's call and direction.

Prayer
Father, may your glory never depart from our hearts, minds, and attitudes. Amen.

Day 813 — Ezekiel 11: The Strength of Hope

> "I, the Sovereign Lord, will gather you back from the nations where you have been scattered, and I will give you the land of Israel once again."
> Ezekiel 11:17 (NLT)

Observation
Chapter 11 continues the narrative of Ezekiel's vision. This portion deals directly with wicked and corrupt counselors who have given Jerusalem's residents bad advice. (The vision comes to Ezekiel while he is in Babylon and transports him to Jerusalem.) In his vision, Ezekiel sees 25 civic leaders who are public and political officials. Several are named individually. These leaders attempted to blend Hebrew and pagan religious practices. They also spoke falsely about the safety of Jerusalem, encouraging new building projects. Ezekiel prophesies that strangers will slay these evildoers. One leader, Pelatiah, is actually struck dead during Ezekiel's vision. This act is proof of the validity of his prophetic words. Verses 22-23 record how Ezekiel watches the glory of the Lord leave the city and rest on the mountain to the east—the Mount of Olives.

Application
In the summer of 1992, presidential candidate Bill Clinton ended his Democratic nomination acceptance speech with the words, "I still believe in a place called Hope." It was a phrase pregnant with meaning. Born in Hope, Arkansas, Clinton spent much of his speech tracing his early roots from that impoverished place to his new place of political prominence. He claimed a belief in the small-town values of hard work, fairness, and respect. The other meaning drawn from his words related to his hope for America. In his speech, he talked about all the things that would lead the nation to greatness and prominence. The rest, as they say, is history. He of course went on to become a two-term American President.

When you gaze out at the current cultural landscape, there is much to bemoan and fear. A sense of meanness permeates many areas of life. There is mistrust, doubt, fear, and violence. Racism is on the rise. A lack of civility is rampant. Selfishness is overwhelming, and greed has brought the downfall of many. Corruption and deception are commonplace. And yet I still believe in a place called Hope. It is not that I possess a Pollyanna worldview or that I choose to turn a deaf ear to the negative dissonance of everyday life. Instead, I choose to walk by faith. My hope is anchored in the person of Jesus Christ: his goodness, his grace, his love, his kindness, and his lordship. I don't deny the negativity of our world; I simply rejoice in the greater power and glory of the Risen Lord. Like the saints of all the ages, I look to the day when Kingdom will come on earth as it is in heaven.

Prayer
Father, let us live this day in the powerful strength of lasting Hope. Amen.

Day 814 — Ezekiel 12: While the People Watch...

> "Dig a hole through the wall while they are watching and go out through it." Ezekiel 12:5 (NLT)

Observation
Chapter 12 begins a long section in the book of Ezekiel composed of various oracles of judgment. (Ezekiel speaks to those already exiled and to those who will soon follow them as Jerusalem is destroyed.) Because the people have displayed a hardness of heart and a refusal to listen, Ezekiel is told to proclaim a number of messages, some of which are harsh. In this chapter, God instructs him to act out his prophetic words. He is told to pack his bags out in the open, as though he is heading off to captivity. That night, he is to dig a hole in the city wall, put his baggage on his back, and head away from the city. He is to do these things where all the people will see him. His example will show how all of them, even the king, will be taken away. He is then told to tremble as he eats his food and shake with fear as he drinks his water. This will symbolize the way the people of the city will one day eat and drink with fear and despair.

Application
All of us live under the scrutiny of being watched. Because of security cameras, cell phones, and computer cameras, we need to assume that nearly every step we take is watched and maybe recorded. Additionally, if you are a parent, you are aware of how little eyes and ears are always watching every step and hearing every word. It is daunting to think that those "sponges" we call kids are soaking up every detail of our lives. During my career as a pastor, I was acutely aware that I lived under the constant scrutiny of our church membership. One of our members even kept a chart each week of the color of my neckties. He claimed there was a subconscious correlation between the sermon theme and the necktie color!

Read our focus verse carefully, and you will notice that God instructed Ezekiel to carry out some of his prophetic actions "as people were watching." God wanted people to see and notice him. I wonder if we are willing to live our lives, hoping to be noticed by others. Most of us want to "fly under the radar" and protect our privacy. But what if God has called us to live openly, publicly, and demonstratively? Guess what? God has. God intends for us to be salt and light. God intends for our faith to be seen. In fact, Jesus said, "let your light shine before others, that they may see your good deeds and glorify your Father in heaven" (Matthew 5:16 NIV). Whether we like it or not, we are called to live in the public arena. We are called to live "out loud." We will testify to the lordship of Christ with both our words and our actions.

Prayer
Father, may my faith be visible to all this day in the things that I do. Amen.

Day 815 — Ezekiel 13: Prophetic Deception

> "This will happen because these evil prophets deceive my people by saying, 'All is peaceful' when there is no peace at all! It's as if the people have built a flimsy wall, and these prophets are trying to reinforce it by covering it with whitewash!" Ezekiel 13:10 (NLT)

Observation
Ezekiel 13 pronounces oracles of judgment on the false prophets of Jerusalem, both male and female, who continually invent incorrect words of prophecy and proclamation. God will judge them for their deceit. Ezekiel states that they are like foxes in the desert that wander amid city ruins. While trying to pass along their own thoughts as coming straight from God's heart, they have built false walls of hope and whitewashed them with rhetoric. But like the once-strong walls of Jerusalem that are about to be destroyed, their walls of falsehood will come crashing down. On many occasions, they have couched their words in God-language, trying to add gravity to their words by saying things like, "The Lord says...," when in fact God has never spoken to them. As a result of their deception, God will judge them harshly, completely obliterating them from the history of Israel.

Application
One of the more popular episodes of the Andy Griffith Show first aired in 1963. Titled "Aunt Bee's Medicine Man," it featured Col. Harvey who came to town selling a Native American elixir that promised to bring "health, zest, vigor, and the joy of living" to anyone drank it. It was actually just an alcohol-infused elixir that caused Aunt Bee and the ladies of the Church Aid Society to get a little "sauced up"! Col. Harvey was a charlatan selling false hope with an alcohol twist. Aunt Bee, who felt a little down because of a recent birthday, got a euphoric lift from the elixir.

There are many charlatans these days who sell a lot of falsehood, many in the name of religion. These modern-day snake oil salesmen can certainly talk the talk. They couch their words in God-speak and proof-text the scriptures to support nearly any cause or contribution they want to promote. The problem is that many who claim to speak on behalf of God have never actually received a word from the Lord. In fact, many of them hardly even know the God they claim to represent. They are betrayed by their attitudes, priorities, lack of civility, and vitriolic rhetoric. Are you interested in truly hearing from the Lord? Look for a preacher/teacher who spends time each day reading scripture. Look for someone who with no agenda who is teachable and pliable by what God reveals. Look for someone who loves God devotedly and people passionately. Look for someone who doesn't whitewash the truth but also speaks with sensitivity and grace.

Prayer
God, may we practice discernment as we listen to those who claim to have a prophetic word. Amen.

Day 816 — Ezekiel 14: Turtle Man

> "Son of man, these leaders have set up idols in their hearts. They have embraced things that will make them fall into sin. Why should I listen to their requests?" Ezekiel 14:3 (NLT)

Observation
Ezekiel 14 pronounces judgment on leaders who practice the idolatry of a divided heart. Some elders of Israel go to Ezekiel seeking a message from God. Ezekiel reveals the deplorable spiritual condition of these leaders. They have allowed the desire to worship idols to overtake their hearts. Because their hearts are hardened by sin, they do not truly want to hear from God; they are simply going through the motions. God never creates evil but does permit the suffering that comes to those who do evil. Thus, Israel's leaders will suffer as a result of their sins. Ezekiel reminds all prophets/preachers/leaders that they are accountable for their words of proclamation. The content of each message is vital. The people's sin is so wicked that God tells Ezekiel that even if Noah, Daniel, and Job were present in the land, even their presence would not be enough to stay God's judgment. The final section of the chapter concerns the four forms of punishing judgment that will come to the land: war, famine, wild animals, and disease.

Application
Years ago, I went fishing more than I do now. I still love to go; I just don't seem to find the time like I once did. But I remember fishing at a farm pond late one afternoon. I noticed a huge snapping turtle slowly easing his way across the water. "I wonder if I could catch him," I thought. I spent the next few minutes trying to catch the large turtle. I decided that the best way to catch him was by trying to snag his arm or neck with a treble hook. After a few near misses, I was able to hook him just behind his head. I dragged him to the edge of the pond, and then I realized something. I now had an angry and dangerous snapping turtle to deal with! His mouth was huge! He would have literally bitten off my finger if I gave him the chance. It was quite an ordeal to remove the hook and ease him back into the water. Is it possible that some of the things we pursue most strongly are the very things that can come back to bite us?

The ancient Israelites stumbled when they pursued false idols and pagan gods. When they "caught" these deities, all they brought upon themselves were the consequences of evil and foolish actions. What are you pursuing this morning? What has captured your attention? Is it worth your efforts? Will it come back to bite you? Sometimes the things we think we want the most are the very things that will hurt us in ways we can't imagine.

Prayer
God, may we fill our lives in pursuit of the things of your Kingdom. Amen.

Day 817   Ezekiel 15: What Makes a Vine Worthless?

> "Son of man, how does a grapevine compare to a tree? Is a vine's wood as useful as the wood of a tree? Can its wood be used for making things, like pegs to hang up pots and pans? No, it can only be used for fuel, and even as fuel, it burns too quickly." Ezekiel 15:2-4 (NLT)

Observation
Ezekiel 15 and 16 contain three parables, all of which state that Israel (Jerusalem) has no possibility of deliverance from the Babylonians. God has declared judgment because of the nation's idolatry. Chapter 15 tells the parable of the Outcast Vine. A grapevine has one purpose: that of bearing fruit. A vine that produces no fruit is worthless. According to the parable, a vine is useless for construction. A craftsman can't even make a peg from the wood of a vine. If used for fuel in a fire, it burns too quickly. The worthless grapevine represents Israel. God had hoped that the people would produce spiritual fruit and turn to God's word and way. But instead, Israel chose the path of disobedient idolatry. Just as the wood of the vine was worthless even to fuel a fire, God's people became worthless as God's representatives. Ezekiel offers no optimism. God will make the land desolate and judge the unfaithful people.

Application
I like a clean car. In fact, I usually give my car a good wash by hand at least once a week, but in the colder months I drive to a local coin-operated carwash and wash it with the scrub brush and high-pressure wand. Last spring, I had an issue at the carwash. I loaded a bunch of quarters and started scrubbing the car with the brush that squirts thick, pink foam. I took the time to make sure I covered every square inch of my car. I let the time expire while foaming up the car. I then began the process of inserting a second set of quarters so I could give it a good rinse. The final quarter, the one that would turn on the water, got stuck in the machine. It would not drop into place. I banged on the machine. I fussed at it. I prayed over it. But nothing happened. The result? No water and one very soapy car. I had to drive home with my car looking like pink cotton candy! The coin machine had one job—receive the coin and turn on the water. In not fulfilling its purpose, it created problems.

    We are on this planet for two reasons. The first reason is to honor God in all that we do. We were created for God's glory. All that we attempt to do should in some way reflect the God who called us into being. The second reason is to help build God's Kingdom. God intends for us to use our talents, our experiences, and our circumstances to help move the Kingdom forward. That's our purpose: glorify God and build the Kingdom. If we fail to live out our purpose, have we not become like a worthless vine (or a malfunctioning coin machine)?

Prayer
God, may we spend this day in pursuit of our God-given purpose. Amen.

Day 818 — Ezekiel 16: Caring for the Marginalized

> "Sodom's sins were pride, gluttony, and laziness, while the poor and needy suffered outside her door. She was proud and committed detestable sins, so I wiped her out, as you have seen." Ezekiel 16:49-50 (NLT)

Observation

Ezekiel 16 tells two more parables about Jerusalem's destruction. The first parable compares Jerusalem to a rescued infant who will become an adulterous wife (vv. 1-43). The second parable compares the fate of Jerusalem to her two sister cities, Sodom and Samaria (vv. 44ff). In the first parable, Jerusalem's sin and punishment are described along with her restoration. Jerusalem was first founded by the ancient Canaanites, particularly the Amorites and the Hittites. Joshua claimed control of the city during the time of the conquest, and David finally conquered it and made it the nation's capital. Through Ezekiel's parable, God reminds the people that God had rescued the city like an abandoned child. God claimed it, cleaned it, nurtured it, and dressed it in splendor. Extending the metaphor of the young girl who would grow to become a beautiful woman, Jerusalem (as a mature woman) turned to idolatry and prostitution by giving herself away to various nations. God would judge her for her sinfulness. In the second parable, the sins of Sodom and Samaria are remembered. The point is that if God judged those "sisters" for their sins, will God not also judge Jerusalem?

Application

Whenever we think of ancient Sodom, we might remember the story in Genesis 19 of God's messengers being treated horribly as the men of the city want to drag them into the town square and commit sexual acts against them. But in reality, Sodom's sins began much earlier than that. In Genesis 18, God's messengers were already on their way to destroy the city because of her great wickedness. In our focus verse, Ezekiel mentions the "pride, gluttony, and laziness" of powerful people in Sodom who ignore the poor and needy.

As I read these words, I think of the huge disparity in our culture between those who live with abundance and those who live with scarcity. I must admit that I am one who lives with abundance. I have a house, plenty to eat, reliable cars to drive, and good job. I don't worry about my next meal or if I will have a safe place to sleep at night. But I am reminded and convicted that those of us with the means to do so must share with those in need. It is a sin to look at a needy neighbor and not act with compassion. The problem may be that we continue to struggle with our definition of "neighbor." If I read the words of Christ correctly, there is no boundary or border to that definition (see Luke 10).

Prayer

Father God, may we possess a heart of generosity. Amen.

Day 819 — Ezekiel 17: Finding Shelter

> "This is what the Sovereign Lord says: I will take a branch from the top of a tall cedar, and I will plant it on the top of Israel's highest mountain. It will become a majestic cedar, sending forth its branches and producing seed. Birds of every sort will nest in it, finding shelter in the shade of its branches." Ezekiel 17:22-23 (NLT)

Observation
Ezekiel 17 is told in the form of a riddle or allegory. Using the image of two great eagles, Ezekiel describes the coming destruction of Jerusalem through a political perspective. In a contest of sorts, God tells the story and asks Zedekiah, king of Judah, to figure out its message. The first great eagle represents the king of Babylon who "plucks" the top-most twig of Judah (royal family) and plants it in a fertile field where it will prosper. The second great eagle represents the king of Egypt. In failing to listen to God's purpose, Zedekiah attempted to form an alliance with Egypt. Because of this, God says that Babylon will no longer protect Zedekiah's royal line; Egypt will destroy it. The chapter closes with a nod to God's final act of redemption, when the majestic branch (Jesus) will be planted firmly in Israel and all the birds of every sort (every tribe and nation) will find shelter in him.

Application
Have you ever found yourself in a fierce storm, desperately hoping to find shelter from its fury? A number of years ago, I was asked to perform a wedding ceremony in the middle of a lake near the community where I served as pastor. The wedding party gathered on two pontoon boats strapped together and decorated for the occasion. Once we were in the middle of the lake, a speedboat brought the bride to the ceremony with her veil flapping in the wind. After she was loaded onto the pontoon boats, the ceremony began. Within a few minutes, the wind started to stir. Soon the water grew rough. Moments later a fierce thunderstorm descended on the lake with a fury of strong wind, heavy rain, and plenty of lightning. I quickly wrapped up the ceremony and we headed for shore. The small engines on the back of the boats were no match for the heavy winds and choppy water. As the lightning danced all around us, we tried to huddle under the small tin roofs of the pontoon boats. Eventually, we made landfall and ran for our cars. (I have no idea if that couple is still married!)

A preacher friend of mine often says, "Either you are headed into a storm, living in the midst of a storm, or walking your way out of a storm." He's right. Life throws a lot of stormy weather our way. And rather than look for a small, flimsy roof to make us safe, we must look to the Lord of the Universe. There we find shelter and security.

Prayer
Father God, teach us again this day to trust in your presence and provision. Amen.

Day 820 — Ezekiel 18: The Second Chance

> "But if wicked people turn away from all their sins and begin to obey my decrees and do what is just and right, they will surely live and not die. All their past sins will be forgotten, and they will live because of the righteous things they have done." Ezekiel 18:21-22 (NLT)

Observation
Ezekiel 18 describes the justice of a righteous God in response to a misinterpretation of an often-quoted proverb. The proverb is stated in verse 2: "The parents have eaten sour grapes, but their children's mouths pucker at the taste." Because of its misuse, God instructs the people through Ezekiel to stop using the proverb. Many had applied it to the ways in which the sins of one generation affected the next. Certainly, parental behavioral choices affect the lives of their children, yet God states that everyone is judged equitably and individually. Only those who sin will suffer the results of their transgression. A righteous man who has an unrighteous son will not be punished for his son's behavior. In like fashion, if the rebellious son then has a son of his own who rejects his father's poor behavior, that son will be judged not by his father's actions but by his own conduct. As verse 19 states, "'Doesn't the child pay for the parent's sins?' No! For if the child does what is just and right and keeps my decrees, that child will surely live."

Application
Everyone loves the story of a second chance. It's why we watch Hallmark movies at Christmas that give us a contented feeling. We enjoy the story of someone who finds forgiveness and redemption. We like seeing a life get turned around and become a beautiful story. No one likes that kind of story better than our Heavenly Father. God grieves at the brokenness sin causes in our lives. God's heart is wounded by our rebellion and disobedience. And like the father of the prodigal son in Jesus' parable (Luke 15), God runs to embrace us and welcome us when we come home. Our Lord is the God of second chances. Though our sins may be destructive, they are not fatal...at least they don't have to be. Notice our focus verse: whenever people turn away from their sins and begin a life of obedience, amazing things can happen. Past sins are forgotten, and the promise of life is restored.

Most of us carry a heavy load of guilt and shame. In fact, for some the shame is so overwhelming that it cripples, limits, and robs us of life. God never intended for us to live with oppression. We are to live with freedom. There is liberation in honest confession and in the reception of healing grace. Maybe you have carried your shame long enough. Why not start this day with a wet-eyed confession and a broken-hearted song? Then watch as the sun rises, the fog lifts, and new life begins.

Prayer
Father God, may we find healing and redemption in your grace this day. Amen.

Day 821   Ezekiel 19: When the Glory Is Gone

> "A fire has burst out from its branches and devoured its fruit. Its remaining limbs are not strong enough to be a ruler's scepter." Ezekiel 19:14 (NLT)

Observation
Ezekiel 19 is a lament or funeral dirge directed at the final kings of Israel prior to the Babylonian exile. This is the first of five laments in the book; a song to sing in grief over the demise of the Davidic dynasty. Ezekiel uses the image of both a lion and a vine. The image of a mother lion, common in depictions of Israel, refers to the nation of Israel who raised many of her cubs to become future kings. This lament points to two specific leaders. One was King Jehoahaz, a corrupt and evil leader, who was captured and deposed by Pharaoh Neco II of Egypt. Jehoahaz was led to Egypt by a hook through his nose and paraded around by Pharaoh as a conquest trophy. The other king was Jehoiachin, also a cruel leader, who was captured and brought to Babylon in a hunting net like an animal and imprisoned for 37 years. The remaining portion of the chapter describes Israel as a vine, once green and able to produce great fruit (leaders). Because of corruption, the nation is now like a "withered" vine that has lost the ability to bear fruit and will be consumed by fire.

Application
Because of poor choices, sinful mistakes, or bad leadership, a group of people can lose the ability to produce Kingdom fruit (changed lives, renewed hearts, impassioned vision). Years ago, I lived through such an experience. I was pastoring a church in Birmingham that had experienced her "glory days" in the late 1950s. The neighborhood had long transitioned, and yet the church had failed to change approach or attitude. A window of opportunity began to emerge in the late 1980s, offering the church the potential to rethink her role in the life of the community. Even though a number of forward-thinking people offered an insightful vision for ministry, others in the church failed to see the movement of God or the potential to do Kingdom work. As a result, the vision was squelched, and in many ways the glory soon departed from the church. What could have been a bold move forward turned into a forgotten dream. In describing ancient Judah, Ezekiel calls her a withered vine who can no longer produce fruit. Her glory days are gone. At times, we may feel that our opportunities to do great Kingdom work have departed from our lives. We feel tainted by our sins and corrupted by our past mistakes. But God has bigger plans and brighter futures for all of us. Refuse to give up on your role in God's plan; God certainly hasn't given up on you.

Prayer
Father God, give us a renewed sense of direction and purpose for your work. Amen.

Day 822   Ezekiel 20: The Power of Regret

> "You will look back on all the ways you defiled yourselves and will hate yourselves because of the evil you have done." Ezekiel 20:43 (NLT)

Observation

Ezekiel 20 records a history of Israel's past rebellion and God's promise of eventual restoration. From a political and historical context, this narrative is set in 591 BC, when King Zedekiah formed a foolish alliance with Egypt against the Babylonians. Exiled leaders of Israel, already living in Babylon, seek a word from the prophet Ezekiel. They long to know if Egypt can in fact save Israel from being conquered by the Babylonians. Ezekiel reminds these leaders that they have forfeited any right to inquire of the Holy God because of their rebellion and pagan worship practices. Their foolish questioning illustrates their foolish thinking. While continuing to practice false worship, they want to hear from God! In the narrative, God recounts the covenantal vows with Israel and the continued mercy extended to the people. God frequently remarks on "my Sabbath." The keeping of Sabbath, or lack thereof, was an important indication of the level of Israel's relationship with God. Were they willing to honor and hallow God by keeping a day of worship and rest? The chapter closes with a prophetic word about the final restoration of Israel as a nation and of Jerusalem as the key place of worship.

Application

All of us live with a little regret. There are things we wish we hadn't said, done, spent, or started. Some of our actions come back to bite us, and we regret the choices we once made. For example, consider the purchase of new car. Imagine convincing yourself that you need to upgrade your current vehicle. You find a nice used car at a local place, and it seems to be a good deal, even though there is no warranty. Not long after you purchase the car, it begins to have "issues," and soon you regret your rush to buy without careful consideration. Making a mistake like this is certainly regrettable, but it pales in comparison to some of the other mistakes we make. Relationally, we can really get it wrong sometimes. We say the wrong thing, make a foolish choice, or let down our guard and allow tempting thoughts into our minds. Poor thoughts can lead to poor actions, and then regret and shame enter the equation. As a preacher, I often preach about the damaging effect of guilt and shame on the human heart. It can certainly lessen our lives and destroy our self-image. But perhaps there is a plus side to feeling regret. Regret can be restorative if we are willing to learn from our mistakes. It can remind us to make better choices. It can correct potential missteps. May we live and learn.

Prayer

Father, as we find healing for our brokenness may we also gain wisdom. Amen.

Day 823 — Ezekiel 21: Wiped Away

> "You will be utterly wiped out, your memory lost to history, for I, the Lord, have spoken!" Ezekiel 21:32b (NLT)

Observation
Chapter 21 is sometimes referred to as "The Song of the Lord's Sword." In this chapter, God tells Ezekiel to offer poetic words of prophecy against Jerusalem that repetitively use the image of a sword for God's destructive force. God indicates that the consequences of the nation's sin will affect everyone living in the land, both good and bad. Great physical and emotional upheaval is coming. The Babylonian army, led by King Nebuchadnezzar, is powerful and moving swiftly. In spite of Israel's hopes, the Davidic line of kings will be interrupted. God instructs Ezekiel to draw a map to indicate the path of the conquerors. He is also told to make a signpost for the roadway that will indicate where the Babylonian army should go. In verse 26, while speaking to Israel God states, "Remove the turban and the crown...." This is a prophetic way of saying that both the priestly and governmental leadership of the nation will be removed.

Application
Recently, I wondered around an old cemetery. I was there to attend the graveside service of a friend. After the service, I took a few minutes to stroll among the various tombstones. Some were extremely old—more than a hundred years—and some were even older. I noticed that time and weather had taken a toll on the oldest markers. In fact, the names and dates on these tombstones were no longer legible; they were completely wiped away. It gave me pause for a moment. I wondered about the lives of those buried beneath my feet. Who were they? When did they live? What kind of life did they once know? In the passage of only a few generations, they were forgotten, and even their names were now lost to the sands of time.

In prophesying to the Ammonites at the end of Ezekiel 21, Ezekiel says they will be "utterly wiped out, their memory lost to history." Most of us live with the uncomfortable knowledge that our lives and influence won't be remembered for long... maybe a few generations. But in terms of God's Kingdom, our names and lives are forever recorded in God's book. Though we will one day be forgotten on earth, we will always be a vibrant part of God's eternal realm. God will never lose sight of even one of us. What will be utterly wiped away is any trace of our former sinfulness. Through the atoning sacrifice of Christ, our sins are erased and our guilty stains washed clean. This erasure of our past mistakes holds the promise for our forever future.

Prayer
Father, let us rejoice today in the hope and victory of our eternal lives. Amen.

Day 824   Ezekiel 22: Show Up, Stand Up, Speak Out

> "I looked for someone who might rebuild the wall of righteousness that guards the land. I searched for someone to stand in the gap in the wall so I wouldn't have to destroy the land, but I found no one."
> Ezekiel 22:30 (NLT)

Observation
In chapter 22, Ezekiel raises specific charges against Jerusalem. The focus is on corrupt leadership, both from the political and spiritual realm. These leaders have destroyed the city's hope through the bloodshed of the innocent and through idolatry. The city will be judged and the people will become objects of scorn and ridicule from every nation. The "princes" of the city ordered the murder of innocent people. They took advantage of the weak and of their parents. They committed a number of immoral sins including rape, incest, and usury. God is angry enough to "beat his fists" against the city. God will pour out wrath on the people like a metalsmith who smelts away silver's impurities. The priests are worthless examples. They have given in to the temptation to exploit and gain wealth falsely. As God looks across the city, there is not a single righteous person to stand in the gap and guard the ways of God.

Application
Politics can be a nasty business. During each election cycle, caustic and false rhetoric is tossed about. Rarely is anyone willing to stand up in a courageous way to tell the truth. Recently, I was reminded of an incident that occurred when John McCain and Barrack Obama were in the presidential race. At a campaign town hall meeting, a McCain supporter told the senator that she didn't trust Obama because he was a Muslim. At that point, Senator McCain stopped the rhetoric and told this woman that he knew Obama well, and though they disagreed on some political points, he knew him to be a decent family man and not a Muslim. Regardless of where we stand on McCain's policies, all of us should admire his willingness to "stand in the gap" as someone who longed for truth to replace falsehood. I hope all of us can be counted as "righteous" people who will help guard our land from falsehood, vitriolic language, and disrespect. If the people of God can't show up, stand up, and speak out, who do we think will carry the banner of godliness, civility, decency, and Christ-like virtue? Many people seem determined to tear apart the fabric of our nation with a "winner-take-all" mentality that insists that the ends justify the means. Sometimes the spoils are not worth the cost of the hunt. As you have opportunity, tell the truth, speak kindness, and love your neighbor.

Prayer
Father, may we this day stand in the gap as righteous people of God. Amen.

Day 825 — Ezekiel 23: Incongruence

> "On the very day that they sacrificed their children to their idols, they boldly came into my Temple to worship! They came in and defiled my house." Ezekiel 23:39 (NLT)

Observation

Ezekiel 23 offers an extended parable of two adulterous sisters who represent the northern and southern kingdoms of Israel and Judah. The first 21 verses describe the sisters' infidelity. Oholah, who represents Samaria and the northern kingdom, and Oholibah, who represents Jerusalem and the southern kingdom, have entered into adulterous relationships in the form of political alliances with pagan nations. The problem is that these two kingdoms failed to trust the Lord for protection and guidance. Instead, they tried to form alliances for security. The northern kingdom tried to form an alliance with Assyria, only to be invaded by her armies. The southern kingdom should have learned from this mistake, but instead they tried to form alliances with Egypt and then Babylon. Ezekiel describes the four-fold punishment for these adulterous nations. Some of the people would be captured. Some would be given into the hands of their enemies. Horror and desolation would result. And finally, they would understand the consequences of forgetting God. The final portion of the chapter offers conclusions about the people's infidelity before God.

Application

Our focus verse describes a sinful practice. The people of Israel had adopted many pagan worship practices from the surrounding nations. In this case, they chased after the Canaanite deity named Molech and offered the fiery sacrifices of their own children. On the same day that they sacrificed their children, they also entered the Temple in order to worship Almighty God. They defiled the House of God with this wicked practice. The incongruence of their actions showed a tremendous lack of respect for God. Though we would like to think we are incapable of such heinous actions, we may not be as far removed from such practices as we imagine. To be sure, none of us are about to sacrifice our children, but we do offer incongruences between our professed faith and daily practices. For example, I am amazed at how many worshippers pull out their cellphones to read scripture in worship because they don't want to "lug" their big Bibles to church. And yet they use that same phone to view racy internet sites, write caustic rhetoric on social media, and send inappropriate texts. Incongruence. Or what about language? Out of the same mouth comes both cursing and praises. We claim to love God, but we are quick to denigrate and disrespect people made in God's image because we don't like their opinions or political positions. Either we truly worship God consistently, or we don't worship God at all.

Prayer

Father, may we strive to eliminate the incongruences in our lives. Amen.

Day 826 — Ezekiel 24: Vindication

> "And on that day a survivor from Jerusalem will come to you in Babylon and tell you what has happened. And when he arrives, your voice will suddenly return so you can talk to him, and you will be a symbol for these people. Then they will know that I am the Lord." Ezekiel 24:26-27 (NLT)

Observation

Ezekiel 24 uses a parable to describe the inevitability of God's wrath upon the city of Jerusalem, including the destruction of the Temple. Ezekiel's prophetic word is tied to a historical date: January 15, 588 BC. On this date, the king of Babylon began his siege on Jerusalem. God told Ezekiel to give these "rebels" a word of judgment. Rebels refers to the rebellious people of Jerusalem. In the parable, Israel is compared to a cooking pot, filled with all kinds of meat, even the choice portions. Like a cooking pot, Jerusalem will boil violently with fire. All will be destroyed, even the key leaders. Just as a consuming fire would eventually cook out everything in the pot, the destruction by the Babylonians will destroy the entire city. As second sign describes the heartache that the people (those already in exile) will endure at the news of Jerusalem's destruction. Ezekiel is told that God will take away his "dearest treasure," meaning his wife. When she dies, the prophet is not to express any outward signs of mourning. If he does not express grief over her death, the people will ask, "What's the message?" Her death is to symbolize the destruction of the Temple, the essential centerpiece of Israel's religious life and worship practices. Such a loss will be incomprehensible to the people. They are told not to mourn at such a moment but to bear the silent remorse as they realize the result of their rebellious actions.

Application

In our focus verse, a messenger from Jerusalem arrives in Babylon to tell those in exile about all that has happened to Jerusalem. God struck the prophet Ezekiel mute for a period of time. Suddenly his voice would return, symbolizing the truth of his prophetic words and the power of God at work in the situation. In many ways, the return of his speech on the occasion of the messenger's report would vindicate his ministry among the people. Ezekiel's words would be proven true. Sometimes a little vindication can be encouraging. Whenever we step out in faith, trusting in the direction that God has given us to go, we can find great fulfillment and joy as God's promises prove true. It is not that we are to enjoy an "I-told-you-so" moment. Instead, we can bear even greater testimony to the trustworthiness of God.

Prayer

Father, how grateful we are for how your ways are proven true again and again. Amen.

Day 827   Ezekiel 25: The Sin of Gloating

> "This is what the Sovereign Lord says: Because you clapped and danced and cheered with glee at the destruction of my people, I will raise my fist of judgment against you. I will give you as plunder to many nations. I will cut you off from being a nation and destroy you completely. Then you will know that I am the Lord." Ezekiel 25:6-7 (NLT)

Observation

Ezekiel 25 begins a series of oracles that describe God's judgment on seven surrounding nations. These oracles extend through chapter 32. God will punish the nations because of the various ways they have afflicted God's chosen people. This chapter contains oracles against Ammon, Moab, Edom, and Philistia. Going back to the Abrahamic covenant, God had promised to bless the nations that blessed Abraham's descendants and curse the nations that mistreated and abused God's people. There was and still remains no excuse for anti-Semitism. The reader will notice a "because and therefore" pattern in each oracle. Each nation's sin is exposed along with the resulting punishment. While God reserves the right to punish God's people for their sins, God also reserves the right to punish those who treat them poorly. In our focus verse, the people of Ammon are punished because of their expressions of glee and gladness when Israel was defeated and the Temple destroyed.

Application

Gloating at the misfortunes of others can be dangerous. In the world of sports, people often talk about bad karma. The line of thinking goes like this: "Be careful about gloating too much when a rival is defeated, for the day will come when they have the chance to gloat over your loss." In other words, always be careful of "payback." Of course, much more is at stake in this passage than trash-talking an enemy. It is a warning against showing utter contempt and rejoicing in the fallen status of others. Scripture reminds us that "all have sinned and fall short of the glory of God" (Rom 3:23 NIV). We should recognize the commonality of transgression and know that each of us will bear the consequences of our poor actions and choices. Surely, to rejoice over those who are mired in the deep mud of guilt and shame is a sin against Holy God. And yet we do this often. When we hear of someone's indiscretion, we can't wait to pass along the rumor and shake our heads at their sinfulness, displaying our disdain and self-righteousness. Feelings of remorse and regret are painful enough to bear. Who are we to add insult to injury? Instead of rejoicing in another's downfall, we should pray for their redemption, healing, and recovery. And maybe, instead of gloating, we can offer our own words of grace and comfort.

Prayer

Father, teach us to be merciful to those who stumble. Amen.

Day 828 — Ezekiel 26: Long Gone

> "I will bring you to a terrible end, and you will exist no more. You will be looked for, but you will never again be found. I, the Sovereign Lord, have spoken!" Ezekiel 26:21 (NLT)

Observation
After four short prophecies against the nations to the east and west of Israel comes a long prophetic word against Tyre. Tyre was a Phoenician city-state on the Mediterranean Coast. Famous for its merchants and sea traders, the city had also become renowned for idolatry. The chief sin that will bring God's judgment is the way Tyre's people rejoice at the fall of Jerusalem. They look forward to new trade and commerce because the trade routes through Jerusalem are disrupted. Tyre greedily rejoices in the suffering of Jerusalem. God promises that like a violent storm crashing against the shore, judgment will crash against Tyre. God promises that siege ramps, swords, and sledgehammers will destroy the city, leaving only a smooth, bare rock. (Historians note that during the Intertestamental period, Alexander the Great used the debris left from the earlier destruction of Nebuchadnezzar to build a mile-and-a-half-long causeway so he could reach the city and finish its destruction.)

Application
Over the past decade, Belmont University has enjoyed upgrades and beautification projects. In order for some of the "new" to come into being, some of the "old" had to be swept away. The Wheeler Science Building is an example. For years, two "sister" buildings stood side by side with a courtyard between them: Hitch and Wheeler. With the construction of a new academic building, the older Wheeler building was no longer needed. And so it was swept away…almost overnight. Literally, within a three-month period, the building was razed, debris was carted away, and beautiful landscaping was planted. Anyone looking at the site today would have no idea that a building ever stood there. It has been completely erased.

Through the prophetic preaching of Ezekiel, God promised that the city of Tyre would never exist again. The prophecy has held true. Even though there is a modern-day city of Tyre, it does not stand in the same location. The former spot is desolate. As our focus verse states, it "exists no more." This story in Ezekiel 26 reminds us, first, that we can count on God's promises. God is ultimately and absolutely trustworthy. What God has promised will always come true. Second, this story also reminds us of the consequences for those who have little regard for the things of God. Judgment will surely come to those who ignore God's boundaries, laws, and instruction. Obedience is always rewarded.

Prayer
Father, we thank you for your steadfastness and unchangeable nature. Amen.

Day 829   Ezekiel 27: Who's at the Helm?

> "But look! Your oarsmen have taken you into stormy seas! A mighty eastern gale has wrecked you in the heart of the sea!" Ezekiel 27:26 (NLT)

Observation

Ezekiel 27 records a funeral dirge or song to be sung over the destruction of Tyre. This poetically written, expanded lamentation begins with Tyre depicted in her glory as a beautiful ship, but she is later described as a catastrophic shipwreck. The first seven verses describe an ornate ship crafted from the finest materials. Verses 8-9 depict the ship's crew as the best on the Phoenician Coast. (The early trading ships from Tyre consisted of 50 oarsmen and were considered to be quite swift. Later, the ships and crews were expanded to more than 200 oarsmen with multiple rows of oars on each side of the craft.) The middle section of this chapter, verses 10-25, describes the military and far-reaching commercial activity of Tyre. The final section describes the wreck of the great ship of Tyre. Ezekiel refers to a strong east wind, most likely a reference to the Babylonian invaders.

Application

What happened to Malaysian Air flight 370 is one of the great mysteries in modern lore. The plane disappeared on March 8, 2014. On that night, the plane lost radar contact over Vietnam, while several tracking stations monitored its unexpected twists and turns. When it never arrived at any location, the mystery began. A number of theories and conspiracies emerged. Through the years, it has become apparent that the plane violently crashed into the Indian Ocean, all but disintegrating into a million pieces. The real question remains, "Why?" As more and more investigators put their resources together, it appears that Captain Zaharie, the pilot in command, was on a suicide mission and forced the plane into the ocean after disabling all communication systems and crew members. A tragic loss of life was caused by having the wrong person in control of the plane.

Using imagery of ships and seas, our focus verse hints at the downfall of Tyre. Her "oarsmen," key leaders both political and religious, had taken the ship into stormy seas. The wrong person at the helm can lead a vessel into the darkest storm. The same result can happen in individual lives when the wrong person takes control of the "ship." As humans, we are flawed, fragile, and often misinformed. We make mistakes. We choose poorly. We are tempted to follow the wrong paths. And sometimes, as we try to direct our own lives, we sail into one storm after another. Soon we find ourselves in great peril. But if we step away from the helm and allow the Spirit of the Living Lord to direct our journey, we may just find calmer seas. Who's at the helm of your life? The Captain makes all the difference.

Prayer

Father, help us this day to relinquish control of our lives so that you may lead us. Amen.

Day 830 — Ezekiel 28: Restored

> "This is what the Sovereign Lord says: The people of Israel will again live in their own land, the land I gave my servant Jacob. For I will gather them from the distant lands where I have scattered them. I will reveal to the nations of the world my holiness among my people. They will live safely in Israel and build homes and plant vineyards." Ezekiel 28:25-26a (NLT)

Observation
Ezekiel 28 opens with the third oracle against Tyre. This time, the judgment is aimed at Tyre's king or ruler. His political and commercial success has led him to declare divine status, saying, "I am a god." But God confronts this false claim. God will bring "strangers" to his door—a reference to the Babylonians. They will defile him and topple his reign. In the verses that follow, Ezekiel offers a lament over the ruler of Tyre. It is directed to more than just a single man who ruled at the time; it is directed to the power and influence of the office. In the lament, Ezekiel makes connections back to ancient Eden where Satan was cast out of the garden because of his overwhelming pride. Both Satan and the ruler of Tyre will be cast down by God's punishment. The chapter then turns to the city-state of Sidon, just 25 miles to the north. It, too, would be judged because of the practice of Baal worship. God would bring both pestilence and sword. The final verses of this chapter, used as our focus passage, describe the ultimate time of restoration that God promises to the people of Israel. The day will come when they will be gathered as a nation once again. (Many see the fulfillment of this prophecy occurring in 1948 when Israel was declared a sovereign nation.)

Application
Recently, I watched a YouTube video of a guy who meticulously restored a 1960s vintage Matchbox car. The video captured his whole process of restoring this toy metal car. First, he completely disassembled the car. Then he sanded it down to the metal. He repainted it, made new wheels and tires, and even put new decals on the sides. Once completed, it looked better than new. But what struck me most was the time and effort he expended in order to restore such a small and seemingly insignificant item.

I am also struck by God's meticulous restoration of our lives. It is humbling to consider that Almighty God takes the time and effort to work on each individual life…each individual heart. God never casts us aside and labels us as worthless. God sees in each of us the image of the Son, Jesus Christ, and works carefully, methodically, and purposefully to transform us into our best selves. If you feel a little ragged these days—a little worn and tired—do not worry. God is in a constant process of restoring your life until the day you will be perfected.

Prayer
Father, thank you for your transformative work in our lives. Amen.

Day 831   Ezekiel 29: Lean on Me

> "When Israel leaned on you, you splintered and broke and stabbed her in the armpit. When she put her weight on you, you gave way, and her back was thrown out of joint." Ezekiel 29:7 (NLT)

Observation
Chapter 29 begins the seventh and final oracle of judgment from Ezekiel. This oracle against Egypt extends through chapter 32. Unlike the oracle against Tyre that focused on economic arrogance, this oracle focuses on Egypt's military power. A connection between Egypt and Israel had existed since the days of Abraham and the Patriarchs. Occasionally, military alliances were made, but they had disastrous consequences. The early verses of this oracle focus on Pharaoh Hophra. Ezekiel compares him to a giant crocodile like those along the Nile River. In fact, the Egyptian god Sohek was a crocodile symbolizing strength and ferocity. Ezekiel prophesies that Pharaoh will be plucked from the Nile with a hook in his jaw. He will be left in the open field and become food for beasts. Egypt's false dealings and treachery against Israel will lead to her downfall. Egypt will endure 40 years of devastation and emerge as the lowest of kingdoms.

Application
Our focus verse highlights the sin of Egypt in regard to Israel. Despite the alliances formed through the years to strengthen and protect Israel, Egypt had proven untrustworthy and ineffective. When Israel leaned on her for support, the alliance proved weak and vulnerable. Egypt was not to be trusted.

My son-in-law Jason recently reconstructed much of his front deck. About a month or so earlier, he was walking on the deck and noticed that one of the boards seemed "squishy." It had slowly decayed and was rotting away. When he went to replace the board, he discovered that several others were in the same shape. Apparently, the original owner of the house had chosen not to use treated lumber. The result was a deteriorating deck. To ensure the safety of his family, Jason bolstered the deck with fresh lumber and supports.

All of us need strong supports to lean on amid life's trying times. We need friends, neighbors, and coworkers who will support us, encourage us, pray for us, and hold us steady. I hope you have a support group like that in your life. I also hope you are the kind of person on whom others can lean. I hope you are a trusted friend, a strong arm, and a supportive person. Being a solid means of support takes time, investment, and a willingness to get involved in the lives of others. I hope you will use your life energy to do that.

Prayer
Father, may each of us become the type of person that gives support and aid. Amen.

Day 832 — Ezekiel 30: Unarmed

> "Therefore, this is what the Sovereign Lord says: I am the enemy of Pharaoh, the king of Egypt! I will break both of his arms—the good arm along with the broken one—and I will make his sword clatter to the ground." Ezekiel 30:22 (NLT)

Observation

Ezekiel 30 continues the oracles of judgment against Egypt. The chapter begins with a lament of this once-great nation. Though judgment was certain, note that Ezekiel is not gladdened by his words; there is no hint of anger or vindictiveness. He offers a sincere word of mourning. Egypt's wealth will be removed. The foundations of power and society will be torn down. Surrounding nations that have allied with Egypt will also suffer destruction—places like Ethiopia, Put, Lud, and Arabia will be caught in God's sweeping punishment. The great canals and irrigation systems that have brought both water and life to the land will be neglected and ruined. Egypt is compared to a soldier whose arms are broken. The warrior becomes defenseless. Thus, Egypt will be broken and defenseless, unable to match the strength of the Babylonian army.

Application

At some point in life, most of us have to deal with a broken bone. It may be a broken arm from a bike wreck as a child, a broken ankle from a sports injury, a broken hip from a fall, or even a cracked skull from a knock on the old noggin'. We immediately feel the impact of a broken bone. The injury affects our daily routine, disrupts our ability to function well, and often causes pain. A number of years ago, a senior adult lady in our church fell down a couple of stairs. I heard her cry out when she fell, and I was the first on the scene. Calmly and almost matter-of-factly, she looked up at me and said, "Dr. Roebuck, would you mind calling my husband and ask him to come? I have just broken by hip and I will need his help." She was right—both about her hip and about her husband coming to help.

Sometimes things get broken, even the bones in our bodies. But other aspects of human life also get damaged. Relationships get broken. Friendships get severed. Peace of mind gets shattered. Secure finances are lost. Restful nights of sleep are destroyed by worry. What do we do when life gets shattered? We can't just place a phone call to a spouse and ask them to come and help. We need something better, more powerful, more authoritative, more redemptive. We need a Father who will bind up our wounds, soothe our broken spirits, and heal our deep cuts. You may be working through a sense of brokenness in your life today. Reach out to God, who will surround you with grace and healing. God's power can mend your brokenness.

Prayer

Father, bind up our wounds and heal our brokenness. Amen.

Day 833   Ezekiel 31: Trim the Tree

> "Therefore, this is what the Sovereign Lord says: Because Egypt became proud and arrogant, and because it set itself so high above the others, with its top reaching to the clouds, I will hand it over to a mighty nation that will destroy it as its wickedness deserves. I have already discarded it."
> Ezekiel 31:10-11 (NLT)

Observation

Ezekiel 31 offers another prophetic word against Egypt, comparing her to Assyria and that nation's downfall. Ezekiel uses the image of a tree to speak allegorically about Assyria. This message condemns Pharaoh Hophra of Egypt, whose arrogance has made him overly confident of Egypt's power and greatness. Ezekiel tells Pharaoh to look to the nation of Assyria as an example. She, too, was strong and powerful, but the Babylonians destroyed her. Ezekiel compares Assyria to a great cedar of Lebanon—one that is tall, strong, and dominate, rising above all the other trees. And yet, because of pride, the once-great tree was felled and its branches stripped of foliage. God judged the nation and brought it to ruin. The great nation of Egypt will suffer a similar fate. God will destroy Egypt for her arrogance and pride. God will use the Babylonians as an instrument of judgment.

Application

I have a huge sweet gum tree in my front yard. Barely six feet in height at the time, it was planted there on the day we moved into the house. Twenty years later, it now soars above the rooftop of our home. In the fall, its leaves turn a brilliant yellow. It also produces thousands and thousands of little prickly balls that must be raked up throughout the winter months. It's interesting how trees grow. Left unattended, the branches extend out in all kinds of directions. In order to keep the limbs away from the house and the front walk, I periodically have to trim the branches. What's true of the tree is true of most of us. If left unattended, we tend to angle off in a number of directions. We chase one line of thinking and then another. We lean into one ideology and then a second. We bend to one temptation only to chase after something else when the first thrill is gone. The tree of our lives can grow dangerously crooked. We, too, could use a little pruning now and then, even though the process of discipline and correction is sometimes arduous. What keeps our lives straight, productive, and meaningful? It is the word of God. We are reminded by its own testimony that the word of God is "alive and powerful. It is sharper than the sharpest two-edged sword, cutting between soul and spirit, between joint and marrow" (Hebrews 4:12 NLT). God's word is the guideline for our journey, the roadmap for our success, and the shepherd's crook that gently guides us in the path of righteousness.

Prayer

Father, may we receive with gladness your correction in our lives each day. Amen.

Day 834   Ezekiel 32: Restoring the Flow

> "Then I will let the waters of Egypt become calm again, and they will flow as smoothly as olive oil, says the Sovereign Lord." Ezekiel 32:14 (NLT)

Observation
Ezekiel 32 describes the final oracles of judgment against Egypt. God tells Ezekiel to mourn for the king of Egypt and pronounce a funeral lament over him. Pharaoh Hophra once described himself as a young lion among the nations, yet God will refer to him as a "monster from the sea," a reference to a large crocodile who "muddies the waters of the Nile with his feet." Pharaoh is called out for his disturbing international policies that brought unrest to the region. Ezekiel prophesies that the crocodile of Egypt will be captured and left to die in the open field. His death will offer a frightening testimony to all other kings. If God's judgment can destroy Pharaoh, who else could bear such scrutiny? The lesser nations will certainly tremble at God's power. Ezekiel then predicts that the waters of the Nile will flow smoothly again after the time of judgment. In a final oracle, Ezekiel insists that the armies of Egypt will join the Assyrians and others in the abode of the dead.

Application
Years ago, when we lived in Gatlinburg, a fierce rainstorm poured huge amounts of water over the area, nonstop, for two days. The local creeks became raging torrents. Water cascaded down from the mountains and brought flooding to the valleys below, including much of the iconic downtown area. As the rain continued to fall, I noticed the carpet in our downstairs den getting soggy. I quickly found the source of the problem. A small stream of water, about the diameter of a pencil, was pouring through the decorative rock wall at the end of the room. Battling the darkness, wind, and rain, I walked around the outside of our home. I discovered that a drainage pipe, all but hidden in the ground, was clogged with dirt and debris. Instead of flowing through the pipe, the water backed up and ran against the foundation of the house, causing the problem in my den. I quickly removed the debris and the water began flowing smoothly again. Through the years, I have spoken with many people who described their prayer life using the language of a stopped-up pipe. They said things like this: "My prayers don't seem to reach the ears of God. I feel like they never get above the ceiling of my room. It's like the flow of my words is stopped up." Do you ever feel that way? Do you ever think your prayers are ineffective, maybe not even reaching the heart of the Father? Maybe you need to remove some of the dirt and debris from your life. Confess your sins and ask for God's grace. You may discover that things will flow freely once again.

Prayer
Father, hear our prayers of confession this day and heal any divide we feel. Amen.

Day 835 — Ezekiel 33: There Is Still Time...

> "None of their past sins will be brought up again, for they have done what is just and right, and they will surely live." Ezekiel 33:16 (NLT)

Observation
Beginning in chapter 33, the book of Ezekiel takes a dramatic turn. To this point, the book has focused on the judgment of God that will come to Israel and the surrounding nations because of their iniquity. But starting with this chapter, the focus turns to the promised restoration of Israel following the destruction. Israel will experience new life. Her enemies will be defeated, and the Messianic Kingdom will be established. The "True Shepherd" will come to guide the people in righteousness. Specifically, in this chapter Ezekiel is appointed as the watchman of Israel. As a watchman who sees the enemy coming—in this case, the judgment of God—he must sound the alarm to warn the people. If they ignore his warning to repent, their destruction is on their own hands. But if he fails to sound the alarm, their deaths are his responsibility. He is charged with speaking to two groups. The first group is people left behind in Jerusalem who have not been carried away into exile. The second group is the remnant of Jewish people now living in Babylon. The message of repentance is the same for both. If they turn from their sins, God will save them from ultimate destruction.

Application
Everyone longs for a second chance. Whenever we fail, make poor choices, or miss the mark, we long for a "do-over," a chance to make things right. If given the chance, we hope our new direction will far exceed our former mistakes. We want to be defined by our best selves and not our past indiscretions. Ezekiel offers his generation and ours a word of great hope. He speaks to the wicked of his day, those who had practiced idolatry and disobedience. He tells them that if they repent of their sinfulness and turn their hearts to God, God will not judge them based on their past sins but will offer them life. That sense of hopeful redemption is available to our generation as well. If we confess our sins and change our path, turning towards God and God's purpose for our lives, we will discover that God is willing to forgive and forget and will judge us based not on who we once were but on who we have become as we pursue righteousness. So there is still time. Your life does not have to be defined by your past mistakes and failures. You do not have to be shackled to your mistakes for the rest of time. Repentance always offers the second chance—the chance to begin again and find grace, redemption, and fellowship with the Father. There is a commonality to our sinfulness. All of us have sinned and fallen short of God's intention for our lives. But God offers us the hope of forgiveness and new life. You and I can have a second chance.

Prayer
Father, may we revel in your grace for our lives this day. Amen.

Day 836   Ezekiel 34: Becoming a Shepherd

> "You have not taken care of the weak. You have not tended the sick or bound up the injured. You have not gone looking for those who have wandered away and are lost." Ezekiel 34:4 (NLT)

Observation
Chapter 34 continues Ezekiel's oracles of restoration for Israel. Throughout this chapter, Ezekiel uses the image of a shepherd in both words of judgment and promise. The first ten verses pronounce judgment on the "false shepherds" of Israel. The prophets and priests of Israel were often called shepherds. They were to be strong, caring, and protective leaders. But the current leadership of the nation proved to be false shepherds. They practiced economic exploitation. Rather than seeing the flock as a trust to protect, the false shepherds saw them as a simple a source of wealth to exploit. They also ignored both the physical and spiritual needs of the nation. Finally, they failed to protect the flock of Israel from danger. They let outside pagan practices continue to influence the people's thinking. Ezekiel pronounces judgment because of their actions. The chapter then turns towards a positive view of the True Shepherd of Israel, referring to the role of the Messiah who will come to care for the flock. From a worldwide dispersion of Jewish families, the Messiah will draw the people back to the land. (Though some see the 1948 creation of Israel as a fulfillment of this prophecy, others point to a time of greater fulfillment that will be realized when Christ, as the Good Shepherd, returns to rule and reign.)

Application
Most of us work under the parameters of a "job description." Our duties, responsibilities, and scope of work are clearly defined. At the time of an annual review, superiors look for the alignment between work performed and the demands of the job description to determine how well we have performed. Have we put in the hours? Have we sold enough product? Did we supervise our employees? In our focus verse, Ezekiel points to the role of a good shepherd. Specifically, the shepherd is to care for the weak, tend to the sick, bind up the wounded, and go looking for any who have wandered away and become lost. What powerful marching orders for the people of God! If we are called into conformity with the image of Christ, then certainly we must see our role as shepherds to the people around us. How well are we doing in terms of fulfilling our job description? Do we care for the weak? Have we sought out those who are marginalized, abused, and forgotten? Have we tended to the sick? Are we striving to care for both the physical and spiritual needs of others? Are we searching for the lost? Are we intentional about their rescue?

Prayer
Father, may be prove ourselves worthy of the title Shepherd. Amen.

Day 837 — Ezekiel 35: The Things of God

> "For you said, 'The lands of Israel and Judah will be ours. We will take possession of them. What do we care that the Lord is there!'"
> Ezekiel 35:10 (NLT)

Observation

Ezekiel 35 offers a word of judgment against Edom. (This is actually the second oracle of judgment against Edom in the book of Ezekiel). Edom is sometimes referred to as Mt. Seir, a mountain range south of the Dead Sea. The judgment against Edom will represent God's punishment against any nation that has mistreated Israel. As the chapter opens, Ezekiel declares the inescapable judgment of God. Edom will be destroyed. Edom had established an alliance with King Nebuchadnezzar of Babylon. The nation acted with particular hatred and cruelty when Jerusalem was attacked. The people's heinous actions would be reflected in the severity of God's punishment. The whole land of Edom would be filled with the bodies of the slain. Most grievous of the sins was that of wanting to take possession of the land of Israel and Judah. Edom boasted that one day she would claim them both. As our focus verse declares, the nation had no regard for the fact that God had claimed possession of this land. In plotting against Israel and Judah, Edom in effect was plotting against Almighty God.

Application

Years ago as a college student, I was victimized by a theft. I had borrowed my father's car for a few days while my own car was being repaired. My father's car was a meticulously kept, late-model Oldsmobile. When I walked out to the car after a day of classes, I noticed that someone had burglarized it, taking all four wheels and leaving the car on cement blocks. The thieves had even broken into the trunk and taken the spare tire. I was angered, of course, by what had happened. But what really angered me was the fact that it was my father's car! I saw the crime as being against him because the car belonged to him.

Ezekiel reminds us that God's judgment was falling on Edomites because they desired to overtake Israel and failed to acknowledge that God had claimed the nation as God's own possession. They were thus plotting against God Himself. This passage offers an important word of warning: we must never ignore, abuse, or trivialize the things of God. We need to pay careful attention to whatever has God's special blessing and promise. Clearly, we must respect God's word. We must value God's church. And we must treat God's prized possession—humankind—with respect, dignity, and civility. To belittle anyone made in God's image is to belittle God. It matters how we treat our fellow human beings. All are precious in God's sight and redeemable through the sacrifice of the Son.

Prayer

Father, may we never neglect, abuse, or ignore the things you value. Amen.

Day 838 — Ezekiel 36: Undeserved Grace

> "Therefore, give the people of Israel this message from the Sovereign Lord: I am bringing you back, but not because you deserve it. I am doing it to protect my holy name, on which you brought shame while you were scattered among the nations." Ezekiel 36:22 (NLT)

Observation
Ezekiel 36 records an oracle of restoration for Israel as the blessed nation of God. It stands in dramatic contrast to the judgmental tone of the previous chapter, in which God's judgment was pronounced against Edom. In chapter 36, the image of mountains speaks of the land and people of Israel. In the first 15 verses, Ezekiel proclaims that the mountains of Israel will prosper. This is a word of hope for both the people and the land. Israel is referred to as God's "everlasting heights," part of God's eternal land grant to the people. God will punish the nations who once abused the mountains, hills, ravines, and valleys of Israel. As Ezekiel describes the restoration of the land, he promises that the trees will bear fruit and the fields will be cultivated. Any disgrace that the land has suffered will cease. In the final verses, 16-30, God promises to gather the scattered people of God once again to the land. God will cleanse them and purify them.

Application
Our focus verse contains an important theological teaching all about how God works with and responds to God's wayward children. The status we have as God's children—protected, loved, and embraced daily—is never a result of what we do. We are frail, flawed, sinful, and broken. We don't deserve a second glance from Holy God. And yet God loves us in ways that defy comprehension. According to Ezekiel, the reason for God's acceptance of the once-wayward people was to protect God's name among the nations. Because the Israelites continued to sin, even in exile, the pagan nations looked upon them with disdain and mocked the God of Israel. In order to reveal God's nature before the nations, God collected the people, restored them, and was honored again through their obedience. The message was not "Look how bad My people are" but "Look how gracious I am as their Father." We must never delude ourselves into thinking that we deserve the grace and mercy of God. We can't build a bridge strong enough to span the chasm that our sinful behavior has created between ourselves and God. We can't earn grace. We can't buy grace. We can't even hope to obtain it. But we can receive it as a gift. As you start this day, take a moment to revel in the merciful embrace of God. We are included in God's forever family, not because we deserve to be included but because God desires us.

Prayer
Father, make us joyful of our grace-caused inclusion. Amen.

Day 839 — Ezekiel 37: Enduring Hope

> "Then he said to me, Son of man, these bones represent the people of Israel. They are saying, 'We have become old, dry bones—all hope is gone. Our nation is finished.'" Ezekiel 37:11 (NLT)

Observation

This is probably the most familiar passage in the book of Ezekiel. It speaks of the restoration of Israel, a promise dramatically depicted by a valley of dry bones. It is an astonishing message of physical and spiritual restoration. The Spirit of God leads Ezekiel to a valley filled with many bones dried by the sun. God asks, "Can these bones live again?" Offering an insightful response, Ezekiel replies, "Only you know, O Lord." He affirms that only God can raise the dead to life. Ezekiel is then told to prophesy over the dry bones. As he does, the bones begin to stir. Suddenly, complete skeletons come together and are covered with muscle and skin. Yet these bodies are lifeless until the breath of God's Spirit calls them to life again. This is a clear message that Israel will never be restored or come to life again apart from the work of God's Spirit. As God explains the vision to Ezekiel, Ezekiel is reminded that for those who feel absolutely hopeless and broken in spirit because of the exilic events, God will offer restoration. To further the message, God gives Ezekiel another object lesson. This one involves two sticks that bear the names of the southern and northern tribes. Ezekiel is to hold the sticks together, emphasizing that God will make the two kingdoms into one nation again.

Application

I have an old baseball glove tucked away on a shelf in my garage. There was a time when I used it almost daily. I played church softball for years, and in those days the leather was soft and pliable. Now the glove only makes an occasional appearance. From time to time, I take it out, oil it up, and play a game of catch. I am always surprised at the healing, restorative quality of the glove oil. That which had become dry and brittle suddenly returns to an almost new condition. Most of us will readily confess that the journey of life robs us of many things. We get jaded in our opinions. We grow rigid, judgmental, and set in our ways. We hold on to grudges and refuse to let old wounds heal. And at some point, we even let the hope and promise of a joy-filled future ebb away, as though it leaks out of our very souls. The question God asks is still valid: "Can these bones live again?" And the answer remains the same: "Yes," if the breath of God inhabits our brokenness once again. In my own pilgrimage, I've discovered that I often need a little renewal. I need an infusion of hope. I need a dose of kindness and grace. I need to feel the fresh wind of God blowing into my life.

Prayer

Father, renew our hearts and lives with a fresh sense of your Spirit this day. Amen.

Day 840 — Ezekiel 38: No Mistaken Identity

> "All living things—the fish in the sea, the birds of the sky, the animals of the field, the small animals that scurry along the ground, and all the people on earth—will quake in terror at my presence. Mountains will be thrown down; cliffs will crumble; walls will fall to the earth." Ezekiel 38:20 (NLT)

Observation
In chapters 38-39, Ezekiel prophesies about a future attack and eventual defeat of the armies of Gog. After foretelling the regathering of the Jewish people to Israel, Ezekiel tells of a final attack by an enemy and God's rescue. After the people return and begin to enjoy a time of peace, the nation of Gog will attack. These were people from eastern Asia Minor, ancestors of the Scythians. (Gog is only mention here and in Revelation 20:8.) It seems that the attack will occur in the era of the end times. It appears that Ezekiel is speaking of a future fulfillment when the nation of Gog will advance into Israel like "a cloud covering the land." Their attack will be unsuccessful. The soldiers will destroy themselves with the sword and God will bring torrential rain, hailstones, and fire and brimstone to destroy this pagan army. Once again, it is clear that God is sovereign and God's wrath on the enemies of Israel will be swift and complete.

Application
My neighbor looks a lot like the Hollywood actor Michael Douglas. In fact, on several occasions he has been mistakenly identified as the movie star while eating in restaurants or attending a concert. Once, when asked to do so, he even signed a few autographs. He's had some laughs along the way, but certainly a mistaken identity can cause problems. In his prophecy, Ezekiel indicates that when God brings judgment on the land, there will be no mistake who is leading the charge. People will quake. Mountains will tumble. Walls will collapse. Everyone will clearly know that God is on the march. There will be no mistaken identity.

The Bible also makes a clear statement concerning those who will be gathered into God's forever Kingdom and those who will not. There will be no mistaken identity. First John 5:12 says, "Whoever has the Son has life; whoever does not have God's Son does not have life" (NLT). It's simple, right? Those who have claimed Jesus Christ as Savior and Lord will be welcomed in the Kingdom, and those who haven't won't. We might cringe a little at that verse. We might want a more inclusive vision of whom God will welcome. And yet God's plan is not contingent on our whims or wishes. It is based on God's eternal truth. Knowing of the importance of the gospel, we must proclaim Christ with boldness, with joy, and with consistency.

Prayer
Father, give each of us a contagious faith so that others will be drawn to you. Amen.

Day 841   Ezekiel 39: Leave No One Behind

> "Then my people will know that I am the Lord their God, because I sent them away to exile and brought them home again. I will leave none of my people behind." Ezekiel 39:28 (NLT)

Observation
Ezekiel 39 describes the slaughter of the armies of Gog. Ezekiel is told to deliver a message to Gog: the Almighty is against them. God will strike them down. This once-strong army will become food for every beast of the field and every bird of the sky. God will even send destruction against their homeland. The people of Israel will gather up the weapons of war left behind from God's slain armies and use them as fuel for their fires. There will be enough weaponry to burn for at least seven years. This is a sign of the finality of warfare against God's people. The Israelites will gather the bones of the slain and bury them east of Jordan to purify the land. Ezekiel reminds the people that God will be glorified, the people's hearts will turn back to God, the people of Israel will return to the Promised Land, and God will bring about a spiritual restoration.

Application
"Leave no one behind" is often repeated among the various branches of the military. It speaks to the comradery and courage of every soldier. Every soldier is to be valued, protected, and defended. Whether wounded, killed in action, or just too weary to go any further, the promise is that he/she will be supported, encouraged, and even carried to safety on the backs of other brave soldiers. No one will be left behind. Such a promise is brought to life in the stories of brave men and women who rescue their fellow soldiers on the battlefield.

Through the words of Ezekiel, God promises that none of the people will be left behind in exile or scattered to the distant nations of the world. God will gather all the faithful and restore them to the land of Israel. God values the people so strongly that God is unwilling to leave any to languish, suffer, or die apart from God's presence. This is the same promise that we, as the people of God, should offer our fellow Christians and church members. Sometimes, we are not willing to do the hard work of redemption, forgiveness, and restoration that the gospel requires. We let people languish in shame, in fear, and in loneliness. It seems that we are willing to leave them behind to wallow in their distress and pain. Surely, we can do better. We need to pay attention to the marginalized, the victimized, and the stigmatized. We cannot cast them aside as those who lack importance or worth. We must claim them again. We must carry them on our shoulders, offering hope and grace and joy. If we are willing to leave the broken, dispirited, and hurting on the battlefield, what have we become?

Prayer
God, may it be said of us that we refused to discount the value of every person. Amen.

Day 842 — Ezekiel 40: Watch, Learn, Teach

> "He said to me, 'Son of man, watch and listen. Pay close attention to everything I show you. You have been brought here so I can show you many things. Then you will return to the people of Israel and tell them everything you have seen.'" Ezekiel 40:4 (NLT)

Observation
Chapter 40 begins a final section in the book of Ezekiel. When all of Israel's enemies are defeated, God will establish a new way of worship for the people. These chapters describe a new Temple that will be built, new worship practices to enact, and a new distribution of land for the people. Chapters 40-43 give special attention to the new Temple, sometimes referred to as the "Millennial Temple." Scholars have interpreted these chapters in three ways. First, some insist that Ezekiel is describing the new structure that will be built on the spot of Solomon's destroyed temple. Certainly, a temple was built in Jerusalem after the exile. Several important stories of Jesus happened in and around this temple. But many are quick to point out that the dimensions of this temple are much smaller than those mentioned by Ezekiel. A second interpretation rests on the idea that Ezekiel was not talking about a physical temple but speaking in a figurative sense. Instead of a building of brick and mortar, God would dwell in the renewed hearts of all God's people. The third interpretation centers on the idea of a future temple, yet unbuilt, that will become the key point of worship in the 1000-year reign of Christ. Whichever interpretation you choose, it is evident that God will establish a visible symbol of God's presence among the people. The descriptive words of chapter 40 give details about the shape and size of this place of worship.

Application
God offers a significant word of instruction to Ezekiel. He is to watch everything that God is about to reveal, learn from the experience, and then teach others what he has learned. I have discovered that one of the best ways God equips us to do ministry with others is by providing us with life experiences. Every life experience can be a teachable moment in which we learn how our faith reacts to various situations that come our way. We learn from the experience so that when opportunities arise, we can offer comfort, insight, and encouragement to those going through a similar experience. For example, several years ago I had bilateral knee replacement surgery. It was quite an ordeal. I learned a lot from the experience. And because I went through that life experience, I am now able to give insight and counsel to others. Consider some of your life experiences. It is possible that God can use your teachable moment to minister to another person? Be open to that possibility.

Prayer
God, may we never waste the opportunities given to us to perform ministry. Amen.

Day 843 — Ezekiel 41: The Holy Place

> "'This,' he told me, 'is the Most Holy Place.'" Ezekiel 41:4 (NLT)

Observation

In chapter 41, an angelic being "brings" Ezekiel to the porch of the Temple so that he can describe it in great detail. In his description, he speaks of the various doorways through which a person must pass to go from the outside to the Holy of Holies, where the presence of God dwells. Each doorway becomes increasingly narrow as if to suggest a careful restriction of access to God. People would understand that they were entering a very special and sacred place. Ezekiel describes side chambers and storage rooms. He also speaks of the wooden table just outside the Holy of Holies where the Bread of Presence is placed. One noticeable difference between this Temple in Ezekiel's vision and Solomon's Temple is that the one in the vision has no cloth curtain between the outer sanctuary and the Holy of Holies. Instead, it has a set of doors.

Application

Think about the most holy or most sacred place you have ever stood. It may be an ancient European cathedral, a church sanctuary, or a spot in nature where the mountains, valleys, and horizon speak of God's majesty. If you have ever made your way to the Holy Land, you may be thinking of a spot where Christ himself once walked. In such places our hearts are moved, our minds are captivated, and our excited words often turn to silence. It is a memorable experience to stand in a place that is holy.

I've had the opportunity to stand in many places set aside for worship, where the faithful have experienced the presence of God. It is difficult to name only one experience or place. I have stood in great cathedrals, ornate sanctuaries, and even Jewish temples. I have walked the streets of Jerusalem and explored the cities where Paul once preached. The truth is that there are many holy places. But notice the angel's declaration to Ezekiel in our focus verse: "This is the most holy place." He is referring to the Holy of Holies in the interior depths of the Temple—the spot where God's presence, sometimes even a visible presence, dwelled. It would seem that there is no other place like it in the world. But maybe there is. Maybe the most holy place is found within each of us…in the depths of the human heart where God longs to dwell. It is humbling and awe-inspiring to think that Almighty God longs to be present in each of us. We see the darkness of our own hearts, the mistakes we make, and the poor directions we choose, and we wonder how God could enter such a place. We need to remember that it is not our goodness that invites God in; it is God's glory that creates a new heart in us for God to inhabit.

Prayer

God, may we create in each of our lives a most holy place for you to dwell. Amen.

Day 844 — Ezekiel 42: Clothes Make a Difference

> "When the priests leave the sanctuary, they must not go directly to the outer courtyard. They must first take off the clothes they wore while ministering, because these clothes are holy. They must put on other clothes before entering the parts of the building complex open to the public."
> Ezekiel 42:14 (NLT)

Observation
Ezekiel 42 is divided into two parts. The first section describes the chamber rooms that lined the inner courtyard of the Temple. The priests were to use these rooms for changing their garments, eating a portion of the food to be sacrificed in the various offerings (Leviticus 2:3), and storing some of the offerings collected in the temple. According to our focus verse, the priests were to change clothes prior to leaving the Temple. Their clothing was considered holy. They wore it while ministering to the people and could not wear it in public away from the Temple complex. The second section of the chapter describes the outer walls of the Temple complex (the Millennial Temple). It was a square area measuring 500 cubits, or 875 feet per side. This huge complex, roughly the size of 13 football fields, was much larger than the areas set aside for Solomon's and Zerubbabel's temples.

Application
Clothes make a difference. What we choose to wear communicates something about our self-awareness and cultural acceptance. In other words, we can dictate the kind of impression we want to make by the clothing we wear. For example, I'm pretty old-fashioned when it comes to Sunday apparel, especially when I am preaching. I still wear a coat and tie. Even if I am overdressed, I hope my choice of clothing commands some sense of respectability. It says something about the importance of what I long to share. If I attend a football game and want to be clear about my allegiance, I wear the proper logo and team colors. Or I if want to give the impression of hard work, I might roll up my sleeves or loosen my collar a bit. Our clothing makes a difference.

The priests described in Ezekiel's prophecy had their everyday clothing and their official "ministry" clothing. Their ministry clothes were considered sacred. In some ways, how well they dressed for their role represented the holy nature of God. They had special clothes for special work. In terms of our practice of worship, are there things we should remove before we head into the Lord's house? I'm not talking about the clothes on our backs but the attitudes of our hearts. Do we dare to enter worship with anger, bitterness, jealousy, or lust in our hearts? Should we not pray for forgiveness, grace, and a higher perspective when we walk into church? If we are going to bring honor to the Great King, let's make sure that our hearts are well dressed.

Prayer
God, create a clean heart in each of us as we enter into worship. Amen.

Day 845 — Ezekiel 43: Absolute Holiness

> "And this is the basic law of the Temple: absolute holiness! The entire top of the mountain where the Temple is built is holy. Yes, this is the basic law of the Temple." Ezekiel 43:12 (NLT)

Observation

Ezekiel 43 describes the scene as the Lord's Glory returns to the Temple. The same angelic being that has directed Ezekiel's movements over the past few chapters tells him to watch as the Glory of the Lord enters through the eastern gate of Temple. The sound of God's coming is compared to that of many rushing waters, full of power and majesty. As the Lord's presence fills the Temple, God speaks directly to Ezekiel. Using anthropomorphic images, God declares that the Temple will be God's earthly dwelling place among the people until the introduction of the new heaven and earth. God promises to dwell among the people forever. As the chapter progresses, God offers specific instructions for how to construct and consecrate the altar of the Temple. For seven days the priests will perform sacrifices and offerings to purify the altar. They are, in effect, wiping or cleansing it so that it is fit for worship. Although sacrifices are no longer needed for sins following the atoning death of Christ, these sacrifices seem to be memorial in nature. With any sacrifice offered, the people will be reminded of their need for atonement.

Application

Holy things are "set apart, distinct, and different." When we speak of the Holy Bible, we refer to a book that is distinctively different from all other books because it contains the very words of God. When we talk about Holy God, we acknowledge that God is without equal, that there is no other god worthy of our consideration. When we speak of a holy moment, we refer to a specially ordained moment when we feel God's presence and carry forward God's purpose. And when we speak of a holy people, we point to God-followers who doggedly pursue Almighty God and God's Kingdom demands.

When God is revealed to Ezekiel, God tells him that the basic law of the Temple is holiness. Everything about that place is to be sacred, distinct, and set aside for worship. Every detail is important—the clothing worn, the size of the altar, the purity of every worshipping heart. Holiness is not only a descriptive quality of the Temple; it should also become a descriptive word for God's people. Everything about us should reflect our profound allegiance to God. We should be holy in demeanor, in language, in thought, and in character. Yes, that's a lofty goal. But does our God deserve anything less of us?

Prayer

God, make us into a holy people whose hearts long for you. Amen.

Day 846 — Ezekiel 44: One and Done

> "And the Lord said to me, 'This gate must remain closed; it will never again be opened. No one will ever open it and pass through, for the Lord, the God of Israel, has entered here. Therefore, it must always remain shut.'"
> Ezekiel 44:2 (NLT)

Observation

The next three chapters of Ezekiel describe the details and the holy standards God expects as the people worship. The same angelic being directs Ezekiel to the outer gate of the Temple area, the one that faces east and the Mount of Olives. Ezekiel has just watched the Glory of God enter through this gate before inhabiting the Temple. Now God declares that this gate must be shut. No one is allowed to enter the Temple through this gate because God has passed through there. (Many confuse this gate with the smaller Golden Gate that stands in present-day Jerusalem, sealed shut by an Islamic Sultan in the sixteenth century in an attempt to keep the Messiah out of Jerusalem.) God tells Ezekiel that a "prince," probably a representative of the Messiah, will sit in this gate rendering judgments and settling affairs. Ezekiel is then brought to the front of the Temple. He is told to "mark well" all of the statutes and laws of God. And then God highlights the roles of the Levites and priests. Because of their faithfulness during the preexilic time when many priests had corrupted worship practices, the descendants of Zadok receive the special honor of offering sacrifices to the Lord on the people's behalf. Every aspect of their lives is outlined in this passage.

Application

Manufacturers and designers want to create efficient products that can be used many times. Electric car designers create long-lasting batteries that can be recharged hundreds of times. Bridge builders want to construct safe bridges that span a waterway for decades. Airplanes are manufactured to last for thousands of safe flights. But some items are made for only a "onetime use." For example, my wife uses disposable contact lenses. She wears them only once and then throws them away. Coffee drinkers use K-cups once in their Keurig machines. Items like disposable diapers and fireworks are a one-and-done proposition. Notice that the Eastern Gate, described in Ezekiel as part of the Millennial Temple, is to be used only one time—the moment when God's glory passes through on its way to fill the Temple. After that, it is to be sealed shut because the Lord's presence has made it too holy for anything or anyone else. In the same way, our lifespans are used only once. Because we are created for God's glory, shouldn't our lives reflect a desire to honor God in all we do? This is a one-and-done opportunity. Let's take advantage of it.

Prayer

God, may it be said of us that we used our disposable lives well. Amen.

Day 847 — Ezekiel 45: Sinning in Ignorance

> "Do this also on the seventh day of the new year for anyone who has sinned through error or ignorance. In this way, you will purify the Temple."
> Ezekiel 45:20 (NLT)

Observation
Ezekiel 45 begins with a careful division of the land, prescribed by God. The first relates to land allotted for the Temple and the priests who serve there. A six-by-eight-mile portion will be deemed as holy or sacred land. The people are to construct the Temple on this portion of land and devote the remainder to the priests' homes. Another section will become the cities where the Levites will dwell. Unlike the time of Joshua when the Levites came from all the regions of Israel, this instruction indicates that they are to live close to the Temple where they will perform their duties. The city of Jerusalem is allotted a two-by-eight-mile section of land. This will become the central area of worship and eventually the capital of the nation. The prince of Israel (think of a religious rather than political leader) will be given land to the east and west of this sacred strip devoted to the Temple. As the chapter continues, Ezekiel gives words of warning to the Jewish religious leaders living in exile. They are admonished to repent and to use honest weights and measurements in regard to offerings brought to the Temple. They are not to exploit the people but to treat them fairly once they return to lead them following the exile.

Application
Most of us are more than familiar with the sins we commit. We know when we act in a disobedient way. We are aware of our poor choices and bad decisions. We feel guilt and remorse and shame, so we confess our sins and hopefully repent of our foolish ways. But is it possible that we sometimes sin in ignorance? In other words, is it possible to commit a sin while not being aware that we are doing so? Of course, it is possible. It happens all the time. We may have a blind spot to a sin we continually commit. We may be unaware of something offensive that we have done before the Almighty. Maybe there is a thought, an action, or even some word that we simply don't recognize as being sinful. When God offers instructions for the leaders who govern the work of the Millennial Temple, part of those instructions involves a yearly sacrifice to atone for sins committed in ignorance. By making such sacrifices, God ensures the purity of the Temple. What about our sins committed in ignorance? In addition to specific confessions of the sins we knowingly commit, we must be open to the possibility that we have sinned in unknowing ways. We must ask God to help us see them and to forgive us once again. This prayer of confession acknowledges that we may not even know the extent of our need for grace.

Prayer
Father, forgive us of both our known and unknown sins. Amen.

Day 848 — Ezekiel 46: Given without Fail

> "The lamb, the grain offering, and the olive oil must be given as a daily sacrifice every morning without fail." Ezekiel 46:15 (NLT)

Observation
Much of Ezekiel 46 is devoted to God's instructions for daily worship. Everything is to be done according to proper methods, rituals, and directions. The prince of the people will have a special role. On the Sabbath day, the Eastern Gate of the courtyard will be opened, and the prince will offer sacrifices for the people. In detailed instructions, God even outlines the way the people are to process through the Temple for worship. Worship is not left to happenstance or to a haphazard methodology. The year of Jubilee is also mentioned. As a reminder, every 50th year, all the property given to others will be returned to the original owner. In his vision, Ezekiel is taken to the holy chambers where the sacrificial meat is boiled and where the grain offering, consisting of flour and olive oil, is baked. There are four kitchens to use in preparing both fellowship meals and sacrificial food.

Application
One of the by-products of growing older is the need to take certain daily medications. Several years ago, I suffered a bout of thyroiditis. My thyroid became inflamed and was damaged to the point that it no longer produces enough thyroid hormone. So, like many others, I have to take a small thyroid pill every day. This pill regulates the levels of thyroid-stimulating hormone in my bloodstream, and I feel no ill effects. The problem is that I have to take the pill every day…for the rest of my life.

When God prescribed worship practices for the Millennial Temple, God declared that the religious leaders were to give a daily sacrifice "every morning without fail." Every single day, they were to make these sacrifices in order to atone for the sins of the people. Things are different in our time. Rather than the sacrifice of animals, the sacrifice of Christ has been offered on our behalf. And although his sacrifice was a onetime event on the cross, the need for his sacrifice is felt every day. As hard as we try, we will never live a day without sin. We are too flawed, too fragile, and too broken. And yet the blood of Christ cleanses us anew and we are made righteous in the sight of God. God's love, grace, and mercy are given without fail. What we should offer in return is our gratitude, bolstered by a sense of confession and repentance. We should offer our own lives as "living and holy sacrifices" each day so that we honor God in our experiences with our words, thoughts, and actions.

Prayer
Father, may we offer the daily sacrifice of our lives in obedience to you. Amen.

Day 849 — Ezekiel 47: The River

> "There will be swarms of living things wherever the water of this river flows. Fish will abound in the Dead Sea, for its waters will become fresh. Life will flourish wherever this water flows." Ezekiel 47:9 (NLT)

Observation

Ezekiel 47 focuses on the description of a great river that will change Israel's topography during the millennial kingdom. Ezekiel's words are not intended to be metaphoric. He describes an actual river that will nourish the land, beginning as a small trickle that flows from beneath the Temple. As the chapter begins, the same angelic being transports Ezekiel once again, this time to the Temple door. Water flows beneath the threshold. It begins as a trickle but soon becomes a river too wide to cross. The river flows both east and west. Lush, fruit-producing trees, which will produce fruit each month, grow along the riverbanks. The western flow will spill into the Dead Sea making the now lifeless body of water fresh. Fishermen will catch an abundance of fish, like those found in the Mediterranean Sea. As our focus verse indicates, life will flourish wherever this water flows. The final portion of the chapter mentions the division of land among the various tribes and the specific boundaries of the land.

Application

I grew up in the town of Rome, Georgia. It was established where the intersection of two rivers formed a third. In the heart of the city, the Etowah and Oostanaula rivers meet to form the Coosa. As you can imagine, these waterways were essential to life in the region's early beginnings. There are numerous Native American influences where the population of the town first grew. Much later, it became an import city of commerce as steamboats and trading ships made their way up and down the waterways. Though no longer used for commerce, the rivers still define the interior of the city, and when the occasional flood occurs, the water overtakes its surroundings. A century ago, engineers built a levee system that continues to protect the downtown area of Rome.

Ezekiel describes a river flowing from the Temple that will dramatically change life in Israel. It will give life to all the regions through which it flows. It will water crops, produce vegetation, supply fish, and nourish the parched areas. Everywhere it flows, life will flourish. I hope the same can be said of God's people wherever they dare to be the presence of Christ. What a wondrous thing to think that wherever God's people go, life will flourish. It begins with each of us. Can we impact our culture with the grace of Christ?

Prayer

Father, may we give hope, life, and mercy to all the lives we touch this day. Amen.

Day 850   Ezekiel 48: A New Name for a New City

> "The distance around the entire city will be 6 miles. And from that day the name of the city will be 'The Lord Is There.'" Ezekiel 48:35 (NLT)

Observation

This final chapter of Ezekiel focuses on the division of land given to the descendants of Israel's 12 ancestral tribes during the millennial kingdom. It does not parallel the division of land during the time of Joshua. In this division, all of the 12 tribes will receive an allotment of parallel strips of land running the entire width of the nation from east to west. One-fifth of the land will be devoted exclusively to the city of Jerusalem and the sacred land surrounding it. The priests and Levites who inhabit this region are forbidden to sell or exchange any portion of the land. A region surrounding the sacred land will be available for pasture and farmland for those living in Jerusalem. The book closes with a description of the 12 gates of the city—3 on each side—named for the 12 tribes. Ezekiel also points out that the glorious presence of the Lord will dwell in the city and the city will have a new name, Yahweh Shammah in Hebrew, which means "The Lord Is There."

Application

Several world cities have changed their names through the years. Bombay is now Mumbai. Canton is now Guangzhou. Saigon is now Ho Chi Minh City. Constantinople is now Istanbul. St. Petersburg is now back to being called St. Petersburg after being changed to Leningrad. These name changes reflect changes in political atmospheres and temperament, different controlling nations, and even different times, as when a former name reflected a dark history. It is rare for a large city to be renamed, and yet it happens, even in the Promised Land. The name Jerusalem means "City of Peace." But when the millennial kingdom comes, it shall be named "The Lord Is There." The change of name reflects the fact that God's abiding, glorious presence will now dwell permanently in that place.

Also reflected in scripture are numerous individual name changes due to a person's experience with God. Abram (exalted father) became Abraham (father of a nation). Jacob (the heel holder) became Israel (one who wrestles victoriously with God). Simon became Peter (the Rock). Believers also claim a new name…the name Christian. Our identity is wrapped up in that name. We belong to Christ. We love in Christ's name. We minister in ways that reflect his grace and mercy. We have been made new. No longer are we defined by our past. We name claim a bright future because his presence now indwells our lives. We become as a new city…a new dwelling place for the Living Lord to forever reside.

Prayer

God, make us worthy this day of the precious name of our Lord that we claim. Amen.

Day 851 — Daniel 1: A Disciplined Faith

> "But Daniel was determined not to defile himself by eating the food and wine given to them by the king. He asked the chief of staff for permission not to eat these unacceptable foods." Daniel 1:8 (NLT)

Observation
The book of Daniel is set against the backdrop of Babylonian captivity after King Nebuchadnezzar's first siege of Judah in 605 BC. (He would assault Jerusalem again in 597 BC, when 10,000 people were taken captive, and then again in 587 BC, when the city, including the Temple, was destroyed.) Daniel becomes a prophet to the nation and will speak of hope during the time of the exile when the Gentile population of the world is in control. His words contain history, prophecy, and apocalyptic visions. Chapter 1 serves as an introduction to the entire book. Daniel and his friends demonstrate that a person should maintain faithfulness despite the presence of a pagan society. The king orders that they be trained as leaders. Daniel was probably about 15 years old when taken into the king's court for training. An early faith decision was made when he and his friends chose not to eat the king's food because it violated Jewish laws. To honor God, they ate only vegetables and drank only water. God made them healthy. God also gave them special wisdom and a special place of service in the life of Babylon.

Application
I played high school football. It was one of the greatest joys of my life. I loved being on the team and getting the chance to play on Friday nights. Our team had various rules that governed our behavior and actions. For example, in order to get to the practice field, players had to cut across the end of the main stadium. We were told to run when crossing that field out of respect for playing on it on Friday nights. We also had a rule about post-practice pull-ups. Before leaving the field, all the players had to do 25 pull-ups. Another rule involved our team apparel. Jerseys were always tucked in, and cleats were only to be black…no exceptions. Those where some of the rules that were important and helped define what it meant to be on the team.

Daniel understood that God had certain parameters in place to govern the people. When first instructed to eat the food from the king's table, Daniel refused because it violated the rules of his faith tradition. He wanted to respect God's boundaries for how the people were to live. We too live under restraint because of our faith tradition…or at least we should. Because we follow Christ, there are rules, boundaries, and parameters that govern what we do and what we don't do. We live to honor God in all things.

Prayer
God, may the disciplines of our faith honor you and bear witness to your lordship. Amen.

Day 852   Daniel 2: The Eternal Kingdom

> "During the reigns of those kings, the God of heaven will set up a kingdom that will never be destroyed or conquered. It will crush all these kingdoms into nothingness, and it will stand forever." Daniel 2:44 (NLT)

Observation
Daniel 2-7 reveal God's continued ultimate reign over the world despite pagan dominion. These chapters are written in Aramaic (not Hebrew), which was the international language of the day. Chapter 2 deals with a troubling, reoccurring dream that King Nebuchadnezzar of Babylon experiences. The dream robs the king of sleep, so he calls in the wise men of his royal court and asks them to reveal and interpret the dream. He does not tell them about the dream, testing their supernatural ability to make the dream known. They, of course, cannot tell the events or nature of the dream. The king is angered and orders the slaughter of all the wise men of the court, which includes Daniel and his friends, although no one ever consulted them about the dream. When the executioner comes for Daniel, Daniel declares that he is able to do what the king had asked. He, along with his friends, prays to God for wisdom, and God reveals both the nature and meaning of the dream. The dream is of a great statue representing the next four great empires of the world: Babylon, Persia, Greek, and Rome. The statue is crushed by a huge stone that represents God's eternal Kingdom and will destroy all the powerful kingdoms of the world. The king recognizes that Daniel's God has given him supernatural abilities.

Application
In the world of sports, we sometimes talk of dynasties. Baseball fans remember the Big Red Machine of the early 1970s when the Cincinnati Reds were so dominant. Pro football fans will think in terms of the Patriots from 2001-2014. Certainly, the Chicago Bulls dominated the NBA from 1991-1998. And who could forget the UCLA men's basketball program in their success of 10 national championships in 12 years during the 1960s and 1970s? As a University of Alabama fan, I could certainly raise the success of the team during both the Bryant and Saban eras as possibilities. But here's what is interesting about all those sports dynasties: they all came to an eventual end. It's one thing to reach the top; it's another to stay on top for very long.

    Such is the message that Daniel offers to the king of Babylon. He clearly tells him that one day his kingdom will fall to another, which will fall to another, which will fall to still another. There is only one great Kingdom that will become a forever Kingdom…a dynasty that will last for all of time. That Kingdom is God's eternal reign that will come on earth as it is in heaven. It will never be conquered or destroyed. We place our hope and trust in that Kingdom.

Prayer
God, may we be loyal citizens of your Kingdom that will never fail. Amen.

Day 853 — Daniel 3: Even if He Doesn't...

> "If we are thrown into the blazing furnace, the God whom we serve is able to save us. He will rescue us from your power, Your Majesty. But even if he doesn't, we want to make it clear to you, Your Majesty, that we will never serve your gods or worship the gold statue you have set up."
> Daniel 3:17-18 (NLT)

Observation

Chapter 3 contains one of most remembered stories in the book of Daniel: the fiery furnace. According to historians, Nebuchadnezzar survived a revolt during the 10th year of his reign. That incident may have brought about the test of loyalty described in this story. The king made a huge golden statue, either of himself or of his favorite pagan god. It was 90 feet high and completely covered in gold. (Covering the entire statue in gold may have been an answer to his troubling dream described in chapter 2, where gold represented the Babylonian empire.) The officials were ordered to attend the dedication service of the statue. At the sound of musical instruments, all of them were to fall down in an act of worship. Those who did not would be incinerated in a furnace...perhaps the one used to smelt the gold for the statue. The three young Jewish friends of Daniel (Shadrach, Meshach, and Abednego) refused to worship a pagan god. They were brought before the king, who ordered them to be burned in a super-heated furnace. When the king looked in, he saw four men instead of three. The fourth had the appearance of an angelic being. The faithful young men escaped without even a hint of fire on their bodies or clothing. Nebuchadnezzar was forced to admit that there was no other god like that of the Israelites. The confession of Daniel's friends, listed above as our focus verse, is one of the strongest declarations of faith in the Bible.

Application

Most of us have read this passage many times, in awe of the faith of three young Jewish men. Though they believed in the impossible and declared that the sovereign God could deliver them, they defiantly praised God and were willing to become martyrs if that would honor God and further the Kingdom. They believed that even if God didn't write the script for their lives in the way they wanted, God was still worthy of praise. They affirmed the sovereignty, majesty, and authority of Almighty God and would not depart from their faith stance. We have much to learn from their experience and testimony. We are often quick to praise God when life goes our way, when our circumstances are pleasant and our blessings abundant. Anyone can offer such a response to a contented life. But can we offer our praises in the face of life's fiery trials? With absolute trust and unwavering commitment, we must remain steadfast and loyal with God's praises continually on our lips.

Prayer

God, teach us to be faithful amid any and every trial. Amen.

Day 854 — Daniel 4: A Humbling Experience

> "But the stump and roots of the tree were left in the ground. This means that you will receive your kingdom back again when you have learned that heaven rules." Daniel 4:26 (NLT)

Observation
Daniel 4 describes the pride, madness, and repentance of King Nebuchadnezzar. The narrative centers on another disturbing dream in the mind of the king. As in the past, the wise men of the king's court cannot interpret the dream, so he summons Daniel to decipher it because, as the king states, "the Spirit of Holy God is in him." He has dreamed of a large tree that reaches into the heavens. It gives fruit to the entire world. The birds nest in its branches, and the beasts of the field rest in its shade. Then an angel descends from the heavens and declares that the tree is to be cut down, but the stump will remain rooted in the soil. Daniel interprets the dream, telling the king that he is the great tree, the ruler over all the world. Because of his overwhelming pride, he will be brought low. He will be struck with a mental illness for seven years, which will force him to live in the wilderness like a wild beast. Only when he repents of his pride will he once again regain his kingdom. The dream is fulfilled, and after seven years, the king repents of his pride. The mental illness leaves Nebuchadnezzar, and he is restored.

Application
Have you ever had an especially humbling experience—a moment when life taught you a valuable lesson? I've had more than a few. We all have. During my high school days, I took a required Bible class. Because I had grown up in church and in a pastor's home, I breezed through the class. I aced every test and quiz. At the end of the year, on Awards Day, I was certain that I would win the Bible Class award over all the other students. When they called the name of the winner, the Headmaster said, "Our Bible award goes to John R. _____." I never heard the last name. I assumed that "John R." would be followed by "Roebuck." I even stood up anticipating the walk to the podium. But alas, the award went to a different student, and I had to scramble back into my seat. How humiliating!

Daniel takes the discussion of pride to a higher plane. He speaks about God's ability to humble each of us until we learn that "heaven rules." Sometimes we need a little reminder that we live in God's world and our lives are governed by God's will and purpose. We are not in charge, and no one has called us to be savior of the world. We need these humbling reminders at times to depend on God and not on our own intellect, wisdom, or life experiences. Though the discipline of the Father is not always enjoyable, it is necessary. A little humility helps us all.

Prayer
God, forgive us when we fail to humble ourselves under your authority. Amen.

Day 855 — Daniel 5: The Handwriting Is on the Wall

> "Suddenly, they saw the fingers of a human hand writing on the plaster wall of the king's palace, near the lampstand. The king himself saw the hand as it wrote, and his face turned pale with fright. His knees knocked together in fear and his legs gave way beneath him." Daniel 5:5-6 (NLT)

Observation

The events of Daniel 5 took place 23 years after the events described in the previous chapter. Nebuchadnezzar is long dead, and Belshazzar is now the coregent of the empire with Nabonidus, who rules in Arabia. Belshazzar holds a great feast to bolster the morale of the people after Nabonidus suffers a defeat at the hands of the Persians. Modern archaeologists have discovered a banquet hall in the ruins of ancient Babylon that could seat more than 1000 people—possibly the site of this event. Belshazzar orders the gold and silver vessels to be brought to the banquet and used for wine. These were the holy items taken from God's Temple during the days of conquest. Suddenly a hand appears, writing words on the wall. The king is frightened and asks for his wise men to interpret the words. Only Daniel is able to translate the words and explain their meaning. The three words, written in Aramaic, are "numbered, weighed, and divided." The message is clear. Because of his blasphemous actions, the king's days are numbered and weighed out, and soon the kingdom will be divided. That very night, Darius of Persia overtakes the city of Babylon and King Belshazzar is killed.

Application

On a local sports-talk radio program this week, the host used this familiar sentence when speaking about an under-performing SEC football coach. "The handwriting is on the wall," he said. "[The coach] will not make it to the end of the season." It is always interesting to mix a little football and faith. Of course, the commentator meant that the decision was already made in the minds of those who mattered. There was no turning back; the issue was settled. When King Belshazzar saw the hand literally writing on the wall, God's judgment was already in place. Belshazzar would be punished for his insolence and disrespectful ways. There was no turning back, no changing the mind of God. The message was clear, plain, and evident. This is one of the more memorable stories in the Old Testament. But even more memorable are God's promises offered to all of us who claim Christ as Savior and Lord. The handwriting is on the wall. The decision is made. The matter is settled. We will be ushered into God's forever Kingdom, not because we are worthy but because we are God's. God claims us as children. The promise is that no one can "snatch them out of the Father's hand" (John 10:29 NASB).

Prayer

God, we thank you that our destiny has been set in stone. Amen.

Day 856 — Daniel 6: Godly Defiance

> "But when Daniel learned that the law had been signed, he went home and knelt down as usual in his upstairs room, with its windows open toward Jerusalem. He prayed three times a day, just as he had always done, giving thanks to his God." Daniel 6:10 (NLT)

Observation
The story of Daniel in the lion's den is a familiar Old Testament story. What may surprise many readers is Daniel's age. Although often depicted as a young man, the various time markers in the narrative make it likely that Daniel is 82 years old! The story focuses on a decision made by King Darius of Persia to appoint 120 governmental leaders over the provinces of the empire. Three key leaders are appointed as commissioners over these 120 rulers to ensure no corruption takes place. Daniel is selected as a commissioner and distinguishes himself above all others. The other leaders grow jealous and make false claims about his leadership that cannot be proven. They trick the king into making a law that no one can worship or pray to anyone but the king for a period of 30 days. Daniel, in defiance of the law, continues to pray faithfully to God. The king is tripped up by his own law and has to throw Daniel, his best commissioner, in the lion's den. But the next morning, Daniel emerges completely unharmed. God "has shut the mouths of the lions." Those who accused Daniel falsely are thrown into the pit and devoured, along with their wives and children.

Application
Sometimes a "conflict of conscience" occurs at the intersection of faith and culture, or even between faith and government. Sometimes God-followers are forced to choose between godly obedience or adherence to a corrupt and immoral law. What is the path to follow? In the story of Daniel, the prophet was steadfast in two ways. First, he trusted in the Lord's deliverance. Even beyond human comprehension, he believed in the power of God to bring a resolution to his crisis. Second, he remained steadfast in his faith stance. Knowing that the king's irreversible law would surely bring about his arrest, Daniel continued to pray three times a day to God, as was his custom and as was dictated in Mosaic law. He felt that it was more important to show allegiance to God than to obey the law of the king. Sometimes our faith puts us in a bind. Sometimes the ways of God and the ways of the world stand in stark contrast and we have to make decisions. To whom will we offer our greatest allegiance? The answer should be an easy one, right? After all, who is the Keeper of our Soul? But sometimes faith fizzles in the face of persecution and punishment. The challenge is to be strong and courageous while seeking godly wisdom.

Prayer
God, as we are forced to make daily choices, may they always be God-led. Amen.

Day 857   Daniel 7: The Eternal Kingdom

> "He was given authority, honor, and sovereignty over all the nations of the world, so that people of every race and nation and language would obey him. His rule is eternal—it will never end. His kingdom will never be destroyed." Daniel 7:14 (NLT)

Observation

Beginning with chapter 7, the book of Daniel records a number of prophetic visions that will later become the "centerpiece" of Old Testament revelation concerning the Messiah. These visions give ultimate hope to Israel as Daniel declares the rise and fall of worldwide empires that will eventually be crushed when the Messiah comes. Chapter 7 contains a vision of four beasts. The imagery is vivid. Four winds blow and stir up the great sea. This is a reference to four great world empires that will stir up the inhabitants of earth. (These are the same ones described previously in chapter 2.) Daniel identifies four beasts representing Babylon, Persia, Greece, and Rome. As they come in succession, the final beast—Rome—will be defeated when the Messianic age or Kingdom comes. In this passage, God is referred to as the "Ancient of Days." This reference speaks of the eternal nature of God. God's wrathful punishment will be poured out on the wicked, but the covenant people will receive the Kingdom.

Application

It's hard for the human mind to think in terms of what is eternal. We tend to think in chunks of time, decades, lifespans, centuries, etc. To say that something will last or remain forever boggles our minds. For example, I recently purchased a simple and inexpensive Casio watch on Amazon. All it does is show the time. There is no day or date or fancy dials. Just two hands, a white face, and a battery that will power it for 10 years without replacement. It cost about 12 dollars. What a bargain, right? I mean, 10 years is a longtime. I will worry about a replacement when that day comes. Also, in 10 years, I will begin my trek through my 70s. What madness is that?

Daniel speaks of the great Messianic Kingdom of God. It is surely coming. It will endure. It will never be conquered. I don't know about you, but I am excited about being on the right side of history, or should I say the right side of eternity. The God in whom I trust, and the Kingdom for which I long, will never vanish, be destroyed, or fail. And because I have received the Messiah into my life, I am connected to the permanence of that Kingdom. Something about my connection to God, something about my existence, and something about my salvation will linger forever. I don't know all the details. I don't know what glory will resemble. I just know that I am included in the Kingdom's forever embrace.

Prayer

Father God, we thank you for our secure, glorious, and eternal destiny. Amen.

Day 858   Daniel 8: Waiting on the World to Change

> "The other replied, 'It will take 2,300 evenings and mornings; then the Temple will be made right again.'" Daniel 8:14 (NLT)

Observation
Chapter 8 continues the description of Daniel's prophetic visions. His vision involving a ram and a goat focuses on events that will take place in the sixth to second centuries BC. The vision places Daniel at the city gate of Susa, the future capital of the Persian Empire. He first sees a ram that is powerful, strong, and dominant. This represents the Persians. But next he sees a goat with a conspicuous horn. This represents the Greek empire, specifically Alexander the Great. In Daniel's vision, the goat attacks and defeats the ram. Four other horns represent the generals over the four corners of the empire. Another small horn appears on the goat's head, symbolic of Antiochus Epiphanes who will dominate the land of Israel in a cruel and blasphemous reign. In fact, Antiochus Ephiphanes will not only compare himself to God but will also offer pagan sacrifices on the altar at the Holy of Holies in the Temple. In our focus verse, an angel tells Daniel how long the time of Temple desecration will last. It will end with the dedication of the new Temple in 164 BC, an event celebrated with the Jewish holiday of Chanukah. Daniel has trouble understanding the meaning of the vision and is aided by the angel Gabriel.

Application
Waiting can be a difficult discipline. In our hurry-up, instant-access world, we want quick answers and immediate results. It pains us to wait for test results, a key decision at work, or even a text update from a family member or friend. We say things like, "I had a blood test, and I have to wait until tomorrow for the results"; "I submitted a proposal at work, and I have to wait two weeks for a response"; "I need my car serviced, but I have to wait until next week to get an appointment." At such moments, we are reminded that the world does not revolve around us. Sometimes we simply have to wait… wait on others, wait on schedules, or even wait on God's timing for our lives. Look back at the biblical record and you will discover that many characters were called to wait. Moses waited a lifetime before God called him into leadership. Noah waited a hundred years before the first raindrop fell. The ancient Israelites waited a thousand years for the Promised Messiah to come to earth. My rabbi friend often reminds me of the important discipline of waiting. He says that such a discipline is woven throughout the narrative of both the Hebrew Bible and the New Testament. As we wait this day on the movement of God in our lives, let us do so with anticipation and patience.

Prayer
Father God, teach us the discipline of waiting patiently for you to act. Amen.

Day 859   Daniel 9: Learning from the Word

> "During the first year of his reign, I, Daniel, learned from reading the word of the Lord, as revealed to Jeremiah the prophet, that Jerusalem must lie desolate for seventy years." Daniel 9:2 (NLT)

Observation
Chapter 9 begins with Daniel offering a prayer for his people. According to our focus verse, Daniel has learned from the writings of Jeremiah, recorded just a generation earlier, that Jerusalem will be desolate for 70 years. The 70 years are almost complete as Daniel experiences this particular moment. He offers a heart-felt prayer for the nation, consistently using the name "Yahweh" for God to emphasis God's covenantal nature. He prays strong words of confession, admitting that the people have failed to obey God's commandments and thus suffered the calamity of the exile. He speaks of the desperate need for God's compassion and forgiveness. As he finishes his prayer, the angel Gabriel appears to him for a second time and refers to a period of time defined as 70 years of 7, or 490 years. This timespan will mark the years between the rebuilding of the Temple and the coming of the Messiah. A careful recording of the dates places the end of the timespan on the exact day when Jesus will walk triumphantly into Jerusalem at the beginning of Holy Week, thus initiating the Messianic age.

Application
I do a lot of casual reading. I enjoy the work of a number of writers. I have read all of John Grisham's books, all of David Baldacci's books, and many others, including a long novel by Stephen King about the Kennedy assassination that a friend recommended. I mostly read for enjoyment rather than education. I read for entertainment value. But I do read some books to gain wisdom and insight. Often, when tackling a difficult topic for my work as Director of the Curb Center, I read books to increase my knowledge and understanding of topics like racism, LGBTQ issues, leadership strategies, biases, etc. In other words, I read with the intent of increasing my understanding of key issues. And I read God's word daily. Notice what happens in Daniel's life when he sits down to read Jeremiah's words: he makes a discovery about God's timing for Jerusalem and the way it relates to the exilic period. This is a reminder that all of us can glean a great deal by investing in God's word. We can learn life lessons, gain insights, realize corrections, and find promises on which to anchor our lives. God's word is truly active and alive. It will speak powerfully to each of us if we invest time with it, approaching it with open minds and obedient hearts.

Prayer
God, may we be willing this day to be taught through the reading of your word. Amen.

Day 860   Daniel 10: Precious in His Sight

> "'Don't be afraid,' he said, 'for you are very precious to God. Peace! Be encouraged! Be strong!' As he spoke these words to me, I suddenly felt stronger and said to him, 'Please speak to me, my lord, for you have strengthened me.'" Daniel 10:19 (NLT)

Observation

Chapters 10 through 12 tell of Daniel's final vision, which speaks of future events that will result in war and great hardship. As this vision unfolds, Daniel, who is probably 84 years old at the time, is enduring a three-week period of mourning. He is probably grieving the pitiful state of the former captives who are now returning to Israel. He is fasting to give greater depth and power to his prayers. As he stands on the banks of the Tigris River, he sees a man in glorious apparel. Only Daniel can to see him. Others can feel a powerful presence, and they flee from it. Daniel is weakened by this vision and falls into a deep sleep. The angelic being comes to strengthen him and to tell him that God has heard his prayer. (Biblical scholars debate whether this vision is of the Messiah or of some other prince in heaven who possesses great authority and power.) The angel also reveals to Daniel much of the meaning behind the visions he has seen. Our focus verse contains a word of encouragement this special messenger gives to Daniel.

Application

As human beings, we all long to be precious in the sight of someone else. We want to be important, valued, loved, encouraged, and needed. This deep longing reaches to the core of who we are. Many people find a sense of belonging and value in their spouses. Knowing that we are precious to someone is meaningful and affirming. But even in the best marriages, there are days of discord when such assurance is hard to find. Some of us may never fully experience such a relationship on this earth. As human beings, we are all flawed, fragile, and imperfect. We have our better moments, soon followed by our darker days. At times we get our relationships right and at other times we struggle. But read again the promise from God's word in our focus verse and apply it to your life, as though it is written from God's heart directly to yours: "You are very precious to God." What an important word of affirmation to know that you are loved, valued, and precious to God. And there is nothing you can ever do to make yourself less precious in God's sight. God loves and values you because God made you. You are God's special creation, crafted in love and kept in grace. You have always been precious in God's sight, and you always will be.

Prayer

God, though we can't comprehend the depth of your love, we gratefully receive it. Amen.

Day 861   Daniel 11: Finding Our Strength in God

> "He will flatter and win over those who have violated the covenant. But the people who know their God will be strong and will resist him."
> Daniel 11:32 (NLT)

Observation

This is another chapter in which Daniel shares predictive prophecy. In fact, chapter 11 contains some of the Bible's more precise predictions. The first part deals with political events that began during Daniel's time lifetime in 536 and then extend to 164 BC. The second part is a prediction of the end-times when a corrupt king, interpreted by some as the antichrist, will rise in power and the final world battles will occur. In a careful reading of this text, combined with a study of world history, the reader can trace the ongoing warfare of the Ptolemaic and Seleucus dynasties, referred to here as the kingdoms of the north and the south. The text refers to the story of Seleucus IV, whose own tax collector poisoned him for forcing him to collect oppressive taxes. It also tells of Antiochus IV, who would destroy the Jewish temple in 169 BC and slaughter 80,000 Jewish men during the Maccabean period. Verses 36-45 focus on the End of Days.

Application

Some of you are old enough to remember Flip Wilson, a comedian who was popular in the 1970s. He often performed a funny routine titled "The Devil Made Me Buy this Dress," which featured a female character named Geraldine. In that old comedic bit, Wilson described how the devil slipped up behind Geraldine and kept whispering into her ear the reasons she should buy a particular dress. She gives in to the temptation and spends the money.

Though we may occasionally joke about temptation, its voice is strong and powerful in our minds. To use Daniel's words, it flatters us until it wins us over. The intent of temptation is always destruction. When the devil lures us in, he desires to cause us to sin and thus drive a wedge between ourselves and Holy God. The subtle, persistent voice keeps whispering in our ears until we begin to give in to the siren sound of evil. New Testament writer James describes the process in this way: "Then, after desire has conceived, it gives birth to sin; and sin, when it is full-grown, gives birth to death" (James 1:15 NIV). But Daniel offers a word of counsel. In our focus verse, he teaches that "those who know God will be strong and will resist...." Sometimes we try to rely on our strength and wit to defeat temptation. "I can handle it," we say. "Things will never go too far." And then it happens. We get caught in an inescapable web. Before this day goes any further, commit your ways to God.

Prayer

God, may our relationship with you be so profound that we are not led astray. Amen.

Day 862   Daniel 12: Is Your Name in the Book?

> "At that time Michael, the archangel who stands guard over your nation, will arise. Then there will be a time of anguish greater than any since nations first came into existence. But at that time every one of your people whose name is written in the book will be rescued." Daniel 12:1 (NLT)

Observation
This final chapter of the book of Daniel provides the clearest statements concerning resurrection in the Hebrew Bible. Chapter 12 offers this important word of hope to Israelites who suffer persecution and exile. Daniel is told that the archangel Michael will rise to the defense of the Jews. Despite the horrific nature of their persecution, those whose names are written in the book of life will be delivered. The idea of names written in a book was a familiar concept. Often cities and villages kept lists of everyone who lived there. Daniel insists that a faithful remnant of God's people will rise from the dust to new life. The faithful will shine like bright stars, leading others to faith. At the close of the chapter, Daniel is told to seal up the words of prophecy until God is ready for them to be revealed. Daniel is not to worry about the timetable of the predicted events. He and others will receive insight from the Holy Spirit. And though Daniel will die and be buried, he too will rise again to receive his inheritance, according to the last verse.

Application
Most of us looked to see if our names appear, correctly spelled, in a number of books. For example, high school and college students often purchase yearbooks. The first thing many do is turn to the class pictures section and make sure their photos and names are there. In the days of phone books, many of us flipped through the pages until we found the list that started with our initial, checking carefully for our names and numbers. And at graduations, we certainly wanted to make sure our names were on the list!

Daniel, whose thoughts are later reflected in the book of Revelation, speaks about a book of life written by God's own hand. Everyone whose name appears in that book will be rescued. It's a list of the faithful, the obedient, the forgiven. We must be careful to remember that what puts us on the list is not our life accomplishments, our wealth, or even our good deeds. It is our faith in Christ Jesus as the Savior and Messiah of the world that makes us worthy. It is by God's grace and forgiveness that we are healed of our brokenness and redeemed of our sinfulness. If you are ever curious about whether or not your name is included, look through the lens of faith. Your name is there.

Prayer
Father God, thank you for our forever inclusion through the work of Christ. Amen.

Day 863 — Hosea 1: Object Lessons

> "When the Lord first began speaking to Israel through Hosea, he said to him, 'Go and marry a prostitute, so that some of her children will be conceived in prostitution. This will illustrate how Israel has acted like a prostitute by turning against the Lord and worshiping other gods.'"
> Hosea 1:2 (NLT)

Observation
Hosea 1 clearly announces Hosea's prophetic role and the time frame for his ministry. He is called as a prophet during the last stages of the northern (Israel) and southern (Judah) kingdoms. God often asks prophets to perform difficult and sometimes humiliating object lessons to complement their messages. No exception, Hosea is told by God to marry a prostitute named Gomer. Her eventual unfaithfulness to the prophet will illustrate Israel's unfaithful behavior towards God and the covenant. Three children will come from their union. The first will be a son named Jezreel. This name will become a reminder of the location, the Jezreel Valley, where the military might of Israel is eventually destroyed. Second, a daughter named Lo-Ruhamah will be born to the family. Her name means "not loved," again a message to the Israelites who have broken their covenant with God. The third child, a son, will be named Lo-Ammi, which means "not my people." The message is clear. God is bringing judgment on the wayward people. Yet they are not without hope. God will not reject them forever. The names will later be connected to God's redemptive work. Jezreel means "God will plant," and people will one day rejoice in God's repopulation of the nation. The Israelites will be talked about as Ammi, "my people," and Ruhamah, "the ones I love."

Application
Object lessons can be tricky. Years ago, I used a magic trick as a prop for a children's sermon. It involved a handkerchief and a cane. The plastic cane would collapse into a tiny roll that could be hidden in the palm of one's hand. When it sprung into shape, the handkerchief would disappear inside. After making a biblical application (which must have been quite a stretch), I threw the handkerchief into the air, and in the blink of an eye it became a cane…at least, that was the plan. But the cane shot out of my hand and hit a kid right in the eye! He immediately started crying, and his mother had to come and rescue him. In the case of Hosea, God used his marriage as an object lesson to the Israelites to illustrate how disruptive unfaithful behavior could be. What if God chose to use your life as an object lesson to others? What would your life story teach others? Would they see gentleness, faithfulness, and noble character? Or would they see how not to behave?

Prayer
God, may we live in such a way that you are honored by our actions. Amen.

Day 864   Hosea 2: The Gifts from God

> "She doesn't realize it was I who gave her everything she has—the grain, the new wine, the olive oil; I even gave her silver and gold." Hosea 2:8 (NLT)

Observation
As chapter 2 opens, God directs Hosea to bring charges against Israel as an unfaithful wife, just as a husband would do in a legal proceeding. "She is no longer my wife!" God declares. However, God is not severing the relationship forever; by the end of the chapter God will seek to bring her to repentance. Hosea speaks of Israel being "stripped naked in public," which was a common Near Eastern practice for those caught in adultery. The shame of stripping was often a prelude to stoning because adultery was punishable by death. God will send her (Israel) out into the wilderness, where she will experience famine and want. Yet God will deal with her through discipline. God will set up a barrier to keep her from wandering and will withhold provisions until she learns dependency on the Lord. According to the text, Israel has acted like a woman who dresses herself with sensuous attire to seduce men. This is a reference to Israel's participation in pagan worship. Yet God promises a door of hope to Israel. Israel will awaken to the truth she once neglected. God will be her betrothed once again.

Application
Sometimes I sit at my desk at home in a quiet moment of reflection, surrounded by the comforts I enjoy and the possessions I claim. And I think, "Everything that I see before me is something that I have purchased at some point. I earned the money and paid the cost." It might be my desk, the painting on the wall, the carpet below my feet, or the house in which I live. Then I think, "How foolish to boast or brag about such a thing!" All that I have, all that I possess, all that I think I "own" is not because of who I am or anything I have done. It is all a gift from the Father. God has created me, gifted me, and positioned me to have the ability to work. God is the giver of talents, opportunities, and even employment. I would do well to reflect the words of Hosea, who reminds me in our focus verse that everything I have is a result of what God has given to me. As I occasionally sit and stare, I should never think, "Wow, look how important I have become!" Rather, I should think, "Wow, look at what a great Heavenly Father I have. And who am I that I should be claimed by God's grace? Who am I that I should enjoy sonship in God's household?" As you embark on a new day, take a moment to consider the materials blessings that surround your life and family. Count your blessings and acknowledge the God who gives you all things.

Prayer
Father God, may I begin this day with a heart of gratitude. Amen.

Day 865   Hosea 3: The Price of Redemption

> "So I bought her back for fifteen pieces of silver and five bushels of barley and a measure of wine." Hosea 3:2 (NLT)

Observation
In this short chapter with only five verses, Hosea is described as a faithful husband redeeming and reclaiming his wayward wife. This illustrates God's reinstatement of Israel after the nation continually rebelled against God and chased after pagan deities. The text indicates that Hosea and his wife Gomer have separated. She has committed adultery with another lover, just as the people of Israel had turned to other gods. Hosea pays a large sum to redeem her or to "buy her back." The reason he has to pay a price is not clear. It could be that she had accrued debts. It could also be that she had sold herself into slavery and needed to be purchased from her current owner. Either way, Hosea has to settle the debt. The large price he is willing to pay indicates Gomer's worth and value to her husband. Following her return, she must undergo a period of purification to cleanse her of immorality. Next comes a period of restoration, just as God promises to restore Israel.

Application
I had a weird conversation recently that people sometimes have with strangers. I was talking with a guy at a local fast-food restaurant as he took my order. He randomly asked if I was Andrew's father. "I am," I answered. And then he replied, "I once bought him as a slave so this crazy girl couldn't buy him." That response needed some explanation! He told me that he was in the marching band with my son. During my son's freshman year, the new band members had to participate in a "slave auction" where the upperclassmen could purchase a "slave for a day" and make that person carry their books, get their cafeteria tray, or even wash their car. He paid a price for my son so that no one else would enslave him. I thanked the guy and felt sure that Andrew would still remember the day.

    Most of you reading this devotional will never serve as someone's slave. No other human being will own you and force you into a life of poverty, abuse, and servitude. But all of you will know the oppression of slavery, for surely slavery takes many forms. We are enslaved by financial pressures, job demands, and family responsibilities. We are held captive by over-burdened schedules and the toils of everyday life. Even more oppressive is the weight of guilt and shame that rests on our shoulders. We feel the pain of an imperfect past. We flinch at the thought of our mistakes and poor choices. And yet we are redeemed by Christ's sacrifice. We are forgiven, set free, liberated.

Prayer
Father God, may we walk in freedom this day, knowing that we are not slaves to sin. Amen.

Day 866   Hosea 4: Passing the Buck

> "Don't point your finger at someone else and try to pass the blame!"
> Hosea 4:4a (NLT)

Observation
Chapter 4 contains a warning: Hosea proclaims God's charge against the northern kingdom of Israel for their covenantal unfaithfulness. Hosea acts much like an accuser in a legal proceeding between two parties. God has a "case" against Israel. The people have been unfaithful to God and immoral towards one another. They are accused of swearing, deception, murder, stealing, and adultery. The punishment against them will have trickle-down effects on the plants and animals. All of the nation will feel the effects of their sinful behavior. Hosea gives particular condemnation on the priests. They have neglected their responsibilities. They will experience shame and know the same punishment as the people. Hosea even indicates that the wind will add to the people's affliction.

Application
The internet is filled with funny animal videos. A recent one made me laugh out loud. Two dogs were being chastised by their owner. In the background, I saw a pillow chewed to shreds. The owner spoke sternly to the dogs. "Molly and Sam, did you do this?" One dog nodded his head towards the other dog as if to say, "It's was him!" The video was priceless.

    It's also an illustration of the way most of us handle our sinfulness. When accused of wrongdoing, we want to pass along the responsibility to someone else. Not wanting to be held accountable for our sins and mistakes, we try to push the blame onto others. Our behavior is as old as the story of Adam and Eve. The moment when God questions him about eating the forbidden fruit, Adam says to God, "That woman that you gave to me…she is the one to blame." In other words, he fails the accountability test. "It's her fault!" For most of us, it's always someone else's fault. We can find plenty of people to blame. "It's my stupid husband…my crazy kids…my boss." Hosea says it's time to stop pointing our fingers at someone else and accept blame for our own poor behavior. Have you noticed that when you try to blame someone else, thinking to shift the weight of responsibility off your shoulders, you actually create more layers of deceit? Keep up the blame game long enough, and soon you will find yourself standing all alone in a wilderness devoid of any friendships or relationships. The biblical promise is clear: confess and you will find grace, forgiveness, and even healing. Pass the blame and you will find loneliness.

Prayer
Father God, may we learn to take responsibility for our own actions. Amen.

Day 867 — Hosea 5: Fair-weather Faith

> "For as soon as trouble comes, they will earnestly search for me."
> Hosea 5:15b (NLT)

Observation

Hosea 5 condemns Israel's leaders who have failed the nation. It contains an indictment against priests, political leaders, and members of the royal family. Hosea lists various cities where many injustices have occurred. In places like Mizpah, Tabor, and the Acacia Grove, the people have been led to worship pagan deities where they should have honored God. Some of the leaders, in their pride and arrogance, hoped that God would simply overlook their sins. They committed spiritual adultery against God. Some of them even moved property boundaries and thus committed theft against their neighbors. Hosea warns of impending destruction, indicating that even the land will be made desolate.

Application

The expression "fair-weather fans" refers to sports fans who support their team only when things go well. This happens all the time. As soon as a team starts to have success, everyone jumps on the bandwagon. Merchandise sales increase, water-cooler conversations become more frequent, and everyone starts showing team pride on casual Fridays by wearing team colors. But when the team starts to "tank," many fans tend to lose both their enthusiasm and allegiance. When the local college team was having a down year, for example, stores had a lot of excess inventory that no one would buy, even at a discounted price.

Do some of us have a fair-weather faith mentality? When life goes well and blessings seem abundant, many people are quick to praise God and offer testimony to God's greatness. But when life turns sour and dark, what happens? Are we as quick to praise God for God's faithfulness and unfailing love? Is the tenacity of our testimony as strong when we live in moments of uncertainty? The fair-weather mentality also shows up when we suddenly need a bailout. Hosea speaks of a pattern of religious behavior that many seem to embrace. As soon as hardship comes, they quickly turn to God, desperate to seek God's favor. But when life is smooth and the journey is easy, are they as intentional to express their faith? Our faith should not depend on the ups and downs of everyday life. Like Shadrach, Meshach, and Abednego, our resolve should be steadfast. "We are confident that our God is able to deliver us," they said, "but even if he doesn't, we will still praise him." There is nothing you can do this day to make God love you any more or less than God already does. All you can do is choose how your faith will respond when the days aren't perfect.

Prayer

Father God, we pray for faithfulness no matter our circumstances. Amen.

Day 868   Hosea 6: To Know the Lord

> "Oh, that we might know the Lord! Let us press on to know him. He will respond to us as surely as the arrival of dawn or the coming of rains in early spring." Hosea 6:3 (NLT)

Observation

Hosea 6 is a call to repentance. The prophet exhorts the nation to repent of her sins and turn once again to the Lord. If she does so, God will heal the nation, bandage the wounds, and restore both land and people. The turnaround can happen quickly through God's might and power. Hosea's goal is to help the nation become "relational" to God. More than simply knowing about God or who God is, Hosea pleads for them to see God as a relatable Being who is intimately acquainted with their ways. God's faithfulness to Israel will be as certain as the dawn and the seasonal rains. The nation will prove her repentance through obedience. Obedience is always the true sign of repentance and loyalty. Disobedience is the mark of rebellion. Hosea also reminds the people that their sins need to be uncovered before restoration can occur. In the same way, our journey to wholeness with God must always include confession.

Application

Let's be honest: most of us are not prepared to share a quote from the book of Hosea. Memory verses seldom come from the minor prophets of Israel. But I can remember our focus verse well, and here's why. Kate Campbell is a friend of more than forty years and is married to my best friend, Stan. She is a singer/songwriter with unique gifts as a lyricist and musician. Years ago, she set this verse to song on one of her CDs. To this day, as I read this verse, I can hear Kate's voice and hum the tune. Her challenge, which echoes that of Hosea, is to press on in knowing the Lord.

    How do we do this? How do we "press on" in establishing a relationship with a God we can't see or audibly hear? We step forward in faith. We trust that God exists and that God longs to relate to each of us. We practice disciplines through which God is revealed to us—the disciplines of reflective listening, honest confession and prayer, and the reading of the word of God. This "pressing on" builds a relationship. We soon begin to hear God's words echoing through our minds at critical moments. We feel a prompting of the Spirit in key situations. We witness the answers to our fervent prayers. We hear God's counsel through the preaching of God's servants or through our conversations with friends. Our longing should not be to have a factual understanding of theology or the books of the Bible. Our longing should be to know the God behind those things. What may begin as an arduous journey of discipline will soon become a glorious relationship with Almighty God.

Prayer

Father God, may we be burdened with a longing to know you fully. Amen.

Day 869   Hosea 7: The Scrutiny of God

> "Its people don't realize that I am watching them. Their sinful deeds are all around them, and I see them all." Hosea 7:2 (NLT)

Observation

In chapter 7, Hosea decries Israel's love for wickedness and rebellious behavior. The sins of the nation are great, and God has seen them all. In fact, when God looks at Israel, all God sees is sin. Hosea speaks of two-faced political leaders who have plotted against the monarchy. They practice political scheming and deceit, which leads to a rapid succession of kings due to assassination. Because the kings are unwilling to confront the evildoers within their political circles, they become vulnerable to the spread of wickedness. Part of Israel's sin is bound to her assimilation with foreign nations. Those alliances have religious, political, and cultural ramifications. Like a silly dove that has left home and cannot find its way back, Israel has slowly but surely wandered away from God and will have trouble finding her way back.

Application

When I was young, my father, brother, and I often went to antique car shows. We even traveled to Atlanta to attend some of the bigger events. The judges at those car shows carefully scrutinized every vehicle to determine the "Best of Show" awards. I recall one show that featured a row of Model T Fords, all painted black and all in pristine condition. To the casual observer, not a single detail would distinguish one car as being the best over the others. But then the judges put on white gloves and literally wiped the bottom of the engines to see which car was absolutely spotless. That's scrutiny!

Hosea reminds the Israelites that God has seen all of their sins. We would do well to remember God's scrutiny. Nothing about our lives is overlooked. God sees every transgression, hears every wayward word, and observes even our deepest thoughts. Nothing is hidden from God's sight. Yet we attempt to hide our sins from God. In fact, all we are doing is fooling ourselves. We want to ignore our sins and hope that maybe God will miss something in scrutinizing our lives. To scrutinize is to be closely watched and carefully examined. Truthfully, none of us can survive the "white glove" test. Whether we want to confess our sins or not, they are there. But here's the good news: though God is able to see our sinfulness, God looks beyond our mistakes and sees the person we will one day become. Does God have a casual attitude about our sins? No. Do they grieve God's heart? Yes. But God's gaze sees more than transgressions; it also sees our worth.

Prayer

Father, thank you for loving us this day, in spite of our sinfulness. Amen.

Day 870 — Hosea 8: The Rules Don't Apply to Me

> "Even though I gave them all my laws, they act as if those laws don't apply to them." Hosea 8:12 (NLT)

Observation
Hosea 8 opens with a call to sound the trumpet. Like an eagle flying over Israel, an enemy is coming that will bring destruction and judgment. The trumpet, or shofar, was used to signal danger. Hosea is rightly telling the nation that her sins will soon bring punishment. One of the sins revealed in this passage is the practice of appointing kings to rule without the consent and approval of God. Many of these kings were "as strangers" before God, meaning they did not know or worship God. Hosea refers to a "calf idol" of Samaria. This was most likely a golden statue used in Baal worship. Like the golden calf once shattered during the time of Moses at the base of Mount Sinai, God will crush this false deity. God clearly states that human-made idols cannot make divine, prophetic announcements. The people had called on Baal for abundance and blessings but instead received infertility and political turmoil. The nation, according to Hosea, will be swallowed up by other nations, partially because of her assimilation of other cultures and worship practices. And even though Israel is building strong fortresses, none of them will withstand the wrath that God is about to bring on the nation.

Application
Have you ever encountered someone who seems to think the rules don't apply to them? Maybe someone speeds past you on the interstate and you hope they will receive a ticket. Maybe someone cuts to the front of the line at the self-checkout station at the grocery. Maybe someone tries to board a plane before his section is called. We all know that there are rules and laws to govern behavior in a civilized society, and we are incensed when someone doesn't play by those rules. We look on such a person with disdain, believing them to be rude and arrogant.

According to the words of Hosea, God condemns the people of Israel for the same reasons. God has given them the law, and yet they act as though it doesn't apply to them. I wonder if the same words could be spoken of us at times. We know what God's word says about any number of things. Don't steal. Don't envy. Don't commit adultery. Don't lie. Don't fashion false gods. And yet we sometimes violate a rule, somehow believing that we are exempt and that the rules don't apply to us—only to "those people." We use the situational ethic that says, "It's okay to break the rules in this situation because…." Is it, really? Are we ever given a pass on God's rules? God is Lord of all, or God is not Lord at all.

Prayer
Father, forgive our arrogance that sometimes tricks us into bad behavior. Amen.

Day 871   Hosea 9: The Foolishness of Preaching

> "The time of Israel's punishment has come; the day of payment is here. Soon Israel will know this all too well. Because of your great sin and hostility, you say, 'The prophets are crazy and the inspired men are fools!'"
> Hosea 9:7 (NLT)

Observation
In chapter 9, Hosea announces Israel's harsh punishment for their worship of false idols and pagan deities. Hosea tells the people not even to think about the usual harvest celebrations. Because they have prostituted themselves with pagan gods in order to seek an abundant harvest, God promises to cut off their harvest. God will withhold blessings, and there will not be enough produce to sustain the land. The people will return to oppression and be forced into exile to Assyria. Because of the exile experience, they will not be able to celebrate various festivals, like the Festival of Booths that was normally set at the time of the harvest. Often, rebellious people declare that the prophets are fools and their words are empty and trite. In this chapter, Hosea declares that if he is a fool, it is because the people have made him crazy with their sins. He announces that God's glory will depart the land. Infertility and premature death will be the result.

Application
"The prophets are crazy and the inspired men are fools!" That's a harsh word for anyone attempting to speak on God's behalf or offer inspired teaching to others. The Apostle Paul once spoke about the "foolishness of what was preached" (1 Corinthians 1:21 NIV), indicating that some have come to salvation even through words that the world deems foolish. It is important to remember that many mysteries of God can seem like foolishness to those with little or no spiritual understanding. People think we are crazy to believe in a God we cannot see or hear. And yet there is such power in the gospel story and in our faith. Even though some may think our words are foolish, we are still bound to tell God's truth, because in God's words are found power, grace, and salvation. Maybe the problem is that we have tended to preach and teach more judgment than grace. We can easily condemn people for their improper behavior, but it is more difficult to speak and live out forgiveness and redemption. It is countercultural to offer others a second chance or to remind them that even the worst sinners get invited to the Table of Grace. But it is better to call ourselves fools for the sake of Christ than to neglect telling the story of his grace. Don't be surprised if someone ridicules or mocks the testimony of Christ you attempt to share. Just keep sowing the seed and let the Spirit do its work.

Prayer
Father, may we share our faith even if doing so makes us seem foolish. Amen.

Day 872 — Hosea 10: Breaking Up the Hard Ground

> "Plow up the hard ground of your hearts, for now is the time to seek the Lord, that he may come and shower righteousness upon you."
> Hosea 10:12b (NLT)

Observation

Often in the pages of the Old Testament, Israel is compared to a vineyard that God manages and causes to bear good fruit. Hosea presents this image once again in chapter 10. However, instead of a luxurious vine, Israel is depicted as a degenerate vine unable to bear the fruit of righteousness. She is judged for her many sins, especially idolatry. The extent of her idolatry is exemplified by an idol at Beth-aven. Later in the chapter, a second agricultural metaphor is described. Israel is compared to a trained heifer taught to bear the yoke of God and sow seeds of righteousness. She was trained to sow with obedience that would lead to good fruit. However, her sins have forced her to be judged harshly. She will bear only wickedness and injustice. One of her other sins is also described: that of trusting in her military power and not in the power of Almighty God.

Application

I've never been much of a farmer. I've never had to till the soil and break up a lot of hard ground. But I have dug a few holes in my time. In fact, the hardest soil I remember digging was in a small community in Central Brazil. Our team was there on a mission trip to build a church, and part of my role was to dig out and form up the front sidewalk leading to the church building. The soil was a mixture of clay, gravel, and dirt. What should have taken only an hour or so to excavate took the better part of two days. I used a pickax, a shovel, and a post-hole digger. But at the end of the week, the concrete was poured, and I am confident that the walkway still exists today.

In his prophetic words, Hosea tells the people of God to plow up the hard ground of their hearts. Certainly, the challenge would be difficult. And it remains a formidable task. Over time, our hearts get jaded, hardened, set in their ways. We let past experiences, defeats, and mistakes slowly destroy the pliability of our hearts. But as always, God longs to do a new thing in our lives. God wants to take away our hearts of stone and give us hearts of flesh, ones that feel compassion and empathy, ones that want what is best for others, ones that forgive and seek the restoration of others. If I were to run a scan on your heart this morning, what would I discover? Would I find hard ground that seems impervious? Or would I find a heart always open to change, new perspective, and transformation? Expose your heart to God and see how God longs to change what is found there.

Prayer

Father God, create in us a new heart and a new spirit. Amen.

Day 873   Hosea 11: The Proof of Allegiance

> "For my people are determined to desert me. They call me the Most High, but they don't truly honor me." Hosea 11:7 (NLT)

Observation

Hosea 11 speaks of God's stubborn love for Israel. Even though the people have fallen into a long pattern of disobedience, idolatry, and pagan worship practices, God still refuses to completely abandon them. In this passage, Israel is depicted as the "firstborn" of God whom God has raised, mentored, nurtured, and taught. And yet, despite God's care and compassion, the nation has run after other idols. God's effort has gone underappreciated. God will punish them by plunging them into captivity. Just as the nation was once oppressed by Egypt, they will now be held captive by Assyria. God will turn away from Israel for a season as a means of discipline. Yet God will limit the punishment. This chapter speaks of hope as God promises to reclaim the people and bring them home from exile.

Application

As mentioned earlier, I experienced double-knee replacement surgery a few years ago. It was quite an ordeal. I was on blood thinners and pain meds for a while and endured physical therapy for almost four months. If you have ever rehabbed a joint replacement (knee, shoulder, hip, etc.), you will remember going through the work of PT. I had all kinds of exercises, machines to manipulate, and stretches to work out the kinks. It doesn't take long to develop a love-hate relationship with your therapist. One the one hand, they are helping you to recover, but on the other hand, they push you through a lot of pain. My therapist was named "Angel." Though she was certainly an angel of mercy, there were days when she seemed more like an "angel of death"! I called her my therapist because she helped me through therapy. But she could only function in that role as long as I obeyed her instruction and worked hard at her prescribed exercises. It's one thing to call someone by a title; it's another to honor the title by responding appropriately.

    Most of us readily call Jesus Christ our "Savior and Lord." That phrase seems to roll off the tongue. But do we take the title seriously? Or are we just honoring Jesus with our lips? Lordship implies authority, submission, surrender, and loyalty. Christ will not be our "Lord" unless we are willing to yield all things under his command. "All things" refers to every facet of our lives—our words, our actions, our purses, our thoughts, our generosity, etc. Unless we are willing to claim that we are fully Christ's servants, then the title "Lord" seems hollow. As Lord, he has the right to govern our days, direct our thoughts, and motivate our actions. This day as you proclaim his title of lordship, vow to respond to his guidance.

Prayer

Father God, teach us to surrender our lives, lovingly and willingly, to our Lord. Amen.

Day 874 Hosea 12: Love and Justice

> "So now, come back to your God. Act with love and justice, and always depend on him." Hosea 12:6 (NLT)

Observation
In chapter 12, Hosea continues to speak words of judgment against Israel for her sins of idolatry. She has been unfaithful in her covenant with God. Contrasted with her infidelity, God is depicted as being deliberately faithful. Hosea suggests that part of Israel's sin is her "pursuit of the east wind," a reference to a foolish alliance with Assyria. Like the severe, scorching heat, this alliance will undo Israel. The story of Jacob is also briefly remembered in this text. His story illustrates that just as Jacob overcame disobedience and received the blessing of God, so, too, Israel can rediscover God's blessing with a repentant heart. Hosea reminds Israel that the harsh punishment coming her way should not be a surprise. Many prophets have predicted and proclaimed God's judgment through the years. Yet, even amid this turbulent period of judgment, God will shepherd the faithful people through the preaching and actions of servants like Hosea.

Application
Remember the childhood game of Simon Says? We all played it. The leader stood in front of a group of players and commanded them to do certain things like "pat your head, raise your hand, stand on one foot." Players were instructed to ignore any command that didn't begin with the words "Simon Says." If Simon commanded it, the player was to obey. "Simon says, 'Nod your head,' or "Simon says, 'Take a step forward.'" Anyone who acted without Simon's instruction was eliminated from the game.

As Hosea calls the nation to repentance, he urges them to "Turn back to God by acting with love and justice." God longs for God's people to act with love and justice. Love must be the fundamental bedrock, the first step we take as we approach others. We love first and argue about differences later. Love becomes the motivation. Because we care about, respect, and value the person before us, we treat them with civility, kindness, and compassion. When we establish love as a first step, we are then to act with justice. God is not calling us to judge others or to condemn their behavior. Instead, we are called to act justly. That means we pursue the injustices of our culture that oppress, demean, and harm our fellow human beings. We must speak to the systemic evils around us. We must decry racism, abuse, exploitation, and sexism. We must fight against hunger, poverty, and the ill treatment of the oppressed. To come back to God implies that we return to the noble struggles to which God's Kingdom first called us. We engage the battles of the King.

Prayer
Father, as we live this day, may we act with love and pursue justice. Amen.

Day 875   Hosea 13: Disappearing Act

> "Therefore, they will disappear like the morning mist, like dew in the morning sun, like chaff blown by the wind, like smoke from a chimney."
> Hosea 13:3 (NLT)

Observation
Hosea 13 speaks vividly about God's impending destructive judgment on the nation of Israel for her idolatry. It is a frightening look at how brutal the attacks of foreign nations like Assyria will be. The chapter begins with a specific look at the past, present, and future history of the tribe of Ephraim, the most prosperous of the tribes. Hosea speaks of her sins and idol worship and the resultant judgment that is coming. By extension, these words are also meant for all of Israel. Hosea briefly recalls Israel's history in Egypt when God recued the nation from oppression and provided for the people's needs in the wilderness. And yet, even with God's provisions, the nation soon forgot God and worshipped the golden calf at the foot of Sinai. The same series of events is unfolding again: in spite of God's multiple blessings, the people have turned towards false idols. No political leaders are capable of leading the nation against the attacks of other nations. The chapter ends on a somber and scary note; the nation will feel the brunt of God's judgment.

Application
A couple of decades ago, my family lived in Gatlinburg, right in the heart of the Great Smoky Mountains. In fact, our home was less than a mile from the boundaries of the National Park. We enjoyed hiking the trails, seeing all kinds of wildlife, and watching the beautiful display of fall leaves each year. The nickname "Smoky Mountains" is drawn from the early-morning mist that often hovers in the valleys, exposing only the highest peaks. I always enjoyed the peaceful, serene view as this mist gently covered the hills and valleys. It was also fascinating to watch the mountains as the sun's warmth began to hit that morning mist. Within a few brief minutes, the mist would totally dissipate. The heavy blanket of white fog would quickly disappear.

    When describing the tribe of Ephraim, Hosea suggests that the people will disappear like the morning mist. He is speaking of the effects of God's judgment on the land. Today, I want to tweak the meaning a little. Let's think not of one of the tribes disappearing but of what God causes to disappear from our lives. Through the atoning death of God's Son, God has caused our sins to disappear. They vanish. They dissipate. They are forever eliminated because of Christ's sacrifice and God's offer of grace. Many of us labor under the guilt and shame of our past, but God has a better future planned for each of us. God removes our sins like the vanishing mist of morning and makes us whole.

Prayer
Father, we remain debtors to your grace. Thank you for our salvation. Amen.

Day 876   Hosea 14: Good-luck Charms?

> "O Israel, stay away from idols! I am the one who answers your prayers and cares for you. I am like a tree that is always green; all your fruit comes from me." Hosea 14:8 (NLT)

Observation
This closing chapter of Hosea offers a final call to return to God. Repentance will bring about the forgiveness and restoration of Israel. In calling the nation to repentance, Hosea even gives the people the words they should use to pray. First, offer God a word of praise from your lips. Second, admit your misplaced faith in political alliances, military might, and pagan idols. Third, affirm the mercy of Almighty God. In response to Israel's contrition, God promises to heal and love the nation. God will be like a dew bringing refreshment to a dry land. God will restore the beauty of the nation, and new growth will become evident. The people will flourish once again. The book closes with a last call from God to move beyond idolatry and a postscript telling the wise to understand these things.

Application
Sports fans are among the most superstitious people on the planet. In order to bring good luck to their teams, they will do almost anything. I have friends who wear the exact same clothes, eat the exact same food, and sit in the exact same chair each week in order to help their team win. Another friend won't allow himself to attend a game. The last time he went to a game back in 1997, his team lost, and he is convinced that he was the reason why. In order to help his team win, he must stay at home and watch on television. I know one guy who will not shave during the season, believing that doing so will bring his team bad luck.

The people of ancient Israel had their own set of good-luck charms. In order to gain prosperity, health, and abundant crops, they would pray to and bow down before any pagan idol they could find. They believed inanimate objects could bring a special karma over the land. By trusting in false deities, they turned their hearts away from God. In our focus verse, God is reminding the people that their trust and dependency must be in God alone. God is the One who answers prayer. God is the source of all blessings. God is the giver of life and the keeper of Israel. Success will come to the nation, not through a good-luck charm but through contrite hearts, fervent prayers, and faithful obedience. Sometimes we treat God like a good-luck charm. We call on God when we need a favor. We dust off the Bible when we are desperate. We go to church and give an offering to please God. We often forget that we are already the objects of God's grace and love. God does not desire flippant prayers or coins in the plate but the allegiance of our heats and the loyalty of our confessions.

Prayer
Father, forgive our foolish idol worship and call us once again to faithfulness. Amen.

Day 877 — Joel 1: Telling the Story of God

> "Tell your children about it in the years to come, and let your children tell their children. Pass the story down from generation to generation."
> Joel 1:3 (NLT)

Observation
God called the prophet Joel to speak to the people of Judah and Jerusalem just prior to the Babylonian invasion of the region. He speaks to the priests and elders of Judah. Written in Hebrew poetry, his words are rich in imagery and emotion. He calls his listeners to repentance in light of the coming Day of the Lord. The book opens with a description of a plague of locusts that overwhelmed the land. Joel sees this as God's judgment. He will use the image of destruction to talk about the future Day of the Lord, most likely an eschatological prophecy. The destruction wrought by a swarm of locusts was a familiar scene in the Middle East. In this case, the destruction was total. As a metaphor for God's judgment, the locust plague illustrates the severe judgment coming to the nation of Israel. The people are called to weep and wail over their losses. Joel instructs them to cry out to the Lord for salvation and hope.

Application
My dad has begun a process writing down many of his life stories, some of which I have never heard. As he ages, he is fearful that some of the stories will be lost to time, and therefore some of the family heritage and history will be forgotten. He is writing them down so the stories will live on. It is a meaningful discipline for him as he writes and also for us who will one day read and remember.

The prophet Joel reminds his listeners to pass down the stories of God from one generation to the next. In this particular case, he wants his listeners to remind their children and grandchildren of the great locust plague. We know the value of passing along great stories. All of us have a canon of stories that we carry with us through our lives. Some of them are stories we inherited from our parents and even grandparents. And some are experiences we have had along the way. We tell them when time and occasion allow because we think they are meaningful and important. It's the same with the stories of faith. We should talk to our children and grandchildren about the moments when our faith intersected with our lives in a powerful way. Remember the day you first confessed Christ? Remember your baptism experience? Remember the answer to a specific prayer? Don't let the memory fade and the story go untold. Just as we would tell the story of a great and memorable experience, we should tell the story of the ways God is present in our lives. Pass along the stories of faith. They are important to us all.

Prayer
God, may the stories of our faith be important enough for us to tell them. Amen.

Day 878 — Joel 2: Gender Equality

> "Then, after doing all those things, I will pour out my Spirit upon all people. Your sons and daughters will prophesy. Your old men will dream dreams, and your young men will see visions. In those days I will pour out my Spirit even on servants—men and women alike." Joel 2:28-29 (NLT)

Observation
As Joel describes the coming Day of the Lord, he outlines two components. The "evening" is a time of judgment described in the first 17 verses of this chapter. The "morning" is a description of God's blessing following judgment, described in verses 18-32. The poetic language is so stylishly written that it is hard to distinguish the object of Joel's words. Is he continuing to describe a plague of locusts, or is he using that metaphor to describe the onslaught of an invading army? Read through an eschatological lens, the powerful plague is merely a description of the swift and terrible future Day of the Lord. Joel is told to "sound the alarm" and call the people to repentance. The people are challenged to return to the Lord. God is gracious and kind and will relent from destruction. The second half of the chapter, in fact, indicates that God will respond to the people's repentance and will bless them. God's blessings will come like "the early rain." This period of blessing will coincide with the sending of the Messiah.

Application
Gender equality is often discussed in various contexts in our culture. There are a number of inequalities in terms of salary scales, job access, and upward mobility. Women are often predestined to lesser employment opportunities and lesser pay. In some cultures, the roles of men and women are distinctively different. Men are seen as the wage earners, while women are relegated to stay at home, raise the kids, and cook the meals. Fortunately, in American culture, many gender roles are slowly being redefined. Though there is still a long way to go, the lines of distinction between gender roles and opportunities are beginning to soften, and that's a good thing.

Yet one of the places where gender equality seems stuck in an earlier time is in the life of the church and in the work of ministry. Many still hold to a view that only men can preach from the pulpit, while women are to keep silent in the church. But take a look at the prophetic words of Joel: "My Spirit will be poured out on all people. Your sons and daughters will prophesy." It seems that in the eyes of God, there are no second-class citizens. God will enable, equip, and call whomever God chooses to move the Kingdom forward. Rather than argue about gender politics, why don't we affirm all of those whom God calls?

Prayer
God, thank you for sending your Spirit upon all people…male and female. Amen.

Day 879   Joel 3: Turning Weaklings into Warriors

"Hammer your plowshares into swords and your pruning hooks into spears. Train even your weaklings to be warriors." Joel 3:10 (NLT)

Observation
In this third and final chapter of Joel, the prophet speaks specific words of judgment on certain Gentile nations for their mistreatment of Israel. As he closes his words of prophecy, Joel once again pronounces God's blessing and deliverance on the nation. In the opening section of the chapter, God uses the pronoun "my" seven times. This indicates God's personal relationship with the people of Israel. All of the Gentile nations will be brought to the Valley of Jehoshaphat (which means "Yahweh judges"), where they will muster into one great army at the end of the age. Rather than successfully attack Jerusalem, they will be judged for their former theft of Israel's treasures and the enslavement of her people. All the armies will be drawn into the battle; "the harvest of judgment will be ripe," declares Joel. The Lord will defeat these foes and bless Judah and Jerusalem forever.

Application
One of my fondest memories of high school is playing football. I played on the varsity team for three years as a wide receiver and a defensive back. During my senior year, I was privileged to start all of the games. It was an exciting time in my life and for our team. We were successful that final year and actually made it to the playoffs. I attribute that success to Coach Charlie Davidson, who inspired us to play beyond our abilities and believe in the possibilities of success each week. Looking at us on paper, you wouldn't think we would be very successful. We were a small team; only three players weighed more than 200 pounds. Most of us were scrawny and scrappy but determined. Coach Davidson formed us into warriors who offered our best each Friday night when we stepped out onto the gridiron.

God speaks through Joel, reminding the leaders of the nation to train even the weakest to become warriors. I like that image. Faith offers each of us the opportunity to attempt great and mighty things through the leadership of God's Spirit. As the expression states, "Attempt great things for God…expect great things from God." When anyone looks at us, they will see that we are not much of a fighting force. We are weak, flawed, and insufficient. Who are we to dare take on the challenges of our age and culture? But God calls us, equips us, and positions us to make a difference. Though our bodies may be weak and our minds sometimes unclear, God is able to turn us into warriors. What makes us strong is not our abilities, intellect, or actions. It is the power of God at work in us and through us. Though we are merely human, God calls us to be warriors. And in God's strength, we will become victors.

Prayer
Father, though we are weak, train us into warriors for the sake of your Kingdom. Amen.

Day 880   Amos 1: The Sin of Slavery

> "This is what the Lord says: 'The people of Tyre have sinned again and again, and I will not let them go unpunished! They broke their treaty of brotherhood with Israel, selling whole villages as slaves to Edom.'"
> Amos 1:9 (NLT)

Observation
Most Bible students are somewhat familiar with the preaching of Amos. The book's themes and metaphors are well known. Amos was a Judean farmer and a shepherd of his own sheep. He also tended a grove of Sycamore trees that produced a fig-like fruit. In the growing season, every individual piece of fruit had to be pierced so that it would grow to maturity—a labor-intensive and tedious job. Amos was from the city of Tekoa, about five miles Southeast of Bethlehem. His prophetic ministry was short but powerful. His key theme is God's passionate concern for justice. Amos calls the leaders of Israel who live in Bethel to repentance and reformation. Bethel had become a center of pagan worship. Amos begins by proclaiming judgment on Israel's surrounding nations that have committed grievous sins in the eyes of God. It is as though Amos is drawing a noose around Israel, slowly encircling the nation in order to pronounce judgment on the people for exhausting God's patience.

Application
Slavery has always been a problem. In our twenty-first century contextualization of the subject, most of us reflect back to the United States' early history when unscrupulous men brought people in chains from Africa and sold them as slaves to work on plantations and large estates. But the problem goes much deeper and has a longer history. In our focus verse, Amos describes the enslavement of Israelites who were sold to the wealthy in Edom. More than half of the world's population during the time of Christ lived in slavery. And today, more people are enslaved (numerically) than at any other time in human history. It was, it is, and it will always be morally wrong for any person to control, manipulate, own, or possess another human being. We should not hide our eyes from the problems of slavery, human trafficking, and bondage that are alive and well in our modern culture. It is easy to ignore the problems of slavery from our privileged positions of wealth, power, and security. But we have a responsibility to work towards justice, to end violence, and to strive for the well-being of every person. Just because you don't own slaves doesn't mean you can ignore those who do. When good people are silent, evil prospers.

Prayer
God, may we become angry and active against the things the make you angry. Amen.

Day 881 — Amos 2: Misplaced Trust

> "On that day the most courageous of your fighting men will drop their weapons and run for their lives" Amos 2:16 (NLT)

Observation

Amos 2 opens with a description of the sins of Moab, a nation located just to the southeast of Israel. Among her sins was the desecration of the bones of Edom's king. The nation had also practiced idolatry by worshipping their national god, Chemosh. Then Amos's attention turns to Judah (southern kingdom) and Israel (northern kingdom). God held them to a higher standard because there were God's covenant people. God's words of condemnation on Israel are particularly harsh and specific. The Israelites have corrupted the courts and sold many of the poor into slavery. Those without power or influence are denied justice. They are left to a life of poverty, oppression, and insecurity. Amos lists other unlawful behaviors. The people have forgotten that God is the source of their strength and prosperity. But the prophet clearly warns them that even the strongest warriors among them cannot save them from God's punishment.

Application

Have you ever been disappointed by a car to the extent that you sold it? I have. As a car owner, it's important to have a sense of trust in your car. The vehicle should start when you need it to start. It should get you from point A to point B safely and securely. It should offer reliable service for years…at least that is the expectation. But sometimes you get a "lemon." I once owned a Volkswagen Rabbit. It was the worst car I ever owned. It always seemed to have trouble starting. Some days the electrical system didn't work. The radio fell out of the dashboard on one occasion. I remember the day it left me stranded in the middle of the street in Harrodsburg, Kentucky. (That wasn't the first time.) I spoke these words to the car (along with others): "You have disappointed me long enough. I've got to let you go." I sold it the next day.

Sometimes we place our trust in things that will inevitably disappoint us. We trust in simple machines. We trust in medications. We trust in advice. We trust in our health. We trust in our weapons. And yes, we often trust in human beings who are as flawed as we are. And we wonder why life doesn't go the way we hope. The ancient Israelites discovered that trusting in their mighty men of valor and in their superior weapons was foolish in the face of God's sure and swift justice. Where are you placing your trust today—in your own wisdom, your savings account, your friends? If so, reconsider. "Trust in the Lord with all your heart; do not depend on your own understanding. Seek his will in all you do, and he will show you which path to take" (Proverbs 3:5-6 NLT).

Prayer

Father, may our dependency and trust be ultimately in you alone. Amen.

Day 882　　　　　　　　　　Amos 3: Great Expectations

> "From among all the families on the earth, I have been intimate with you alone. That is why I must punish you for all your sins." Amos 3:2 (NLT)

Observation
As Amos 3 opens, God refers to Israel as "family"—an expression of a close and personal relationship with the people. In the following verses God says that the relationship with Israel is exclusive and unique; no other nation has received God's favor or covenant relationship. But because the nation has not responded in faithfulness, God will judge her. God asks a number of rhetorical questions that indicate the certainty and authority of God's judgment upon Israel. God is sovereign and will do as God wills. The people are told that there is no value in trying to silence the words of the prophet, for he speaks only what God has directed. His words of judgment are hard for the people to hear. Other nations, Philistia and Egypt, are called to gather on the surrounding mountains and witness the judgment of Israel. At least they have not received and then ignored a relationship with God the way Israel has. Later in the chapter, God promises to cut off the horns of the pagan altars in various Israelite cities. This action will reveal the weakness of the pagan gods and the futility of worshipping them.

Application
Years ago, I served as a summer youth intern at my home church in Rome, Georgia. One night, the youth group gathered for a fellowship event behind the Youth Center. We played volleyball and ate pizza. As the night wore on, a water balloon battle broke out. I became a ringleader and soaked a lot of people. Several of the girls got a little angry…something about their hair and makeup. The next morning, I was summoned to the Youth Minister's office and called out for my actions. I used the old excuse: "Everybody else was doing the same thing." He said, "But you are a leader, and I expected more of you." Ouch. Sometimes it hurts to be corrected.

One of the reasons Israel would receive God's judgment was because of the people's privileged relationship with God. They were chosen, blessed, set aside, and made special. Yet they acted flippantly with the influential leadership role that God had given them. Rather than embrace the relationship, practice faithfulness, and become a light to the nations, they ignored the covenant and acted like the other pagan nations surrounding them. How well have we taken on the mantle of responsibility to truly be the "people of God"? Do we act with kindness, forgive lavishly, and serve faithfully? Do we care for the marginalized, uplift those who struggle, and seek justice for all?

Prayer
Father, help us to value our calling and live it out well. Amen.

Day 883   Amos 4: Stubborn Hearts and Closed Minds

> "'I brought hunger to every city and famine to every town. But still you would not return to me,' says the Lord." Amos 4:6 (NLT)

Observation
Amos 4 describes Israel's failure to learn from past mistakes and take corrective action. The nation continues to sin, though God has sent warning after warning. The chapter begins with a condemnation of the rich women of Bashan who oppress the poor and crush the needy. Covered with grasslands, the region of Bashan was renowned for its sleek, well-fed cattle. Amos calls these women the "Cows of Bashan." He also describes the extent of devastation that will befall the cities of Israel as a result of God's judgment. The walls will be breached, and as people are led away into exile, there will be no need for them to walk through the city gates; the holes in the walls will be large enough. Verses 6-11 describe five calamities that have already affected the Israelites as God attempts to bring them back to repentance: exhaustion of food and supplies, drought, locusts, plague and warfare, and destruction of cities.

Application
Some people just don't get it. They can't seem to take a hint. For example, take the poor fellow who has his heart set on a certain young lady. He calls her. He sends gifts. He tries his best to impress her. But she turns him down. She tells him that she is not interested and already has a boyfriend, but he keeps hanging around until he becomes a pest. Or consider the petulant child who wants to stay up late and play video games. He asks and pleads and begs and promises, but the parents remain steadfast in their resolve and send him to bed. He goes to bed angry and disappointed, and the parents go to bed frustrated by his behavior. Some folks are just stubborn.

    Take the case of the ancient Israelites. God longed to reestablish a relationship with them. God sent prophets to proclaim God's intentions and created guidelines in scripture. And yet they continued to choose disobedience and rebellion. Even when they got a taste of God's judgment, they still made poor choices. Admittedly, we are not much better. We struggle with stubborn hearts and closed minds. Even when a prayer is answered or a sin is forgiven, we fall right back into the pattern of disobedience and idolatry. Why can't we get it right? Because of our human nature. As the old hymn states, "Prone to wander, Lord I feel it, prone to leave the God I love." You are going to make some mistakes today. You are going to disappoint the Father. So am I. But God will not love you and me any less. Rather than abuse God's grace with stubbornness, let's allow gratitude to rule the day.

Prayer
Father, take away our bent to sinning and make us obedient in all things. Amen.

Day 884   Amos 5: What Pleases God

> "But let justice run down like water, And righteousness like a mighty stream." Amos 5:24 (NKJV)

Observation

Amos 5 is similar to a funeral dirge. It speaks of the certainty of judgment. The land was a gift to Israel, a place where the people could live and prosper. But because of their idolatry, they had turned it into a place of death and burial. If Israel attempted to send out armies to fight the ones God sent to bring about justice, their armies would return decimated. Verse 7 mentions "wormwood," a plant with a bitter taste. It appears frequently in the Old Testament as a metaphor for sin and bitterness. The people's transgressions had left a bitter taste in God's mouth. One of their sins was worshipping the stars. God reminds the people that God alone created the heavens and set the stars in their courses. Rather than worship God, the people worship the things God created. Other sins are also described. Amos speaks of the unfair taxation and exploitation that the rich have enacted upon the poor. They continue to sin as though fidelity to God does not matter. Many welcome the coming "Day of the Lord," thinking it will bring prosperity and restoration to Israel, when in fact it will mean destruction.

Application

God desires a lot of things from us: loyalty, obedience, compassion, and honest worship. God desires time with us. God wants to hear our prayers, know our thoughts, and interact with the desires of our hearts. God also wants us to represent the Lord before the nations. In other words, we have to care about the things that God cares about. We have to show compassion to the marginalized, feed the hungry, clothe the naked, and tell the story of God's Son Jesus. It is clear to me that God wants us to be engaged with culture, attempting to share truth, model God's forgiveness, and extend grace to others. God wants us to work on justice issues and righteous living. Notice our focus verse. In a couple of his speeches, Martin Luther King, Jr., made these words popular in our culture. God wants justice to roll down like water and righteousness to wash over our land like a mighty stream.

Justice and righteousness, especially in the context of the American legal system, is not always fair and equal to all races, ethnicities, and religious preferences. Some are denied fair representation. Some are denied access to good legal counsel. Some are treated as guilty long before they are ever tried. We have a role to play as God's representatives on earth. We have to champion the marginalized. We have to work for equality and justice. We must make the causes of the poor and underserved our causes.

Prayer

God, burden us with the responsibility of bringing justice and fairness to our land. Amen.

Day 885 — Amos 6: A House of Cards

> "When the Lord gives the command, homes both great and small will be smashed to pieces." Amos 6:11 (NLT)

Observation

Amos 6 offers words of warning and woe to those living in Zion and Samaria. Zion (Jerusalem) was the capital of Judah, the southern kingdom. Samaria was the capital of Israel, the northern kingdom. At the time of Amos's prophecy, both kingdoms enjoyed military might and economic prosperity. The leaders of these capital cities considered themselves "notable persons." Those in Samaria boasted that no other nation was as strong as Israel. But this idea that they "were too strong for destruction" was a false notion. The Assyrians would soon overrun their land. Amos warns about the extravagant lifestyles of the rich who profited by stealing the wealth (livestock and crops) of the poor. In an ironic twist, those who were the "leaders" would soon be "led" into exile, where they would be powerless and pitiable. Their luxurious strongholds and palaces would be destroyed. Amos uses two metaphors to describe the impossibility of escape from judgment: "Can a horse gallop up a cliff? Can oxen plow solid rock?" Israel will soon be defeated on all borders.

Application

Have you ever constructed a house of cards? You take one card and lean it against another. Then you add a few more and maybe even attempt to construct a second level to your "house." But from the beginning, you know it is a tenuous process. One false move, one sudden breeze...and the house will collapse.

We spend a lot of time constructing our own houses—not the ones of brick, mortar, and lumber but the strongholds where we place our attitudes, prejudices, and opinions. We carefully build layer upon layer until our minds are too jaded, our thoughts too rigid, and our beliefs too unbending. We get set in our ways. We build huge walls that distance us from those who are different in opinion, in thought, in gender, and in skin tone. We cloister ourselves away and hope not to encounter the outside world. We build mental structures and allow ourselves to reside only in those places.

Maybe it's time, as our focus verse suggests, for God to smash our "homes" to pieces. Maybe it's time for us to be open to the fresh wind of the Spirit who longs to transform our thoughts, reprioritize our actions, and reorient our values. Do we need to let our foolish houses of cards come crashing down? Is it time to tear down the structures created by our negative humanity and dark emotions so that Christ can do a new work in us?

Prayer

God, tear down the walls of resentment, hatred, and selfishness we have created. Amen.

Day 886   Amos 7: The Call of God for the Ordinary Man

> "But the Lord called me away from my flock and told me, 'Go and prophesy to my people in Israel.'" Amos 7:15 (NLT)

Observation

Chapter 7 begins the final section of Amos in which the prophet announces a series of five visions, all of which describe the punishment of Israel. Amos starts with a vision of a great locust plague. These insects will strip every green leaf and twig throughout the land and cause many of the trees to die. Amos makes the case before God that such a plague would bring a crippling economic blow to the land because Israel is "small and weak." He prays that God might halt the destruction. God responds to this prayer and chooses to extend grace by not bringing the plague. Then Amos describes the next vision, a fierce and terrible fire that God will bring upon the land that will consume all of Israel. Again, Amos prays for leniency and God again relents. The next vision is one of a plumb line. Like a skilled craftsman who uses a plumb line to measure the careful, straight construction of a wall, so God will judge Israel to see how obedient and true the nation has become. Amos' words anger a priest named Amaziah, who reports to King Jeroboam. Amaziah tells Amos to go back to Judah and prophesy there. Amos, however, affirms that the Lord alone has called him to prophesy. In response to Amaziah's treachery, Amos pronounces judgment on Amaziah and his family.

Application

From the time that I was a high school senior, I began to sense a strong calling to enter the ministry. I headed off to Samford University in pursuit of that sense of calling and in the prayerful hope that I would gain clarity. And I did. About halfway through college, God's calling for my life focused on the role of a pastor. When I finished college, I headed to seminary for further study and later began a 32-year career as a pastor. For many who serve in professional ministry, the story is much the same. God calls a person out of their current vocation and life pursuits and prepares them for full-time work as a pastor, youth minister, or other ministry. Many of us pull up roots and head to grad school to learn how to minister effectively. But for most people, God's calling does not require a complete reorientation of life; it requires a reorientation of purpose. Amos was a shepherd and farmer. God called him for a season to go and preach to Israel. God used him amid his day-to-day life. Most people will never be called to professional ministry, but they will be called to bear testimony to Christ in their everyday pursuits. God still calls the ordinary to do extraordinary work.

Prayer

God, today may each of us bear testimony to you in the day-to-day stuff of life. Amen.

Day 887 — Amos 8: Starved for a Word

> "'The time is surely coming,' says the Sovereign Lord, 'when I will send a famine on the land—not a famine of bread or water but of hearing the words of the Lord.'" Amos 8:11 (NLT)

Observation

Amos 8 contains the fourth vision of God's judgment upon Israel (after the locust plague, the fire, and the plumb line). This time, Amos sees a basket filled with ripe summer fruit. The message is simple: the time is ripe for the impending judgment of God to fall upon the land. Like the fresh fruit contained in the basket, Israel will soon be consumed. The palace singers, who once composed songs of praise and gladness, will turn to wailing as bodies of the slain begin to cover the land. So many will die that citizens will bury them in silence because there is no time to mourn. God's harsh judgment is due to many sins like the oppression of the needy, religious hypocrisy, and the use of unjust scales by merchants. "Waves" of terror and destruction will sweep across the land. Darkness will cover the earth. (Two solar eclipses occurred in 784 BC and 763 BC) The people will suffer, not merely from famine caused by a lack of food but also from famine cause by a lack of spiritual instruction from God. God will no longer be revealed through the words of the prophets. The people will crave a word of hope from God but will not receive it.

Application

On two separate occasions, I have taught a group of bi-vocational pastors in a rural region of Honduras. I taught this group with the help of an interpreter. I speak absolutely no Spanish, and they spoke absolutely no English. Each afternoon, following the teaching session, my translator left the camp and headed back to his home in Tegucigalpa. Throughout the evening and overnight hours, I had no interaction with the pastors because of the language barrier. I could gesture and wave, but I desperately craved a conversation. This pattern continued during my stay in Honduras. I remember how excited and relieved I felt to arrive back in the United States, where I could understand the language and join in dialogue.

Sometimes we crave a word of conversation. Sometimes we want to talk with others, to hear their voices and know their thoughts. Imagine how desperate the ancient Israelites felt when Amos told them God was sending a famine of words. God had repeatedly warned them, but because of their insolence, no further words would come from the Lord. Perhaps we take for granted how exciting and important it is for us to hear a word from God. God speaks through scripture, through servants, through songs, and through creation. Daily, we know of God's closeness and care. Let us rejoice this day that God chooses to speak to us.

Prayer

God, may we be reminded this day that you desire to share yourself with us. Amen.

Day 888 — Amos 9: The Blessings of God

> "'The time will come,' says the Lord, 'when the grain and grapes will grow faster than they can be harvested. Then the terraced vineyards on the hills of Israel will drip with sweet wine!'" Amos 9:13 (NLT)

Observation

This closing chapter of Amos reveals the fifth and final vision of Israel's impending destruction. In this final vision, Amos sees the Lord standing beside the altar at Bethel. God commands that the supportive columns be destroyed so that the entire structure will collapse. Any people surviving the destruction will be found and killed. Whether the sinful idolaters try to escape by hiding in the earth or on the highest hill, surely the righteous wrath of God will find them. Amos again expresses God's sovereignty over all the earth. God will uproot both people and place in this judgment. The final portion of chapter 9, however, is not devoted to judgment but to God's eventual restoration of the people. A faithful remnant of the people will survive. In the coming Messianic age, the dynasty of David will be restored, and the land, along with its people, will flourish.

Application

Many years ago, while I served in my first pastorate in a rural community in Middle Kentucky, well-meaning church leaders decided that I needed a garden in my backyard. Early one Saturday morning, I was awakened by the sound of a huge John Deere tractor plowing up the yard. The jet-black soil was turned over and seeds were planted…many seeds. An older gentleman asked about our favorite vegetables. His plan was to plant a little of whatever we wanted. He planted corn, potatoes, squash, watermelons, green peppers, and tomatoes. In fact, he planted 140 tomato plants! We had so many tomatoes that summer that we couldn't give them away fast enough. Every day brought hundreds of ripe tomatoes. We supplied the whole town!

In describing the restoration of Israel, God mentions that grain and grapes will grow faster than they can be harvested. The image is one of great abundance and overflowing blessings. Let's consider our blessings for a moment. Your blessings today may or may not consist of too many grapes and too many tomatoes. But you and I both live amid great abundance. God's blessings are fresh each morning and overwhelming to consider. The fact that you are alive today and have the ability to even read this devotional is a sign of God's blessing. You have life…you have family…you have friends…you have possessions…you have work…you have clothing…you have food…you have shelter. But most of all, you have hope—the hope of eternal life and the hope of God's continual presence.

Prayer

God, may we be reminded this day of the abundance of our blessings. Amen.

Day 889　　　　　　　　　　Obadiah: Your Brother's Keeper

> "When they were invaded, you stood aloof, refusing to help them. Foreign invaders carried off their wealth and cast lots to divide up Jerusalem, but you acted like one of Israel's enemies." Obadiah 11 (NLT)

Observation
Obadiah's prophetic words fill a single chapter. This is the shortest of all Old Testament books. Obadiah was an obscure prophet who spoke to the people of the southern kingdom of Judah. His words, however, focus primarily on the nation of Edom. Edom was situated to the southeast of Judah, and the two nations shared a common border along with a common heritage. The Edomites were descendants of Esau. The conflict that arose during the time of Jacob and Esau continued through many generations. Even though they shared a common ancestry, the nation of Edom had refused to act as a brother to the nation of Judah. When Jerusalem was attacked and the people scattered, Edom did nothing to help. Obadiah, whose name means "Worshipper of God," had the conviction that God would intervene in human history and bring justice to the world. The first portion of the book (vv. 1-18) declares God's judgment on Edom. The second portion (vv. 19-21) speaks of God's full restoration of Israel. The Edomites, who felt that they were militarily invincible, would be judged harshly for their mistreatment of the Israeli exiles.

Application
Am I my brother's keeper? This question has been asked literally since the beginning of time, when Cain offered such a response to God about Abel, the brother he had slain. Every time this question is raised in scripture, God's response is always the same: "Yes!" It seems that we are responsible for the well-being of our fellow citizens. God spoke through Obadiah to express anger at the way the Edomites treated the Israelites in their time of trouble. Rather than offer comfort, relief, or human compassion, the Edomites tended to pile onto the suffering and pain of the demoralized Israelites. God was angered by their lack of intervention or care.

This narrative has remarkable relevance for our time. All across the globe, there are huge humanitarian needs. Millions are displaced because of war and violence. Others suffer from disease and drought. Still others endure poverty, hunger, and a lack of basic healthcare. For those of us who live in affluence and safety with plenty to eat and safe places to live, it is easy to ignore the plight of others. I fear that our judgment one day will be harsh not because of the things we did to others but because of the things we failed to offer to those who are hurting, demoralized, and underserved. God have mercy.

Prayer
God, may we become those who respond to the needs of hurting humanity. Amen.

Day 890　　　　　　　　　　　　　　　　Jonah 1: Honest Confession

> "'Throw me into the sea,' Jonah said, 'and it will become calm again. I know that this terrible storm is all my fault.'" Jonah 1:12 (NLT)

Observation

God uses Jonah in a prophetic role to call the Ninevites into repentance because of their sinful behavior. Jonah lived during the end of Elisha's ministry and was a contemporary of Hosea and Amos. His story represents the plight of Israel. Like Israel, Jonah was sent to be a witness to the world, and like Israel, Jonah was disobedient. In fact, he tried to run as far away from God as he could. But God preserves both in the end. This story displays the sovereign nature of God, who is able to compel humans into service and control the winds and waves of nature. Jonah is called to preach to Nineveh, a great city within the Assyrian Empire that would soon become her capital. In Jonah's mind, blessing Nineveh meant cursing Israel. Though some see the story of Jonah as metaphorical, compelling evidence indicates that he is a historical character. He is mentioned in 2 Kings 14:25. All of the events in his story are repeated in the pages of scripture. The calming of the seas, the appointment of an animal to do the work of God, the deliverance of a sinner, and the repentance of a city are found in other situations and other narratives. Jonah receives a clear call from God and runs 2000 miles in the opposite direction. His rescue from the belly of a whale is both supernatural and plausible through the power of God.

Application

I have a pastor friend who once said these words in a sermon: "All of us are standing in one of three places. We are either walking into a storm, living in the midst of a storm, or walking out of storm." He's right. We tend to live in such places. But often we place ourselves in the storms through rebellion, bad choices, or poor associations. Many of the storms we encounter are the result of our own making. Look again at our focus verse. When confronted by the sailors about the life-threatening seas, Jonah states that he is to blame for the storm. He confesses that his disobedience has placed all of their lives in peril. And when he has a moment of reflection, he will pray and confess his sins, repenting of his rebellious response to God's call.

We often play the "blame game" when it comes to our mistakes and failures. Not wanting to admit that we are imperfect or that we are responsible for our actions, we try to shift blame onto someone else. We blame associates, spouses, strangers, or even circumstance. This merely slows the process of grace and redemption in our lives. To confess is to honestly admit sin and commit ourselves to the hard work of repentance.

Prayer

God, teach us to make honest confession when we have "missed the mark." Amen.

Day 891　　　　　　　　　　　Jonah 2: Merciful Listening

> "I cried out to the Lord in my great trouble, and he answered me. I called to you from the land of the dead, and Lord, you heard me!"
> Jonah 2:2 (NLT)

Observation

Chapter 2 tells of Jonah's prayer and God's deliverance. The narrative shifts away from the sailors and the ship and focuses only on Jonah, the fish, and God. In his distress, Jonah cries out to God, just as the sailors had earlier told him to do. His prayer is retrospective, describing his deliverance experience with words of thanksgiving. He uses words and phrases from scripture that are embedded in his mind from a lifetime of following God. In his prayer, Jonah describes the despair of being out of sync with God's purpose for his life. He was surely descending to his grave, he says, "but God" (a phrase used occasionally in both the Old and New Testaments) miraculously delivers Jonah. Because of his rescue, Jonah offers vows of repentance and fidelity to his calling as a prophet. His deliverance is completed as the fish spews him out upon the dry land. Though the location is not mentioned, it is interesting to consider where the prophet finds himself. I suggest that maybe God deposits him on the coast of Israel, near the spot where his rebellion from God first began.

Application

"Are you listening to me?" This is a frequently asked question. Sometimes our spouse asks it, desiring to know if he/she has our full attention. Often, we ask it of our children when we want to ensure good communication. At other times, we might say it to an audience, a classroom full of students, or even a group of friends who seem distracted as we spin a funny tale. "Are you listening to me?" Ask that question of Almighty God, and the answer is always yes. Always. The story of Jonah teaches us that there is no place, physically, relationally, or spiritually, that is out of God's earshot. God listens to every prayer we pray, regardless of circumstance or emotional distance. Yes, God hears even the prayers of sinners. Jonah willfully and deliberately turned his back on God's direct calling for his life. Tarshish was the last known inhabited city to the west. Located in modern-day Spain, this city was nearly 2000 miles in the wrong direction. Jonah also prayed in the depths of the sea from the belly of a fish. And yet his connection with God was loud and clear. God heard Jonah and Jonah heard God. In our self-inflicted circumstances and even in our willful disobedience, God listens for our cries for help. God's desire is never to punish our insolence but to redeem our brokenness. God listens out of love, compassion, and mercy.

Prayer

Father, we praise you this day for your constant listening vigil. Amen.

Day 892   Jonah 3: Responding to Our Actions

> "When God saw what they had done and how they had put a stop to their evil ways, he changed his mind and did not carry out the destruction he had threatened." Jonah 3:10 (NLT)

Observation

Chapter 3 tells of Jonah's re-commissioning by God to go and preach to the city of Nineveh. God offers this second opportunity for Jonah to respond without giving him a rebuke for his earlier rebellion. Nineveh was 500 miles away from Israel. It was a great city with more than 1,500 towers within its walls. The inner wall of the city was more than 100 feet thick. Three chariots could ride abreast over the top of this wall. Jonah enters the city and proclaims God's coming judgment. Written between the lines is the understanding that judgment will come unless the people are willing to repent. Perhaps the greatest miracle of the story is the Ninevites' response to Jonah's preaching. They believe his words and believe in his God. They fast and wear clothing indicative of sorrow and repentance. Even the king dresses in sackcloth and sits on ashes. He pronounces a royal decree telling all of the Ninevites to repent. As a result of Jonah's warnings, the nation is spared from judgment…at least for now.

Application

This chapter sparks an interesting theological question. Does God's mind change? Does God change plans at our responses and prayers? This story seems to indicate that God is willing to relent from the destruction of Nineveh because the people repent and declare allegiance to God. So, was God's mind changed? The God whom we declare to be all-powerful and unchanging? That's a great question. Here's my response. I affirm that God is absolutely sovereign. This world and its circumstances are always under God's authority and discretion. God may choose to do whatever God wills to do. I do not believe that God changes purpose or will. What God longs to accomplish will be accomplished. God's will trumps all human intercession, suggestion, or circumstance. What can change, however, is the way in which God responds to our actions. God is affected by a repentant heart. God is moved by our actions of obedience and loyalty. God offers grace and mercy to us, though none is deserved. God's response to us is always consistent with God's love for us. As God consistently and unfalteringly moves the arc of history towards the Kingdom, God allows humanity to bear the fruit of repentance and loyal discipleship. While God's ultimate will is always accomplished, our response to God's leadership can affect the way we move through this life.

Prayer

Father, we acknowledge your sovereignty and will strive to live obediently. Amen.

Day 893 — Jonah 4: Angered by Mercy?

> "I knew that you are a merciful and compassionate God, slow to get angry and filled with unfailing love. You are eager to turn back from destroying people." Jonah 4:2b (NLT)

Observation

This final chapter speaks of the theological lesson Jonah learns through his anger. What pleases God so much—the repentance of Nineveh—angers Jonah. He had predicted the destruction of the city and is angered by God's merciful acts. He sinks into self-pity and self-interest. It is ironic that one who was shown amazing mercy amid his rebellion is not pleased when God shows mercy to others. Jonah is shocked by the fact that God shows mercy to the undeserving. In a strange twist, he now prefers to die rather than see his prophetic words come to naught. But just as God desired to save the Ninevites, God now wants to save Jonah from his poor attitude. A plant shades Jonah's head in the scorching heat. When a worm destroys the plant, Jonah is angry. God uses these events as a teachable moment. Just as Jonah had compassion for a plant, God showed compassion for thousands of people who were once destined for destruction. The pure heart best discerns God's character. As Jonah understands the nature of God, he too will gain wisdom.

Application

The theme of this passage is repeated in the story of the Prodigal Son (see Luke 15). In Jesus' parable, the older brother is angered by the father's generosity and extravagant mercy. The father reminds him that all he has belongs to this son. When the father divided the estate at the younger brother's request, he distributed his wealth to both sons. According to Jewish law, the older brother would receive two-thirds of the father's estate. So the older brother now owns all the land, the livestock, and the servants. Nothing about the father's mercy will change any of that or lessen its value. And yet the older son is angered by his father's actions. Most of us could place ourselves in the story of the Prodigal Son because of our wayward insolence and rebellion. We see ourselves as the wayward child. But truth be told, most of us are more like the older brother than the one who wandered away. We sometimes sit in judgment of those who have made poor choices. We get angry when a "sinner" receives grace and forgiveness. We would rather everyone get "exactly what they deserve." But is that really what we desire? If we all get what we deserve, none of us will know the bliss of living in the Father's house. How can those of us who know God's mercy dare to deny it in the life of another? We should celebrate it instead.

Prayer

God, knowing the commonality of our sins, may we rejoice in every act of mercy. Amen.

Day 894 — Micah 1: Sin Cities

> "And why is this happening? Because of the rebellion of Israel—yes, the sins of the whole nation. Who is to blame for Israel's rebellion? Samaria, its capital city! Where is the center of idolatry in Judah? In Jerusalem, its capital!" Micah 1:5 (NLT)

Observation
Micah was a prophet of God from the town of Moresheth, located near Jerusalem. He is mentioned in the book of Jeremiah for his effective preaching. God called him to prophesy to both the northern and southern kingdoms, and his ministry spanned the reigns of King Jotham, Ahaz, and Hezekiah. His messages emphasize social justice, practical holiness, and the ultimate reign of the Messiah. The book of Micah is divided into three messages following the introduction. As the book opens, it states that Micah's words are from the Lord God Almighty. The people are told to listen, to pay attention to what God is declaring. As Micah proclaims the coming judgment of God because of people's idolatry, he emphasizes that all the land will feel the effect of God's wrath. The people have acted in ways that are contrary to God's holy standards. Now God will obliterate their idols and places of worship. As a sign of the people's utter spiritual humiliation, Micah will preach while barefoot and naked and will scream like a "howling jackal." The text contains an interesting word play with the city names. Micah pronounces a judgement on each city that is the opposite of what the town's name means. For example, he mentions the name of Gath, which means "place of telling." But in his preaching he says, "don't tell anything in Gath."

Application
Just as key leaders are tasked with setting standards, modeling proper conduct, and leading with integrity, so too the capital cities of the northern and southern kingdoms were to serve as examples of proper worship and spiritual conduct. And yet, in the places where God was to be most honored, the people practiced idolatry. The sins committed in these cities flowed forth like a flood into the surrounding regions. The capital cities of Samaria and Judah were no longer the places where people traveled to discover God and worship with integrity. Whether or not we see ourselves as leaders, all of us affect the lives of the people around us. Our coworkers, families, children, and friends all pick up on the attitudes that we display. Our pessimism, anger, bitterness, and prejudices have a way of seeping out of our bodies and flowing into the lives of those nearby. In other words, we positively or negatively influence those close to us. Our dark emotions destroy not only our lives but also the lives of others. Let's be leaders. Let's set the standards.

Prayer
God, may our faith so shine before people that they may see your good works. Amen.

Day 895 — Micah 2: The Comfortable Lie

> "Suppose a prophet full of lies would say to you, 'I'll preach to you the joys of wine and alcohol!' That's just the kind of prophet you would like!"
> Micah 2:11 (NLT)

Observation
In chapter 2, Micah speaks words of judgment against the wealthy oppressors of Israel. Sorrow and woe will surely come to those who stay awake at night thinking of ways to defraud their fellow Israelites. These wealthy leaders have abused their power. They unjustly seized the inherited lands of others and took the homes of the poor. Micah proclaims that calamity is surely coming. In a reversal of fortune, those who took the land of others will have their own land taken from them by the Assyrian army. They will reap what they have sown. Other false prophets in the land resent Micah's preaching. They are losing face while Micah defends the character of God. These false prophets do nothing to condemn the actions of the wicked. Many unethical practices are described: seizing the clothing of unsuspecting travelers, abusing war veterans with disabilities, and driving widows from their homes. But in spite of all the wickedness, there is still hope for Israel. Micah speaks of the day when God will reassemble God's children and bring them home from exile. (Scholars debate whether Micah was speaking of an immediate fulfillment of prophecy when the exilic period ended or of the coming Messianic age.)

Application
Preachers, prophets, and politicians have always been tempted to speak a comfortable lie rather than deliver the uncomfortable truth. The wicked prophets of Micah's day told the rich and powerful only what they wanted to hear. They were unwilling to confront evildoers with the God's truth. We've all played that game to some extent. We've all told a "white lie" or two to avoid a contentious moment or a difficult conversation. We would rather tell someone what we think they want to hear than tell them the truth. But this often backfires. Take the story of the guy who jumped in his car and sped down the street. Soon, the police pulled him over for speeding. While he waited for the officer to approach the car, he noticed that he had neglected to fasten his safety belt. "Oh no," he thought, "I'm going to get a really big ticket!" He quickly reached over and snapped it into place. "Do you always wear your seatbelt?" the officer asked. "Yes, sir," the man responded. "I never start the car without first buckling up." Knowing he had caught the driver in a lie, the officer said, "Well, do you always loop it through the steering wheel?" It is still true that honesty is the best policy, especially in relationships. Deception will always be revealed. Strive to build integrity in all that you do.

Prayer
God, forgive our lack of honesty. May we never become comfortable with any lie. Amen.

Day 896 — Micah 3: Hopeless Expectations

> "Then you beg the Lord for help in times of trouble! Do you really expect him to answer? After all the evil you have done, he won't even look at you!"
> Micah 3:4 (NLT)

Observation
Chapter 3 marks the beginning of the second of three messages in the book of Micah. Specifically, this chapter offers judgment against the various leaders of Israel. Micah begins with an indictment of corrupt political leaders. He compares their actions against the people to a cruel person who would skin a live animal and chop it into pieces to place in the cooking pot. The warning to all political leaders states that exploiting people for the sake of achieving selfish personal or professional goals is a sin against God. Next, Micah takes on the corrupt religious leaders of Israel. They have led the flock astray. Micah compares them to the setting sun when darkness soon replaces the light. In the final section of the chapter, Micah speaks to a broad spectrum of ungodly leaders. They have perverted justice, practiced violence, and used intimidation to exploit the poor.

Application
One of the undergrad students in a class that I teach has "worn out his welcome with me." Over the course of the semester, he has underperformed. Specifically, he has a habit of turning in assignments after they are due. He always offers an excuse or a sad tale and then pleads to turn them in late. This has happened with every assignment! He's a likable kid but seems lazy in terms of his assignments. I had to cut off the flow of grace this past week. I told him that unless the next paper was turned in on time, he would receive a zero. There would be no more leniency.

Apparently, the political leaders of Micah's day had fallen into the same trap. Time and again they had abused their power and disregarded God's patience. They willingly committed heinous acts and then pleaded for God's help when a time of difficulty arrived. Micah offered a "you've-got-to-be-kidding" response. They couldn't have it both ways. Fidelity to God requires not occasional obedience but consistent obedience. Honestly, we're not much different. I fear that we often get close to exhausting the patience of God. We willfully commit sins and then ask God to bail us out of our trouble. And God forgives. Then we sin again and once more ask for God's help. Rather than devote our lives to God, we only look to God when we need a quick answer to prayer or a miraculous solution to a problem. We don't treat God as a loving Father with whom we long to have a relationship. We treat God like a cosmic Santa Claus whom we beg for another gift. Do we really expect God to keep answering?

Prayer
God, we confess our lack of consistency. Make us better, stronger, purer. Amen.

Day 897 — Micah 4: The Great Age

> "Everyone will live in peace and prosperity, enjoying their own grapevines and fig trees, for there will be nothing to fear. The Lord of Heaven's Armies has made this promise!" Micah 4:4 (NLT)

Observation
Micah 4 expresses a hopeful word to those about to go into exile. It speaks of the future reign of the Messiah in Jerusalem and the restoration of God's people, who will soon become a small remnant during the exilic period. The age will come when God brings a grand era of peace to the world. The Temple, which Babylon will shortly destroy, will once again be seen as the most prominent place of worship in the world. The desire to worship God will multiply exponentially. The crooked paths of injustice will give way to the purposes of God. When the Messiah establishes his Kingdom, all the nations of the earth will submit to him in peace. The faithful of God, scattered to distant lands, will regather in Jerusalem. As the chapter closes, Micah reminds the people that difficult and devastating moments are about to happen in Israel as the armies of the enemy approach, but the time will come when God will rescue and restore the people.

Application
When the world gets overwhelming, the pressure of work is strong, or the news of the day becomes too much to bear, I sometimes retreat to the comfort of my recliner and watch an episode of The Andy Griffith Show. Call it my happy place. Most of us attempt to create such a place of respite. It might be a week-long vacation at the beach, a hike in the woods, or a canoe trip down a lazy river. We long for moments of serenity, peace, and bliss, moments devoid of stress, anxiety, or fear. And sometimes we can, in fact, create such a moment. But it is only a brief moment, for the pressures of life, work, family, and finance soon catch up.

Notice what God promises through the words of Micah in our focus verse. He describes what life will resemble in the great age when Jesus, as Messiah, comes to reign on the earth. Everyone will live in peace and prosperity. Our needs will be met, and our anxieties will dissipate. We will enjoy life in its fullness, with nothing to fear. We won't worry about illness, death, pain, or a lack of prosperity. This coming age is more than the simple longings of an old Hebrew prophet. It is a promise from God. God will bring it to pass. The age of glory will indeed come. And so, when you feel a little stressed, overburdened, and anxious about your life, take a moment to pause and reflect. Find the place in your mind and heart that is guarded with hope, and then remember all that God will do.

Prayer
God, may we live this day with an overwhelming, exciting, and lasting hope. Amen.

Day 898 — Micah 5: The Long Arc of God's Plan

> "But you, O Bethlehem Ephrathah, are only a small village among all the people of Judah. Yet a ruler of Israel will come from you, one whose origins are from the distant past." Micah 5:2 (NLT)

Observation

The opening verse of Micah 5 is a call to arms. The people are told to marshal the troops against the coming enemy who will lay siege to Jerusalem. The narrative quickly shifts, however, to a word concerning the coming of the Messiah. In one of the most remarkable prophecies in the entire Bible, Micah proclaims the coming of the Messiah, correctly predicting Jesus' birth in Bethlehem. Though it is not a prominent city—so insignificant that it is identified by the region of Ephrathah to distinguish it from another town with the same name—it will become the birthplace of Christ. Eight centuries later, the prophecy rings true. In telling the story of Jesus' birth, Matthew 2:6 quotes this prophetic word. Verse 3 of Micah 5 also makes reference to a woman in labor, indicating that Israel will not know peace until the Messiah comes to reign. When the Messiah comes, the faithful remnant of God's people will refresh and give insight to the world like "dew covering the ground or rain falling on the grass." The Lord will prosper the people, but the rebellious enemies will not be spared.

Application

When I was young, my maternal grandparents lived in Orlando, Florida. It was always a treat, during the dead of winter, to travel to Orlando just after Christmas and spend a few days in the Florida sunshine. My grandfather, Sam Blair, was a Pontiac man. He continued to trade up for a new car every couple of years until the day he died. One December afternoon, he took my brother and me on a ride in his new Pontiac to a place south of Orlando. We drove to a vast, swampy wilderness area. He told us that Walt Disney had bought thousands of acres in this spot and would one day build a huge attraction. He was, of course, correct. A few years later, Disney World began to emerge. What is available to people now began as a dream in the mind of Walt Disney a very long time ago.

As Micah describes the coming of the Messiah, he mentions that his origins are "from the distant past." I find that verse intriguing. I am reminded that the coming of Christ to our world, to intersect with human history, was not by happenstance. It was part of God's deliberate plan from the beginning of time. From the start, God planned to offer redemption to the world through the life of God's Son. That means not only that God had always planned to do a great work but also that God had always included us in that plan.

Prayer

God, how we rejoice in the long arc of your plan! Amen.

Day 899 — Micah 6: What God Requires of Us

> "No, O people, the Lord has told you what is good, and this is what he requires of you: to do what is right, to love mercy, and to walk humbly with your God." Micah 6:8 (NLT)

Observation

The final two chapters of Micah contain the prophet's third message to the people. Although it continues to mention impending judgment, this message ends on a hopeful note as Micah describes God's future blessings that will surpass the judgment. The narrative begins with a courtroom metaphor. God challenges Israel to defend her actions. God speaks to the mountains and hills, which will act as a jury. The mountains represent the people of the world who have witnessed Israel's actions. God offers an indictment and challenges Israel with a series of rhetorical questions. God's faithfulness contrasts with the nation's lack of faithfulness. Micah reminds the people that part of showing fidelity to God is offering respect and dignity to one's fellow human. To walk righteously with God is to practice ethical relationships with others. God requires justice, mercy, and humility. The chapter ends with the nation being called out for her corrupt business ethics and idolatry.

Application

"What are the requirements?" That question is asked many different contexts. For example, a student entering a class at the beginning of the semester might ask what is required to achieve a good grade. If you apply for a loan, you may need to determine if you fit the requirements for consideration. I recently wrote a grant proposal here at work. The guidelines for doing so listed 15 various requirements. Requirements are important. In his third and final message to the Israelites, Micah outlines specifically the things that God requires of the people. To live in a right relationship with both God and people, they are to do three things: do what is right, love mercy, and walk humbly. Let's unpack that list. To "do what is right" is a call for justice, fairness, and ethical behavior in our actions. We are to do the right thing whenever we are confronted with options and choices. We are to treat others with honesty, respect, and a sense of decency. To "love mercy" is to extend mercy to others in the same way that God has extended mercy to each of us. Because we find forgiveness and grace, God requires that we offer the same to others. When our human nature wants to pull us towards thoughts of revenge, caustic anger, or bitterness, we are forced to adopt a God-like ethic that demands we respond to others with the mercy God offers us. To "walk humbly" is the call to understand our place in the presence of God and our place among our fellow human beings. We are to treat God as our Lord to whom we offer obedience and to treat others as our equals to whom we offer respect.

Prayer

Father, may we strive this day to fulfill all of your requirements of us. Amen.

Day 900   Micah 7: Gone for Good

> "Once again you will have compassion on us. You will trample our sins under your feet and throw them into the depths of the ocean!"
> Micah 7:19 (NLT)

Observation
In this final chapter, Micah describes his own personal misery and his transformation to hope. "Woe am I," he states in the opening verse. He offers this mournful cry over the impoverished spirituality of his people. They are like a barren vineyard where no fruit is produced. Corruption is widespread. Officials, judges, and the rich are singled out for their heinous corruption. Micah warns that few in the country can be trusted. Beginning in verse 7, Micah's comments turn to a more hopeful tone. He declares that God will eventually lead the people back. Israel's enemies will be humbled. The restoration of Israel will be so complete that the world's nations will be stunned by all that God has done. Micah closes with words of praises for God. God is faithful, compassionate, and protective. God will fulfill the covenant with Israel.

Application
In the world of computers, many go to great lengths to protect data. It is important to safeguard names, account numbers, important documents, etc. But from time to time, computers get old and need to be replaced. What should we do with the hard drive once the data is copied onto a new computer? I like the approach from the IT guys here on campus where I work. They first use a powerful magnet to effectively wipe away most of the data. Then, to be sure that no one can capture any remaining material, the hard drive is placed in a powerful machine that crushes it into pieces. The data is destroyed, never to be read again.

In his closing word, the prophet Micah reminds us of how God deals with our sins. Out of compassion, God wants to forever remove the relational distance-causing sins. God not only removes them from the forefront of God's mind but also crushes them under his feet and casts them into the depths of the sea. In other words, God obliterates them, destroys them, completely removes them from the record of our lives. Or, as Hebrews 8:12 states, "And I will forgive their wickedness, and I will never again remember their sins" (NLT). How freeing and exciting it is to know that God, through the atoning sacrifice of Christ, chooses to remember our sins no longer. Though we struggle with self-forgiveness, and though we often live under oppressive shame, such remorse is not found in the heart of God. Our compassionate God loves us enough to make a way for us to be in God's presence, forgiven, whole, and redeemed. I wish that for at least this one day you and I could regard our past mistakes the way God does.

Prayer
Father, we praise you for your compassionate forgiveness and grace. Amen.

Day 901 — Nahum 1: The Strong Refuge

> "The Lord is good, a strong refuge when trouble comes. He is close to those who trust in him." Nahum 1:7 (NLT)

Observation

Nahum, whose name means "Comfort," is one of the 12 Minor Prophets of the Old Testament. He receives a vision from God that he will pass on to his hearers. He is from the city of Elkosh, whose location is no longer known. His preaching is uniquely directed not towards Israel or Judah but towards the Assyrian capital of Nineveh and her residents. Through Nahum's preaching about the absolute destruction of Nineveh, the Israelites will find comfort. The "iron rod" of oppression will be broken. Though Assyria has overrun the northern kingdom (Israel), Nahum preaches hope to the southern kingdom (Judah). Nahum prophesied around 621 BC when Nineveh was at the height of her power. Some 75 years earlier, Jonah had also been sent to preach to the residents of Nineveh. And although his preaching was effective and the city repented, apparently his message was forgotten and ignored by the time Nahum appeared on the scene. In this first chapter, Nahum describes the wrath of God as a coming storm. By God's power, even the mountains and hills will be shaken, and the land will become desolate. Nahum reminds his listeners that the Lord will protect God's people in the day of their trouble.

Application

Many years ago, the Baptist church in Brent, Alabama, was victimized by a sudden and fiercely destructive tornado. Worshippers headed into the Sunday evening service under dark and ominous skies. As the service progressed, the winds and rain began to rage. The pastor, who had previously experienced a tornado, recognized the tell-tale, train-like sound. He told the congregation to flee to the exits and make their way to the building's basement. Moments later, the tornado ripped through the sanctuary, leaving only the front and back walls standing. The storm literally carved out the middle of the structure. Only one pew was left intact. All of the congregants made it to safety except for a father and his young son, who hunkered down in the sanctuary because there was no time for them to flee. By the providence of God, the father and son had taken shelter under the only pew that remained. Both of them, along with all the others, were safe when the storm subsided.

"The Lord is good," Nahum preached, "a strong refuge when trouble comes." Not all the storms we face are caused by wind and rain. Some are relational, financial, and physical. As they inevitably come to us, let us remember that God is close to those who trust in God.

Prayer

Father, protect us this day from the destructive storms that blow around us. Amen.

Day 902 — Nahum 2: Those Who Slip Away

> "Nineveh is like a leaking water reservoir! The people are slipping away. 'Stop, stop!' someone shouts, but no one even looks back."
> Nahum 2:8 (NLT)

Observation

Nahum 2 describes the fall of Nineveh. It is as though Nahum is able to see from an aerial viewpoint. The advancing Babylonian army will come swiftly and capture the city, plundering the wealth and treasures. Nahum's words taunt the residents. With irony in his voice, he tells them to be strong and courageous as the advancing armies come in terrifying scarlet battle array. Their "chariots of steel" will glisten in the sun as they rapidly break into the city, like "flashes of lightning." Attempts to stop the enemy will be futile. Nahum predicts that part of the city's desolation will result from flooding rivers. This is a historical occurrence that took place just three years after his prophetic word. Nineveh was filled with vast treasuries of silver and gold taken from other nations in times of conquest. These former spoils of war would be taken from them.

Application

Some of us have participated in a relay race that involved running down a field to fill up a bucket with water using only a plastic cup with a hole in it. It took forever to fill the bucket because so much water seeped out of the cup.

As Nahum describes the impending fall of Nineveh, he mentions that the residents of the city are seeping away like a leaking water reservoir. When others attempt to stop them, no one even looks back or listens to their pleas. When I read this narrative, I am struck by the parallels to the modern-day Christian church experience. Over the past 25 years, mainline denominations have lost over 40 million people. These people, known as the "dones" (not done with faith but done with organized religion), have slowly but surely left their churches, and most don't look back or listen to those who attempt to cajole them into staying. The key question is, "Why are members leaving in such numbers?" There are several factors to consider. Many come to church wanting conversations about cultural issues, but rather than conversations they get condemnation for their opinions. Others feel the sting of judgment when their thoughts don't line up exactly with the majority viewpoint. Others see hypocrisy and lack of authenticity as a reason for leaving. Still others have been abused by the church, its judgments, its lack of compassion, and its lack of forgiveness. And so they slip away. How do we respond? Is there an answer? Yes. It's called kindness. It's called being the presence of Christ, authentically and honestly, with the people around us.

Prayer

God, may we be conformed to the image of Christ so that we don't repel others. Amen.

Day 903 — Nahum 3: The Power of a City

> "All this because Nineveh, the beautiful and faithless city, mistress of deadly charms, enticed the nations with her beauty. She taught them all her magic, enchanting people everywhere." Nahum 3:4 (NLT)

Observation
This final chapter of Nahum describes the Lord's judgment against Nineveh. The destruction will be complete. The city will be disgraced, defeated, and abandoned. Nahum speaks words of lament. This great city is filled with lies, treachery, robbery, and deception. Her defeat will begin with the crack of a whip as chariots roll and horses kick up dust. The city has led people away from the truth, encouraging them to wander into false and faithless religions. In Nineveh's day of destruction, no one will grieve over her or comfort her. Nahum compares her destruction to that of the city of Thebes in Egypt…once powerful and proud but suddenly destroyed. As Nineveh collapses, the officials and rulers will flee from the city, leaving residents defenseless. As the book closes, it is clear that Nahum's message is about the certainty of God's judgment towards evil and oppressive people.

Application
Last fall, I had an opportunity to spend a few days in the nation's capital. Each time I visit Washington, DC, I am drawn in by the city's beauty—its layout and design, its great monuments, and its stately buildings. It is an impressive place. It is also a little intoxicating. I can easily get caught up in the power that emanates from the familiar structures. Laws are forged there. Senators shape legislation and representatives push toward reform. Washington, DC, influences the world. It is a place that causes the heart to swell with patriotic fervor and the mind to consider the possibilities. But it is also a place where power corrupts and many are taken in by the lure of wealth and influence. Though I have only visited the city on brief trips, I feel certain that it would not take long to come under the spell of that captivating place.

Cities have a way of impacting their residents. Cities have a vibe, a reputation, a charm…even an emotion. I live in Nashville. It's a booming town with lots of growth and the resultant growing pains. People get swept up in the excitement of Music City. More than 100 new residents claim Nashville as home each day. But I wonder, as people of faith, is Nashville influencing us more than we are influencing her? Are we made better by living here, or are we impoverished of life and soul because of her subtle pressures in our lives? Though each city has a power of its own, the greater power must come from those who dwell within it. We are called to shape, lead, and make better the places we live.

Prayer
God, on this day, may we become noble citizens of our towns so that good is the result.

Day 904 — Habakkuk 1: The God of Amazing Acts

> "The Lord replied, 'Look around at the nations; look and be amazed! For I am doing something in your own day, something you wouldn't believe even if someone told you about it.'" Habakkuk 1:5 (NLT)

Observation
Little is known about the prophet Habakkuk. Scholars believe he was a Levitical musician because of the final verse that reads, "For the choir director: This prayer is to be accompanied by [my] stringed instruments" (3:19). The Apocryphal book Bel and the Dragon mentions Habakkuk as being from the tribe of Levi. His name means "to embrace," and many point to his strong love for God as the reason behind his name. His ministry took place shortly before the Babylonian invasion of Judah (605 BC). He was a contemporary of Jeremiah and Ezekiel. At this point in the history of Judah, the nation has forsaken earlier spiritual reforms and become violent, wicked, and idolatrous. Judgment is certainly on the horizon and will come at the hands of the Babylonians. Though a faithful remnant will survive, it is clear that discipline will precede deliverance. The book opens with a dialogue between the prophet and God. Habakkuk is confused over the disparity of God's love for the people and the promise of judgment. He appeals to God's holiness and wonders why God is silent while the righteous suffer.

Application
We live in a day and age when amazing things occur. Consider the world of technology. We rely on inventions and technologies that were little more than dreams just a few decades ago. We can talk to anyone on the planet using a cell phone that instantly connects us to others. We can "Google" any topic and gain insight and information at the blink of an eye. The other day I was driving home in Nashville's afternoon bumper-to-bumper traffic. A guy drove past me in a new Tesla sedan, literally reading a book from the driver's seat while the car controlled the speed and the distance between his car and the next, carefully braking to a stop if need be. Yes…it's an amazing world.

In our focus verse, God tells Habakkuk that he will be amazed at what God is doing. God is using a powerful pagan nation to bring about justice on Judah. This is an amazing moment in biblical history when God chose to act this way. God continues to do amazing things in our world. God arranges people, places, and circumstances for God's glory. Be assured that the Lord is always at work, bringing about the ultimate fulfillment of the Kingdom. Whenever you catch a glimpse of an unusual God moment, be amazed and grateful at God's involvement with our world.

Prayer
Father, amaze us today. Dazzle us. Intrigue us. And reveal yourself to us. Amen.

Day 905   Habakkuk 2: The Righteous Shall Live by Faith

"Look at the proud! They trust in themselves, and their lives are crooked. But the righteous will live by their faithfulness to God."
Habakkuk 2:4 (NLT)

Observation
As chapter 2 opens, Habakkuk waits to receive a response from God. He has asked questions of God as he tries to understand God's actions—specifically, why God would use the Babylonians as instruments of judgment. God's response is twofold. First, the Babylonians will indeed face punishment for the destruction of Judah. Second, the righteous must trust in God's actions and timing, knowing that judgment will come to the wicked. God tells Habakkuk to write down these words on a tablet to make the message permanent and portable. Others will be able to read what God has declared. History records that 70 years later, the Persians defeated the armies of Babylon. This is a reminder that God's word is always fulfilled, yet often in unexpected ways. Our focus verse, the key verse of the entire book, declares that the righteous will live by faith. It is repeated three times in the New Testament: Romans 1:17, Galatians 3:11, and Hebrews 10:38. There are two possible translations from the original language. Do the righteous live by God's faithfulness to them, or do they live by their faithfulness to God? Or is it both? The chapter continues with a series of "woes" pronounced upon Babylon. Instead of being dazzled by Babylon's power, the world will be dazzled by the power of the Lord God. The final verse is also well known to most readers: "The Lord is in his holy temple. Let all the earth be silent before him" (2:20).

Application
If we can declare that God arranges people, places, and circumstances to God's glory, then we must understand that there is at times a mystery to God's unfolding plan. There are situations we don't understand. There are questions that go without answers. There are prayers with unexpected responses or no response at all. How do we live in the tension of not having all the answers or not having an understanding of all God's ways? We believe in a God who is all powerful and all knowing, who is motivated by a special love and compassion for people. And yet difficult things occur, and we don't know why. Habakkuk's response is important for our faith journey: the righteous live by faith. We live by faith in a God who is wiser, more powerful, and transcendent of time. We live amid life's tensions and unanswered questions by submitting to God's greater plan and purpose. We must believe that in God's providence and timing, all things will work together for good and for the glory of the Kingdom. We live by faith in God's faithfulness to us and by our faith in God.

Prayer
Father, remind us today that faith is the victory that overcomes the world. Amen.

Day 906　　　　　　　　　　　Habakkuk 3: Even Though...

> "Even though the fig trees have no blossoms, and there are no grapes on the vines; even though the olive crop fails, and the fields lie empty and barren; even though the flocks die in the fields, and the cattle barns are empty, yet I will rejoice in the Lord! I will be joyful in the God of my salvation!"
> Habakkuk 3:17-18 (NLT)

Observation
This final chapter reflects Habakkuk's prayers. He will trust in the Lord despite his difficulties and doubts. His words are presented in the form of a psalm, poetic in nature, with embedded musical notes. One of those notations is the word "Selah," which means "to pause" or "to exalt." This is the only place "Selah" is used outside of the book of Psalms, where it appears 71 times. Habakkuk's poem is divided into three parts. The first part reflects praise for God's powerful deeds in the past, particularly the exodus experience. The second part is a series of rhetorical questions focusing on God's actions to bring salvation. The third part reflects Habakkuk's heart of trusting in God while waiting for deliverance to come. The prophet faces the destruction of Judah with fear and trembling. He is shaken. His lips quiver, he is brought to tears, and his bones feel weak. And yet he realizes that he is to wait quietly and rest securely in the slow work of God. God will once again deliver the people.

Application
Some days we win at life. There are days when things seem to go our way. The sun shines, the birds sing, and life moves smoothly. We've all had days when we declare that it's good to be alive. And then there are days that aren't as easy to endure. Poured into every life is a little sadness, tragedy, and disappointment. The problem is that we often think to praise God on the good days. "Thank you, Lord, for my blessings!" But how well do we do on the dark days? Are we as quick to praise God even when things aren't going well? Look at the moment in time in which Habakkuk lived. Devastation was coming. Judgment was knocking on the door. There were no figs, no grapes, no olives. The crops were failing, and the fields were barren. The results of God's judgment were quickly affecting life in Judah. Even so, the prophet declares his praises to the Lord God. Even though things were not good, not happy, not hopeful, he found the capacity to worship. Even though you may be going through a difficult season, even though you may be in a tight financial squeeze, even though your health is not perfect, even though your closest friend just moved away, even though the pressures at work are enormous…you are called to faithfulness. Wait quietly and rest securely in the slow but purposeful work of God. God is praiseworthy.

Prayer
Father, give us the capacity to praise you on both the good and difficult days. Amen.

Day 907 — Zephaniah 1: Not the Time for Words

> "Stand in silence in the presence of the Sovereign Lord, for the awesome day of the Lord's judgment is near." Zephaniah 1:7a (NLT)

Observation

The name Zephaniah means "Yahweh has stored up" and is perhaps symbolic of the prophet's message: the "stored-up" wrath and judgment of God is about to unfold over the land. Zephaniah's genealogy is traced through four generations and is linked to Hezekiah, the renowned king of Judah. It is possible that Zephaniah was of Ethiopian descent. God called him to preach during the reign of King Josiah (640-609 BC). The key theme of this book is "The Day of the Lord." Zephaniah uses this phrase 23 times in just three chapters. This day of the Lord will bring gloom, despair, destruction, and judgment. But it will be followed by prosperity, restoration, and blessing. The reason for God's harsh judgment is rebellion. The people of Judah have rejected the Lord as their God. As the book opens, the prophet first pronounces judgment over all the earth. The remaining section of chapter 1 is a pronouncement of judgment over Jerusalem and Judah. The people are called to be "silent" before the Lord. There is no excuse or explanation to offer for their sinfulness.

Application

Have you been, "fussed at" lately? Let's say that you have messed up on a task, an assignment, or some other instruction and suddenly you are called out for what you have done. Perhaps your spouse, your boss, or your friend is calling you into accountability. In such moments, we often try to make excuses for our poor decision-making. We try to point blame, redirect the conversation, or offer a lame explanation. But rarely do those things work. Sometimes we just have to take it. We have to sit in silence as our poor behavior is brought to our attention.

We find ourselves in the same situation with God. Like the ancient Israelites who were told to sit in silence before God's judgment, offering no excuses or explanations, we have moments when we must do the same in the presence of our Heavenly Father. Our excuses are lame before God. Our explanations are pitiable. God knows our deeds, the thoughts of our minds, and the intentions of our hearts. It is best to sit in silence in God's presence and let our feeble attempts at excuses drift away. It is not that God wants us to wallow in shame; God wants us to realize the depth of our disobedience so we might appreciate the extravagance of God's grace. In the silence we will realize our transgressions, understand the distance they can cause in our relationship with God, and then reflect on God's willingness to restore us when we have failed.

Prayer

Father, today we offer no excuses. We sit in the silent anticipation of your grace. Amen.

Day 908 — Zephaniah 2: A Call to Kindness

> "For the Lord their God will visit his people in kindness and restore their prosperity again." Zephaniah 2:7b (NLT)

Observation
Zephaniah 2 emphasizes God's judgment upon the enemies of Judah. God will bring the nations of the world into accountability. Before pronouncing judgment on these nations, Zephaniah calls the people of Judah to "gather themselves together." This could be a call for collective repentance among the people. It could also be an eschatological calling to gather the nation together again in Judah at the time of the Messiah's return. The people are to seek the Lord in humility. As the chapter progresses, Philistia, Moab, and Ammon are all singled out for the Lord's judgment and destruction. They have all been enemies of Judah for various historical reasons. Zephaniah insists that Moab and Ammon will live in perpetual devastation. As judgment comes, the Lord will end all false worship and all the nations will bow down before God.

Application
Sometimes, when the world is quiet and the house is asleep and we have a few minutes for quiet reflection, we might ponder existential questions or think about the legacy we hope to leave behind. We might long to be remembered for possessing certain great qualities. What an honor it would be for someone to say that we were gentle, or generous, or noble, or gracious. What if people say we were courageous, bold, and passionate? As I muse on such things, the word "kindness" often comes to mind. What a wonderful tribute to be thought of as a kind person. To be kind means that I will have proven myself to be gentle, humble, considerate of others, peaceful, generous, and filled with grace. Those of you who know me well must be thinking, "He's got work to do!" And maybe I do. But at least that's the aspirational goal: to be a kind person.

Part of what drives that desire is realizing that if I am to reflect the heart of my Heavenly Father, then kindness is essential. Notice our focus verse: "God will visit us in kindness." Consider the words of the Apostle Paul as he writes about the fruit of the Spirit: "love, joy, peace, patience, kindness…." Kindness makes the list! Those who embrace faith in Christ discover that the indwelling Spirit of God is at work in our hearts and lives. Part of what God longs to instill in us is kindness. I think kindness is a choice…or maybe many choices we make each day. As you ramble through another day, encountering all kinds of people in all kinds of settings, why not strive to be kind?

Prayer
Father, may we visit others in kindness today. Amen.

Day 909 — Zephaniah 3: Worship with Words

> "Then I will purify the speech of all people, so that everyone can worship the Lord together." Zephaniah 3:9 (NLT)

Observation
The opening verses (1-8) of this final chapter of Zephaniah describe the judgment of Jerusalem. The prophet offers a word of intense woe. The judgment will bring profound pain, calamity, and destruction. The rulers, judges, and priests have acted violently and viciously towards the people. Corruption is widespread. These key leaders have failed to learn from the destruction of other cities and nations. In contrast, the final verses (9-20) focus on God's promise of restoration. The goodness and grace of the Lord will be poured out on the people. God will purify their speech so that worship can be pure and holy. God will remove their sin and the shame of past deeds. God will fill their hearts with joy. And God will regather the people. Though some of these promises will be fulfilled at the end of the exilic period, the greater fulfillment will come during the Messianic age when the Messiah returns to initiate his Kingdom and rule.

Application
When I was a kid, the often-proposed threat of punishment for saying bad words was this: "I will wash out your mouth with soap!" It was a parental pledge to rid a child's mouth of curse words...a purging of the tongue. It makes me think of the scene from the classic movie A Christmas Story, when Ralphie's mother forces him to suck on a bar of soap for saying a really, really bad word. The truth is that all of us could probably do with a little verbal cleansing. Culture continues to creep into our hearts and minds, and sometimes we say something or shout a word that we probably should not say. Our words sometimes betray us, and we end up harming our reputation and character with poorly chosen speech.

But I think the emphasis of our focus verse goes beyond the occasional and accidental use of a curse word. I think it has more to do with how we use our words to inflict pain and abuse on others. James warns that "Out of the same mouth come praise and cursing" (James 3:10 NIV). We use our mouths to condemn, to abuse, to manipulate, to belittle, and to control others. And then we waltz into worship and use the same mouths to offer praise to God as though our tongues are suddenly transformed into a fount of holy speech. In our focus verse, God promises to purify the speech of the people so that they can worship together. It is the inconsistent use of our words that becomes so hypocritical. We choose our words. We control our tongues. Whenever we practice inconsistencies, we betray our faith convictions and our worship suffers.

Prayer
Father, give us a consistent and pure heart, and words to match. Amen.

Day 910 — Haggai 1: Home Improvement

> "Why are you living in luxurious houses while my house lies in ruins?"
> Haggai 1:4 (NLT)

Observation

Haggai's ministry began during the second year of King Darius of Persia's reign, during the postexilic period. He started preaching around 520 BC, about 20 years after the end of the Babylonian exile. (The book of Ezra mentions the prophet Haggai and his work.) God's people had been quick to reestablish the wall of Jerusalem under Nehemiah's leadership. But soon their enthusiasm waned and the proposed work on the Temple became a low priority. They built lavish homes for themselves but failed to provide the Lord with an adequate space to inhabit. The book of Haggai is a series of four messages offering a rebuke for the inverted priorities of the people. They had fallen into a period of spiritual indifference. But as soon as they heard Haggai's prophetic word, they took dramatic corrective action. They began to work on the Temple with great zeal.

Application

For most people, buying a home is the biggest investment of their lives. To protect the value of that home, homeowners go to great lengths to maintain, improve, and maybe even add on to the original construction. Many add granite countertops, screen in a porch, or lay new carpet. Others paint and refinish and carefully manicure the landscape. It is interesting, however, that the same people will fuss and fight over each dime the church proposes to spend on upkeep and maintenance. While many people give to the building fund, it is only a fraction of what they spend each year on their own homes. Such was the case of the ancient Israelites returning from exile. It is possible that some of the expensive lumber acquired for rebuilding the Temple found its way into the people's more lavish homes. The prophet saw such actions as being "inverted priorities." He felt that the people were neglecting God while lavishly constructing their own homes.

Sacred space is important. The house of God should be a place that honors the Lord. It should be maintained, well kept, and appropriately adorned. What message does it send to seekers when we claim to love God with all our hearts while letting the church building deteriorate? Having been a pastor of five different congregations, I can certainly appreciate the ever-increasing costs of maintenance and upkeep. The drain on the church budget can be oppressive. Certainly, a sense of balance needs to be struck between missions giving and building maintenance. But we must be mindful of the stewardship of God's house. As we consider the costs to make our own homes look nice, we must remember the church as well.

Prayer

Father, may we seek to honor you in how well we maintain our sacred space. Amen.

Day 911 — Haggai 2: The Bright Horizon

> "The future glory of this Temple will be greater than its past glory, says the Lord of Heaven's Armies. And in this place I will bring peace. I, the Lord of Heaven's Armies, have spoken!" Haggai 2:9 (NLT)

Observation

Haggai 2 offers a word of encouragement to the Israelites as they begin the process of rebuilding the Temple. The people are distraught as they consider the former splendor of Solomon's Temple and compare it to the small structure they hope to build. God tells them to take courage and continue their work. They are reminded of the glorious past when God led them out of Egypt. That same spirit will lead them in this endeavor. They are to look to the future when the Temple will once again be filled with God's glory. God will shake the heavens, the earth, the seas, and the dry land. In other words, a new world is coming, and the glory of the new Temple will far exceed the glory of the former Temple. Part of Haggai's preaching is a call to spiritual purity. As the new Temple foundation is laid, so too the people need to reestablish a firm foundation in their personal lives. Haggai closes his prophetic words with a merciful promise of blessing.

Application

Belmont University's basketball teams play in the Curb Event Center located on campus. It's an impressive building. When configured for basketball, it can seat about 5,000 fans. It features video screens, state-of-the-art lighting and sound systems, and delicious concessions. It can be configured to host graduation ceremonies at the end of each semester. It is also an amazing music venue where large-scale productions like the CMA Awards have been held. Ryder Cup Tennis matches have been played in that space, and, last but not least, it has housed US presidential debates. I have been around Nashville long enough to remember when the Curb Event Center was built. In order to clear the footprint for the building, the old gym, referred to as "The Barn," had to be demolished. Many hated to see it go because of the memories and the quaint setting it provided. It was difficult for anyone to envision what the future home of Belmont Basketball would resemble. And now, thinking back, who would even compare the two? The future glory far eclipsed the past glory.

God promised the people of Haggai's day that the future glory of the Temple would surpass anything they had known. As we gaze off into the future, we too might wonder how things will turn out. Has the glory of God departed? Will the world ever know God's grace, love, and care? The gospel is always looking forward. It promises that better days are on the horizon, when Christ will return and make all things new.

Prayer

Father, may we find encouragement today as we remember your unfolding plan. Amen.

Day 912 — Zechariah 1: I'll Be Waiting

> "Therefore, say to the people, 'This is what the Lord of Heaven's Armies says: Return to me, and I will return to you, says the Lord of Heaven's Armies.'" Zechariah 1:3 (NLT)

Observation
Several qualities distinguish the book of Zechariah from the other Minor Prophets. Zechariah was both a prophet and a priest of Israel. Additionally, the book is by far the most Messianic, apocalyptic, and eschatological of the prophets. Zechariah talks about the redemption and restoration of Israel that will come about in the Messianic age. The reader will recognize Messianic fulfillment in his words as he speaks about the Messiah riding into Jerusalem on a donkey, being rejected by his own people, and being pierced for the sins of his people. Zechariah began his prophetic ministry about 16 years after the Babylonian captivity. It is believed that he was a young man when he started. The first eight chapters were written well before the final chapters, leading many to think that the latter chapters were written much later, perhaps as late as when the Greek empire began to assert dominance over the Persians. Regardless, as the book opens, the nation finds itself in a time of political peace but national despair. The prophet's words are meant to encourage the returning exiles about God's ultimate plan for the nation. The first portion of the book contains six "night visions" that come to Zechariah on the same night. He speaks of angels who travel across the earth and the rise of four "horns" that will be punished for their excessive abuse of Israel, most likely referring to Babylon, Persia, Greece, and Rome.

Application
To this day, I still do a lot of "waiting" on my kids. When they were teenagers, I always waited up at night to make sure they got in safely from dates, ballgames, etc. Now that they are grown, married, and reproducing, I still wait anxiously every time they plan a visit to our house. I look out the window a dozen times so I will know when they pull up. I like to greet them at the car and grab the first grandparent hug from the kids. In my favorite New Testament passage, I love the image of the waiting father who patiently but perhaps anxiously waits for the prodigal son to come home again (Luke 15). I envision him looking out at the horizon, shielding his eyes from the sun, watching daily with the hope that his son will come home again. I envision his eyes lighting up as he finally spots him and begins his age-defying run down the front path to greet him. Zechariah was careful to remind his people that if they "returned to God," they would find God waiting with acceptance, redemption, and joy. Nothing has changed. If you have lost your way, not to worry; when you turn toward the Father, you will find the Father waiting.

Prayer
Father, we are thankful that whenever we turn to you, we find you waiting. Amen.

Day 913   Zechariah 2: The Importance of Measurements

> "He replied, 'I am going to measure Jerusalem, to see how wide and how long it is.'" Zechariah 2:2 (NLT)

Observation
Zechariah 2 records the prophet's third night vision. In this vision, an angel is sent forth with a measuring line or tape to measure the dimensions of Jerusalem. This indicates that Jerusalem will increase mightily in size. One day there will be so many people and cattle that the city walls will not contain them. Jerusalem will be like a city without walls as it continues its outward creep. (Some commentators suggest that this vision refers to the expansion of the church that will reach beyond borders, race, ethnicities, etc.) The prophet Zechariah addresses three groups. First, he offers words to those who have been dispersed by persecution to the four winds. They will be gathered again to Jerusalem. Second, he speaks to the city itself. The city will be glorified by the presence of God within it and will become a holy place. The third message is extended "to all flesh." When the Messiah returns, all humanity will be silent before him in wonder and awe.

Application
Taking accurate measurements is critical for many industries, endeavors, and events. For example, when engineers take on the process of designing a new car, every aspect is carefully measured for fit, function, and finish. When an architect designs a building, measurements are critical. The builders have to follow those measurements exactly as they construct the building. When prescribing medicines, measurements are important both to the doctor as he/she prescribes the right dosage and to the pharmacist as he/she formulates the correct amount of medicine. Even as we raise our children, we are careful to take measurements to ensure that they are growing healthy and strong. (How many of us have a doorpost somewhere in our homes where we have marked the height of our children at certain ages?)

According to Zechariah's prophecy, the angel of God carefully measured the city of Jerusalem. The dimensions were an important part of God's revealed plan. My concern is not how one might measure a city but how we might measure ourselves—not in feet and inches but in terms of our character, faith, and values. How do we measure what is important? Maybe it comes down to our investments. What we choose to invest in becomes a measure of what is important. How we spend our time and resources says much about our values. How are you measuring up? Are you making a difference in the world around you? Are you investing in the right things?

Prayer
God, as we measure our lives this day, may we discover an increase in our humanity.

Day 914 — Zechariah 3: Clean Clothes

> "So the angel said to the others standing there, 'Take off his filthy clothes.' And turning to Jeshua he said, 'See, I have taken away your sins, and now I am giving you these fine new clothes.'" Zechariah 3:4 (NLT)

Observation

Some people refer to this third chapter as the "hinge" in Zechariah's night visions. Here, the narrative swings from depicting the coming Messiah as King to recording the people's response to prepare for his coming by being purified from their sins. In this vision, the prophet describes a high priest whose name is Jeshua. As he stands before a heavenly court, Satan appears to accuse him. Jeshua represents all the people of Israel and their sinfulness. The sins are depicted as the "filthy clothing" that Jeshua is wearing. The angel in Zechariah's vision is commanded to remove these filthy clothes and replace them with clean, festive clothing. This image indicates that with the coming of the Messiah, God will take away the iniquity of the people. When the Messiah comes, the people will know divine favor, prosperity, and peace if they have walked steadfastly in the ways of the Lord.

Application

I recently had the privilege of spending time with an interfaith group touring the National Holocaust Museum in Washington DC. This was my second time to experience the museum. Our group was given a private viewing of the exhibits and also led in discussions and dialogue by docents from the museum. If you ever go there, you will find it to be a somber, difficult, and emotionally draining experience. Some of the images that continue to haunt me are of men and women in the concentration camps who were mercifully freed by the Allied forces at the end of the war. They were gaunt, emaciated, and dressed in filthy and torn rags. What must it have been like, once liberated, to experience new, fresh, clean clothing? What must it have been like to wear garments that no longer spoke of their oppression but of their freedom?

In his vision, Zechariah depicts a high priest named Jeshua who was dressed in filthy clothing. But by the command of God, his clothes were changed into clean, fresh, and festive garb. We need to see ourselves, like Jeshua, standing with the filth of our sinfulness spattered across our clothing. How we need renewal, grace, and forgiveness. How we need to exchange our sinfulness for the holiness of Christ. The promise made through these prophetic words still rings true today. God once again declares that we be stripped of our sinfulness and shame and instead wear the garments of purity, grace, and mercy through the loving embrace of Christ.

Prayer

Father, like removing filthy rags, may we cast aside our sinfulness as we discover grace.

Day 915 — Zechariah 4: From Small Beginnings...

> "Do not despise these small beginnings, for the Lord rejoices to see the work begin, to see the plumb line in Zerubbabel's hand."
> Zechariah 4:10 (NLT)

Observation

Chapter 4 returns to a telling of the night visions that the prophet Zechariah experienced. These last three visions speak of the empowerment and enabling of Israel that will be brought about by the ultimate and final work of the Messiah. In this vision, Zechariah sees a golden lampstand with seven branches. There is a bowl of olive oil affixed above it with tubes running to each of the seven branches. On each side of the lampstand is an olive tree. These two trees are directly connected to the bowl of oil, providing a continuous flow that keeps the golden lampstand perpetually lit. The prophet asks for an explanation and is told that God's ongoing and ultimate work will be the result not of force or strength but of God's Spirit. The small work (in particular the building of the Temple) that had been started would ultimately result in amazing splendor. Zechariah then asks about the two olive trees. He is told that they represent the roles of the high priest and king. These two offices will be united when the Messiah comes. He will reign with both spiritual and political authority over the lampstand, which represents Israel.

Application

About 20 years ago, a friend moved to Middle Tennessee as a "church planter." His job was to start a new church amid a new but growing area south of Franklin. He prayed, talked with people, and began implementing a strategy. On the first Sunday of the new work, only 17 people came to his home to begin worshipping together. Soon, more started attending. Then additional space was needed, and a small plot of land was purchased. With the land came the first building, which was quickly outgrown. You can tell where this story is headed. As the years progressed the church grew and grew. Today there are 37 staff members spread across two campuses. The small beginning has become a great work.

In our focus verse, the angel of the Lord tells Zechariah not to despise the small beginnings of the structure that will one day become the glorious Temple. The angel reminds him that God rejoices to see the work begun. I believe that God is always pleased and excited whenever we dare to dream a new dream and begin a new ministry endeavor. Though our talents, resources, and fellow dreamers may be small in number, God rejoices in the creation of new beginnings. It's the same in our personal lives. Whenever we take even a small step to change our hearts or start a new spiritual discipline, God is pleased.

Prayer

Father, thank you for small beginnings and great results. Amen.

Day 916 — Zechariah 5: What's in Your Basket?

> "'What is it?' I asked. He replied, 'It is a basket for measuring grain, and it's filled with the sins of everyone throughout the land.'" Zechariah 5:6 (NLT)

Observation

Zechariah 5 contains a vision of a flying scroll and a woman in a basket. Although they might appear as two separate visions, they are actually linked and seem to have been given to the prophet in the same moment. The meaning suggests that God will forcibly and finally deal with sin and rebellion. In the vision, a giant flying scroll appears—30 feet by 15 feet—that represents the Torah or Law of God. Words are written on both sides of the scroll. The curse of disobedience is going forth over the entire land. One side makes reference to the eighth commandment, teaching the faithful not to steal. The other side makes reference to the third commandment, teaching the faithful not to swear falsely. After identifying evil in the land, the vision shifts to that of God's punishment. A large basket appears, symbolically filled with the sins of the people that are metaphorically depicted by a woman named "Wickedness." Two angels carry the basket containing the woman to Babylon, the center of wickedness. Babylon is referred to as "Shinar," the name associated with the city in Genesis 11 where the story of the Tower of Babel takes place. This name connects the contemporary city with its long history of wickedness. In what is probably an eschatological interpretation, as the evil is taken from Israel the nation is made holy once again.

Application

Wednesday is trash day in my neighborhood. It's when the garbage trucks come rolling through to collect their cargo of discarded items. In a model of efficiency, four trucks come by the house each week. One is a large truck with a hydraulic arm that picks up the trash bin, dumps it into the truck, then sets the bin back in place. Another, smaller truck comes by to collect the blue recycling bags. The third truck picks up large odd-shaped items like discarded pieces of furniture or old lawn mowers, etc. The fourth truck contains a huge suction tube that sucks up the leaves that have been pushed out to the curb. I find it intriguing that in just a few minutes, all the garbage, all the trash, and all the debris is quickly removed.

Zechariah describes a large basket containing the sins of Israel. The basket is carried away from the land so that Israel can be holy again. What if you had a basket that would carry away all the stuff you want to discard? What would be in your basket? Guilt? Shame? Remorse? Mistakes? Sins? Though I would never be profane enough to call Jesus our "garbage man," I would describe him as the Lamb of God who comes to take away the sins of the world.

Prayer

Father, cleanse us this day. Remove our sins and make us new. Amen.

Day 917 — Zechariah 6: People Will Come

> "People will come from distant lands to rebuild the Temple of the Lord. And when this happens, you will know that my messages have been from the Lord of Heaven's Armies. All this will happen if you carefully obey what the Lord your God says." Zechariah 6:15 (NLT)

Observation
This chapter reveals the sixth and final night vision of Zechariah. His vision deals with the Lord's final judgment of the nations. It speaks of four chariots drawn by various-colored horses that will patrol the earth to bring God's judgment. These four chariots proceed from two bronze mountains. Some have speculated that these mountains refer to Mount Zion and the Mount of Olives, both of which play pivotal roles in the story of Israel. But others suggest that they are used metaphorically to symbolize the gateway of God through which the chariots go forth by God's authority. (Some have even compared them to the two large bronze pillars that once stood in front of Solomon's Temple.) Following the vision of the chariots, the chapter shifts into a discussion of the role of the future Messiah. He will combine the roles of priest and king, meaning both righteousness and royalty. To remind the Israelites about this role, Zechariah is told to make a crown of silver and gold and place it in the Temple so that the future Messiah will be prominent in the people's minds.

Application
Recently, former President and Mrs. Carter were in Nashville to lead a group of volunteers in a weeklong Habitat for Humanity building project. (My wife and I were privileged to join the Carters for lunch while they were in town.) The group of volunteers was composed of individuals from all across the country. Whenever there is a "Carter Building Project," many of the same people come together to join with the Carters for the week. They come to hammer, lift, saw, sweep, and paint. Collectively, the project moves forward and this mosaic of people construct a number of houses.

Zechariah indicates that people will come from distant lands to build the Temple of God. In my mind's eye, I see people of every tribe, tongue, and race working side by side to do the work of God. It's a vision for what I believe the church is all about. The church, ordained of Jesus Christ, goes beyond barriers of nationality, race, and denomination. Together, each of us who have claimed Jesus in faith comprise his church and build his kingdom. For so long, many saw competition between various churches and denominations. But the Kingdom of God is bigger and broader than that. It's not about competition but about complementing ministries. Together we will usher in the day when the Kingdom will come on earth as it is in heaven. As we strive for that day's appearing, let us embrace our fellow believers and work with joy.

Prayer
Father, gather each of us into a mighty force that will transform our world. Amen.

Day 918 — Zechariah 7: Walk the Walk

> "This is what the Lord of Heaven's Armies says: Judge fairly, and show mercy and kindness to one another. Do not oppress widows, orphans, foreigners, and the poor. And do not scheme against each other."
> Zechariah 7:9-10 (NLT)

Observation
Zechariah 7 and 8 contain portions of sermons offered to the Israelites who were newly returned from exile. Dated around 518 BC, these sermons were based on "messages" the prophet received from the Lord. There were designed to correct the misunderstanding that the return from exile was the total fulfillment of all that God had promised. Yes, the return marked a partial fulfillment, but much of what was promised through the prophets was yet to come and would only be fully realized in the Messianic age. Some of the spiritual leaders raised a question. They asked Zechariah if they should continue to fast and mourn each fall on the anniversary of the destruction of Solomon's Temple. Since the reconstruction of the Temple had begun, was the time of fasting still necessary? Zechariah led the people to understand that moments of mourning and fasting were important because the returning exiles had not fully repented of earlier sins. God wanted repentance and not just rituals. The people were not fasting out of a pure heart. More than merely practicing external rites, God demanded meaning. The people were not to practice "religion" but to exhibit the religious behavior described in our focus verse.

Application
We demand consistency in our leaders, friends, and coworkers. We often express it this way: "If you are going to talk the talk, then walk the walk." We want words and actions to align. We want spoken resolve to be matched with practical action. For example, if the mayor of our community says she is going to be tough on crime, we expect better policing, more officers on patrol, and maybe faster prosecution of criminal behavior. In other words, don't just make a promise or grandiose statement; follow it with action.

The sin of the returned exiles was proclaiming fidelity to God without demonstrating that fidelity through action. They were called to fairness, mercy, and kindness. They were admonished to avoid the oppression of others and treat the marginalized with respect. The same powerful message needs to reach our ears. Our practice of religion cannot be devoid of practical expression. As New Testament writer James reminds us, "Faith, if it has no works, is dead" (James 2:26 NASB) If we are going to proclaim faith in Christ and an allegiance to his Kingdom, then we must allow our declarations to find a place of expression. It matters how we treat others. It matters whether or not we are compassionate, gracious, and kind. Walk the walk.

Prayer
Heavenly Father, may our profession of faith match our practice of faith. Amen.

Day 919   Zechariah 8: Anyone Clutching at Your Sleeve?

> "This is what the Lord of Heaven's Armies says: In those days ten men from different nations and languages of the world will clutch at the sleeve of one Jew. And they will say, 'Please let us walk with you, for we have heard that God is with you.'" Zechariah 8:23 (NLT)

Observation
Chapter 8 contains the words of two messages that Zechariah received from the Lord. Through the prophet's words, the Lord once again declares and affirms love for Israel and indicates wrathful judgment of the nations. God will "dwell" or "permanently reside" in Zion. When the Messianic age occurs, God promises to be present with the people, to purify them, protect them, and collect those who have been scattered to the various nations of the world. Jerusalem will be such a place of peace where children and senior adults—some of the most defenseless of the population—will walk freely and play joyfully on the streets. God will also bring about a spiritual transformation of the people. Zechariah offers encouragement to be steadfast in the task of rebuilding the Temple and not become distracted. In a second message, God promises that the sorrows of the people will be turned to joy. "Fast" days will turn into "feast" days. Though the people once turned others away from God because of their sinfulness, they will now lead people to the Lord. Ten men will cling to the sleeve of every Jew in order to discover the God of Israel.

Application
Think about a group of preschoolers at play in a local park. Sometimes you might see the teacher holding a long rope with small loops tied at certain intervals. The children are told to grab one of the loops so that the teacher can lead them back to the bus or to the classroom. The children faithfully cling to the rope because they want to follow the adult who is safely leading them.

    I love the image that Zechariah offers in our focus verse. Ten men will clutch at the sleeve of a Jew, wanting to walk with him because they believe God is with him. It makes sense that a person of faith would lead others to discover that same faith. It also begs a question: "Is anybody clutching at your sleeve?" In other words, is your faith vibrant enough, active enough, and authentic enough that others want to draw near and discover what motivates and transforms your life? Christ calls us to be salt and light. We are to become transformative people who lead others to discover who God is. Look around. If no one is tugging at your sleeve, maybe it should give you pause. Maybe, rather than being distinctively different, you have assimilated into the mold of culture. Each of us must hear the call to pursue God with all our hearts in the hope that others might join us in the journey.

Prayer
Father God, may our hearts be faithful and our witness become contagious. Amen.

Day 920 — Zechariah 9: A Different Kind of King

> "Rejoice, O people of Zion! Shout in triumph, O people of Jerusalem!
> Look, your king is coming to you. He is righteous and victorious, yet he is
> humble, riding on a donkey—riding on a donkey's colt."
> Zechariah 9:9 (NLT)

Observation

Chapter 9 marks the beginning of a series of oracles or "burdens" proclaimed by Zechariah. They are called burdens because of the weight of his messages and his duty to proclaim them. These messages carry both judgment and blessing. In his words, Zechariah feels the need to continue to remind the Israelites that the ultimate fulfillment of God's promises has not yet come but will take place in a later Messianic age. In the first oracle, the prophet refers to a great king who is coming to conquer a number of lands, including Tyre. Though warfare will occur all around the Mideast, Jerusalem will be protected. Most scholars see the fulfillment of this prophecy in the history of Alexander the Great, who conquered most of this region in 333 BC. But then Zechariah turns his attention to the coming of another king, a greater King. He speaks of the coming of the Messiah, who will offer salvation to God's people. The people are to rejoice greatly in his coming reign. They are literally to offer "exuberant shouts." The language concerning his coming should be familiar to readers of the New Testament. Zechariah speaks of the Messiah coming in humility and peace, riding into Jerusalem on a donkey.

Application

When a new movie is released, an advertisement might say something like this: "Coming soon to a theater near you!" We won't have to travel miles and miles to see the new film; it is coming to us, near to where we live. I am reminded of those words as I carefully read the writings of Zechariah. In speaking about the Messiah, he is careful to say that the Messiah is coming to us. In other words, he moves in our direction. We don't humbly come into his palace; he humbly comes into our world. Or, as the name Immanuel implies, "God is with us." He is indeed a different kind of King. He comes not to overpower us, manipulate us, threaten us, or conquer us. He comes in peace to dwell in us and offer salvation, hope, and endless joy.

I find the idea of the Messiah coming to us to be a unique expression of God's love for us. If anything, we should grovel at God's feet, fearful of even attempting to approach God's presence. And yet God comes to us. God takes on the robe of human flesh and steps into the story of flawed humanity. It makes me even more aware of my need to welcome Jesus graciously, with a pure heart, a clean mind, and an expectant hope.

Prayer

Father God, may we receive King Jesus in both humility and joy. Amen.

Day 921 — Zechariah 10: Stress Relief

> "They will pass safely through the sea of distress, for the waves of the sea
> will be held back, and the waters of the Nile will dry up."
> Zechariah 10:11a (NLT)

Observation

Zechariah 10 speaks of God's powerful restoration of the people. Included in this restoration is the promise of an agricultural blessing. God will bring the spring rains to produce abundant crops. Additionally, part of this restoration will include a purification of the people. God is holding the kings of the land responsible for the spiritual wanderings of the nation. These corrupt leaders will be punished, but the "lost sheep" will be gathered safely and will know the way of the Lord. In this chapter, Zechariah speaks specifically about the role of the tribe of Judah. From Judah will come a cornerstone on which the nation will rest. This cornerstone, understood to be the Messiah, will bring stability and security. Zechariah goes on to proclaim that God will one day gather all of the people back to the land of Israel in an "end times" restoration.

Application

We stress over finances, family, and the future. We let both the great and small things of life cause us worry and angst. For example, what if you go out to your car expecting to drive to work and you discover a dead battery? Stress. What if your cell phone runs out of battery life while you are waiting on an important call? Stress. What if you get to work and notice that your shirt has a huge stain? Stress. What if your kid tried out for the school play but didn't make it? Stress. Each day brings its unique set of stresses and strains. And the stress affects us. It robs us of sleep, disrupts our health, and can even cause disruptive anger in our relationships. But notice what Zechariah says about stress and its relationship to the people of faith: "They will pass safely through the sea of distress, for the waves of the sea will be held back." He reminds us that as God followers, we have a weapon against stress. God's abiding presence offers support, comfort, peace of mind, and victory. In response to worry and stress, the Apostle Paul said, "Be anxious for nothing, but in everything by prayer and supplication, with thanksgiving let your requests be made known to God" (Philippians 4:6 NASB).

Stress and worry are complicated problems, but the solution may be as easy as this: "Pray more, stress less." We need to believe in the promises of God's word. We need to take seriously the call to offer our concerns before God's tender heart. Peter also reminds us, "Cast all your anxiety on him because he cares for you" (1 Peter 5:7 NIV). Today you have a choice to make—endless worry or faithful prayers. Which sounds like a better choice?

Prayer

Father God, teach us this day to rest in your care for us. Amen.

Day 922   Zechariah 11: The Cost of Abandonment

> "What sorrow awaits this worthless shepherd who abandons the flock! The sword will cut his arm and pierce his right eye. His arm will become useless, and his right eye completely blind." Zechariah 11:17 (NLT)

Observation

Zechariah 11 has a twofold theme. First, Zechariah will role-play a depiction of Israel's rejection of the one true shepherd (Messiah). Second, Zechariah will role-play God's rejection of a future false shepherd. The chapter speaks of the coming judgment of Israel that will be like a forest fire consuming the land. This judgment will be caused by the people's rejection of the coming Messianic King. (This prophetic word seems to be fulfilled by the Roman generals Vespasian and Titus during the Jewish revolt of AD 68-73.). The true work of a good shepherd is to pastor the flock. Jesus' earthly ministry of gentle care for the poor and downcast is seen as a fulfillment of Zechariah's words. The rejection of the Messiah, according to Zechariah, is that God will withdraw favor from the land. In keeping with the theme of the Messiah's fulfillment through the life and work of Christ, Zechariah speaks of 30 pieces of silver, the compensation for a gored slave, which is later described in Matthew 27:7. In identifying the false shepherd who will rise and treat the nation poorly (vv. 15-17), most scholars point to the role of King Herod the Great.

Application

Recently, a story appeared in the news from a small town in Canada. In the midst of winter, a mother, obviously suffering mental health concerns, apparently abandoned her two small children, leaving them to fend for themselves with no heat or food in their tiny rural shack. Sensing danger, the four-year-old gathered his little sister in his arms and courageously walked more than half a mile through deep snow to knock on the door of a neighbor. Gratefully, both children survived the ordeal. Whenever we read of such a story, we wonder how a parent could so completely abandon his/her role of care.

Zechariah speaks of the fate of the worthless shepherd who abandons his flock. How shocking to be given the responsibility for the lives of many sheep and fail to provide adequate care. This morning, I hope each one of us will see ourselves in the role of shepherding others. Many people in our sphere of influence need the care that we provide. Our flock might consist of our family members or our close friends. But certainly, our care should be extended to others, like neighbors, coworkers, and people we consistently encounter in our day-to-day routines. Has not God placed those people in our lives for a purpose? We are to give compassionate care, prayerful support, and grace-filled words.

Prayer

Father God, teach us to shepherd well those who need our care. Amen.

Day 923   Zechariah 12: From Whence Does Your Strength Come?

> "And the clans of Judah will say to themselves, 'The people of Jerusalem have found strength in the Lord of Heaven's Armies, their God.'"
> Zechariah 12:5 (NLT)

Observation
Chapter 12 marks the beginning of the final section of the book of Zechariah, which is devoted to the future deliverance of Jerusalem. In this chapter, Zechariah predicts events that will occur at the "end of days" when the Messiah returns to deliver Israel and establish his kingdom on earth. One phrase often repeated in this section is "in that day." This is an eschatological reference referring to a distant future—not something that will occur in Zechariah's day. The chapter begins with a poetic introduction of God as the omnipotent creator of heaven, earth, and humankind. Because of God's power and wisdom, God will control the final outcome of Israel. The prophet speaks of a final great battle that will result in a time of deliverance. Jerusalem will be like a cup of wine that will stagger her enemies with drunkenness. She will be like a stone, so heavy that those who attempt to lift her will injure themselves. In this time of warfare, God will liberate Jerusalem and strengthen the city's inhabitants. This will also prove to be a time of repentance for Israel. The people will once again reclaim a passion for following God.

Application
Where do you find strength? Some would argue that the way to build strength and endurance is through exercise and weight training. Others might suggest following a strict, regimental diet that feeds your body with protein and needed vitamins. Still others suggest that we are strengthened through the books we read or the company we keep. In other words, our encouragement comes from the people with whom we surround ourselves. All of these suggestions hold true. We can fortify our bodies, our immune systems, and our mental health through careful management and healthy relationships. But there is a greater source of strength. As Zechariah reminds us, "the people will find strength in the Lord of Heaven's Armies."

He's not the only one to make such a statement. Consider the words of the psalmist: "I look up to the mountains—does my help come from there? My help comes from the Lord, who made heaven and earth!" (Psalm 121:1-2 NLT). Or recall the words of Isaiah: "Don't be afraid, for I am with you. Don't be discouraged, for I am your God. I will strengthen you and help you. I will hold you up with my victorious right hand" (Isaiah 41:10 NLT). Let us remind ourselves this day that ultimate, lasting strength is found in our fidelity to the Lord. God strengthens our limbs, fortifies our passions, and empowers our courageous acts. Call on God this day.

Prayer
Father God, give us strength in our weakness and power in our resolve. Amen.

Day 924 — Zechariah 13: There Is a Fountain...

> "On that day a fountain will be opened for the dynasty of David and for the people of Jerusalem, a fountain to cleanse them from all their sins and impurity." Zechariah 13:1 (NLT)

Observation
Now that Israel has looked upon the coming Messiah in faith and hope, the Lord will open a fountain to cleanse the people of their sins and impurities. Not only will they be forgiven of their sins, but the Lord will also purge the land of wrongdoing. Idols and the places of idol worship will be removed. Even the names of idols, once worshipped, will be forgotten. With perhaps shocking language, Zechariah declares that those proven to be false prophets will be stabbed by their own parents as a part of this purification of the land. The chapter also predicts some of the future events that will occur as the Messianic age is ushered in. The Messiah "will be pierced" for the transgressions of the people. And the people of God will be scattered for a time, only to be brought home again. (Many see the fulfillment of this prophecy occurring 2000 years later in 1948 when the nation of Israel was reestablished.)

Application
Woven somewhere deeply into my DNA is a "car-washing" gene. I can't explain it any other way. My dad always loved a clean car. When I was kid, I would often see him quickly rinse off the car before heading to work… sometimes while even wearing a tie. When I would come home from college, before I could get my things unloaded, Dad would be in the driveway, hose in hand, giving my car a good wash. That clean car mentality has found its way into both my brother and me. I really can't stand for my car to be dirty. I want the dirt removed and the tires to shine. A clean car looks better and it runs better…I can't explain why, but I know it does.

Removing the dirt, grime, and impurities is always important—not only for cars but for people. Though I certainly crave a warm shower each day, I'm not describing that kind of cleansing. I'm talking about a spiritual cleansing, a washing away of sin, disobedience, and impurities. An old hymn comes to mind: "There is a fountain filled with blood, drawn from Emmanuel's veins, and sinners plunged beneath that flood lose all their guilty stains." Because of our Messiah's "piercing," his sacrifice, and his atoning death, our sins can be washed away. His spilt blood washes clean the dark stains of our iniquities. It is vital to understand two essential truths this day. One, we have a sin problem. "For all have sinned and fall short of the Glory of God" (Romans 3:23 NASB). Second, "While we were still sinners, Christ died for us" (Romans 5:8 NIV). Oh yes, there is a fountain, and we must gladly bathe in it.

Prayer
Father God, thank you for the fountain that cleanses our sins. Amen.

Day 925 — Zechariah 14: One Lord

> "And the Lord will be king over all the earth. On that day there will be one Lord—his name alone will be worshiped." Zechariah 14:9 (NLT)

Observation

This final chapter of the book of Zechariah serves as a last message describing the renovation of Jerusalem that will come about in the great and fearful "Day of the Lord." This day will bring both judgment and restoration. Correctly understood, the Day of the Lord has two parts, evening followed by morning. The evening is descriptive of destruction and judgment that will come when the Messiah returns to the world. The morning is descriptive of the joy that will unfold as God makes all things new. This chapter first looks at the time of judgment. All the nations will gather against Jerusalem. There will be devastation, plundering, and enslavement. Half the people will be taken to exile. Yet God is directing these events to bring about an ultimate good purpose: the restoration of God's holy people whose attention will no longer be divided among idols. The time of deliverance is also described. The enemies will be defeated, and God will be present in Jerusalem. God will stand on the Mount of Olives and the mount will split in two! This will first provide a way of escape for God's people but will then become a river that flows both to the east and to the west, creating a fertile land. The chapter ends with a promise of all people coming to Jerusalem to worship.

Application

Each spring, the world of sport explodes with excitement over March Madness, the 64-team college basketball tournament that ends the season. It's a huge deal to be a part of the tournament. Some teams are automatically included when they win conference championships, while other teams are selected to receive an "at-large" bid. Once the tournament begins, all 64 teams hope to win it all and be proclaimed as National Champions. What I find interesting about the tournament is that there is only one winner, which means there are 63 losers. A vast majority will not play in the championship game, no matter how much they long to do so.

In the long history of the world, there has been a pantheon of gods. Each culture, each empire, and each tribe has discovered something to worship. The Greeks had their gods of mythology. The Romans had other gods to worship, as did the Egyptians, the Minoans, the Babylonians, etc. Many looked to the stars in the sky as gods to worship and appease. But notice what Zechariah says will occur on the great Day of the Lord. There will be only one King, only one Lord, only one name worthy of worship: Jesus. He is the King of all kings and the Lord of all lords. May the names of false deities be forever forgotten.

Prayer

Father God, we praise you as the One true God and worship you always. Amen.

Day 926 — Malachi 1: God's Standard of Excellence

> "You have shown contempt by offering defiled sacrifices on my altar. Then you ask, 'How have we defiled the sacrifices?' You defile them by saying the altar of the Lord deserves no respect." Malachi 1:7 (NLT)

Observation
Malachi, whose name means "My Messenger," was a prophet speaking on God's behalf. It is clear from the opening verse that God has given an important word to Malachi and he is duty-bound to offer it to his people. (The book is postexilic, probably written around 415 BC as the Israelites were reestablishing themselves in the land of Israel.) The opening passage sets the theme of the book as "God's unconditional love for Israel." The people are directed to live in response to God's love. They are to respect God, obey God, and honor God. The people respond to God's declaration of unconditional love by asking, "How have you loved us?" They consider the pains and pressures of their current circumstances and wonder about God's affection. They are reminded of God's faithfulness from the time of Jacob through the present age. As the chapter continues, God will describe Israel's unfaithfulness despite God's love for them. The role of the priests is brought to light. They have failed miserably. They have offered blemished sacrifices and defiled food and have further profaned worship by treating it as a common, ordinary experience. They have even swindled some of the offerings given at the Temple. God expects better in light of unconditional love for the people.

Application
I am a lifelong fan of Alabama football. The past decade has been fun under the leadership of Coach Nick Saban. Coach Saban demands a lot of his players and often speaks of following a "process" for establishing a winning program. He says of his team, "We try to play to a standard of excellence."

Striving for excellence is important in any endeavor. It is critically important in the practice of worship. Certainly, God deserves our best efforts. Worship is not a simple, casual moment. It requires our best attention. Our best thoughts. Our best planning. Our best preparation. We are honoring the King of kings, so why would we treat the moment as being unimportant? Preparation for worship is not shouldered simply by those who lead the experience. Preparation is important for all who attend. As we gather in God's house, our hearts and minds must be prepared to hear from God. Distractions must be banned from our thoughts. Our concerns must be shelved for a moment so that our biggest concern is to praise, honor, and listen well. Let's demand excellence.

Prayer
Father, may we never treat our time with you flippantly. Amen.

Day 927 — Malachi 2: Faithful in Marriage

> "'For I hate divorce!' says the Lord, the God of Israel. 'To divorce your wife is to overwhelm her with cruelty,' says the Lord of Heaven's Armies. 'So guard your heart; do not be unfaithful to your wife.'" Malachi 2:16 (NLT)

Observation
Malachi 2 offers further words of warning to the priests who failed to lead the people effectively. They failed to honor God's name, and because of their lack of focus and fidelity, God promised a strong rebuke upon their words and ministries. They would be treated as being "unclean." By contrast, the faithful priests would receive life and peace because they revered the name of the Lord. They would offer true instruction to the people. The latter part of the chapter focuses on marital unfaithfulness. Many citizens had failed to recognize covenantal marriage, instead marrying pagan women who chased after foreign gods. Some even divorced their wives in order to marry such women. Lifelong marriages are God's intent because such unions provide the best environment for health and happiness. In the strongest words of condemnation of divorce in the Old Testament, Malachi declares the words of God saying, "I hate divorce." The challenge for each man is to guard his heart in order to stay faithful to his wife and thus eliminate the temptation for divorce.

Application
We live in an age and culture where half of all marriages end in divorce. Statistically, there is no difference in marriages that are "Christian marriages" and those that are not. Is this what God intends for marriage? Is God honored as many marriages dissolve? I think it is important to state that divorce is never Plan A with God. It is God's desire that we honor the marriage covenants we make at the altar. God hates divorce because it represents the breaking of a vow that was made before God and in the presence of many witnesses. However, God does offer forgiveness and redemption to those whose marriages have failed. In the case of many divorces, however, what happens is that those who have experienced brokenness in that key relationship fail to seek the forgiveness of God or take time to consider what needs to change in their lives as they approach a second marriage. Relationships are tough. They take a lot of hard work, compromise, and commitment. And sometimes even the best marriages are torn apart by difficult situations and circumstances. I cannot in good conscience tell a husband or wife who is being emotionally and physically abused that they must stay in such a caustic relationship. We must help the hurting, not offer further abusive condemnation. But let's cling to the ideal. Let's work and pray our way in marriage.

Prayer
Father, teach us to love each other enough so that divorce is never an option. Amen.

Day 928　　　　　　　　　　　　　　　　Malachi 3: Testing God

> "'Bring all the tithes into the storehouse so there will be enough food in my Temple. If you do,' says the Lord of Heaven's Armies, 'I will open the windows of heaven for you. I will pour out a blessing so great you won't have enough room to take it in! Try it! Put me to the test!'"
> Malachi 3:10 (NLT)

Observation

As chapter 3 opens, it is clear that judgment and justice are coming on both the enemies of Israel and those within Israel who have acted in disobedience. The beginning verses say that a messenger is coming to announce the appearance of the Messiah. This messenger is Elijah, who will come to prepare the way of the Lord. Later, at the birth of John the Baptist, it is said that John comes in the power and spirit of Elijah (Luke 1:17). Further, in Matthew 11:9-13, John clearly functions in the role of Elijah announcing the coming of the Messiah. Malachi then announces that a second Messenger is coming. This is a theophany. This messenger is the Lord who comes to judge the world. When the Messiah comes, he will purify the people from their sins. One of the sins described in this chapter is robbing God of the tithes and offerings. When confronted, the people ask, "How have we robbed you?" God challenges the people. In response to their gifts, God will reward them with abundancy. As the chapter closes, the people are reminded that God will remember the faithful and reward them.

Application

Many of us have grown up with a mindset and theology stating that it is never a good idea to test Almighty God. In fact, it is never our place to do so. God is sovereign. God is Lord. God alone controls the destinies of our lives. It would be foolish to test God in any way or even attempt to wrangle God into a conditional promise like, "I will do such-and-such if you will answer this prayer the way I want it answered." No. We don't strike deals with the Almighty...unless the Almighty invites us to do so. In our focus verse, God invites the people to "put God to the test." God seeks a spirit of obedient generosity. If the people are faithful to honor God with their tithes and offerings, God promises to respond with abundant blessings. The crops will produce great harvests and the grapes on the vine will ripen and not fall to the ground. You may have heard the old expression, "You can't out-give God." I have found that to be true. I have never known a single person who practiced generosity towards God and then later regretted doing so because of sudden scarcity. In fact, the opposite holds true. Those who give lavishly in order to meet the needs of others and to honor God find amazing blessings. Beyond material sufficiency, such people find lasting joy. God will bless. Test God.

Prayer

Father, forgive our selfishness and fear that limits our generosity. Amen.

Day 929 — Malachi 4: Healing in God's Wings

> "But for you who fear my name, the Sun of Righteousness will rise with healing in his wings. And you will go free, leaping with joy like calves let out to pasture." Malachi 4:2 (NLT)

Observation
This final chapter of the Old Testament speaks once again about the coming day of the Lord that will bring judgment to some and restoration to others. For some, the day of the Lord will come like a burning furnace. The arrogant and wicked will be consumed like dry straw in a raging fire. The day will be different for those who have loved God. Contrasting the fire of judgment, the righteous will know the warmth and healing rays of sunlight. This will be a sign of God's comfort. They will be vindicated over their enemies. The chapter closes with a final word of exhortation. The people are to remember the Law of Moses. They need to recapture the faith of their forefathers. As they do so, they are to look for the coming of Elijah, who will precede the Messiah. His presence will lead them to repentance. In stating that Elijah's preaching will turn the hearts of the children towards their fathers, Malachi is most likely speaking of how present-day followers of God will develop a strong faith like that of the patriarchs.

Application
I have always been intrigued by a New Testament connection to our focus verse, which speaks of "healing in his wings." The Synoptic Gospel accounts tell the story of a poor woman who suffered for 12 years with a hemorrhage. According to Luke 8:43-48, she comes up behind Jesus and touches the fringe of his robe. He immediately feels the power flow from his life to hers. While confronting her about her actions, Jesus says, "Your faith has made you well." In the first century world, people thought a healing effect would come from touching the fringe of a rabbi's robe. The robe was seen as his "wings." Touching those wings would give healing. In a shocking display of faith, the woman reaches out to touch the hem of Jesus' garment. She believes that doing so will provide the healing that her life so desperately needs. The faith that gives her new life, however, is not simply faith in the idea of touching a rabbi's robe; it is faith in the idea that Jesus is the miracle-working Messiah who has come to redeem Israel. Her faith in *who Jesus is* offers her life, healing, and grace.

All of us are broken by life. We stumble, we mourn, we bleed, we suffer, we fear, and we worry. Where will we find a healing balm to soothe and make us whole? We reach out in faith and touch the rabbi's robe, for there is healing in his wings. Christ has come to bind your wounds, soothe your pain, and restore your life. Reach out to him in faith.

Prayer
Father, may we, even this day, catch a glimpse of the healing you provide. Amen.

www.ingramcontent.com/pod-product-compliance
Lightning Source LLC
Chambersburg PA
CBHW051120160426
43195CB00014B/2274